Politics and   s
in
The Age of Walpole

B. W. Last

AVERO

© 1987   B. W. Last

First published in Great Britain in 1987 by
Avero Publications Ltd.

British Library Cataloguing in Publication Data

Last, B. W.
  Politics and letters in the age of Walpole.
1. English literature – 18th century – History and criticism
2. Politics in literature
I. Title
820.9'358   PR 448.P6

ISBN 0-907977-22-7

Printed in Great Britain by
Unwin Brothers Limited
The Gresham Press
Old Woking, Surrey
A member of the Martins Printing Group

CONTENTS

Chapter 1: Introduction: Town and Country   1
Chapter 2: Swift   15
Chapter 3: Bolingbroke   49
Chapter 4: Gay and London Life   67
Chapter 5: Crime – Jonathan Wild   87
Chapter 6: Fielding – the plays   111
Chapter 7: Alternatives and Parallels   133
Chapter 8: Language   147
Conclusion   169
Bibliography   173
Index   183

ACKNOWLEDGEMENTS

I am grateful for the assistance given me by the University Library, Leeds, The University Library, Southampton, the University Library, Nottingham and the British Library. My thanks to Ahmadu Bello University, Nigeria, which awarded me study leave in order to collect material for this work, to Dr D. A. Low of the English Department of the University of Stirling who made many valuable suggestions concerning the study of eighteenth century prose, to Mrs Sally Lockhart of the British Council in Rabat who typed the manuscript and to my wife, Mary, who was always ready to help and encourage in the writing of this study.

PREFACE

This study began after some consideration had been given to two significant aspects of life in the eighteenth century, the increasing importance attached to property and the accompanying growth in the rate of crime. Although the latter was sometimes apparent rather than real, the increase in the use of the metaphor of crime in order to attack a political party indicated that the contrast in political and social ideology between the two rival factions of Whig and Tory was becoming sharper. Amongst the writers who attacked the Whig administration - and Sir Robert Walpole in particular - were all the major writers of the age. Pope, Fielding, Swift and Gay were intensely aware that a new way of governing was being adopted , that a body of monied men was becoming more and more powerful and that they were observing a significant change in the power base of England. From the settled state of the Tory country ideology to the shifting world of the court and the town represented a major shift in power and methods.

Some writers and political commentators felt uneasy in this new world; some, like Bolingbroke, were exiled from it altogether and could only look at England from a distance and attempt to recapture past ideals. The recapturing was achieved in a prose style which asserted the continuing need for a country ruled by the educated and well-bred landed gentry.

But the attempt met with failure. Walpole and the stockjobbers saw to it that England was ruled by the mercantile class, supported by book-keepers. The satirists seemed to be correct; the nation was controlled by a group of men whose main concern was the acquisition of money and property and who therefore had little regard for the past and whose tactics showed a remarkable parallel with those of contemporary thieves. The hope was that this was merely a temporary aberration, that an alternative was still possible and that honour could be re-established.

This study examines several writers in the light of the above general comments and indicates the intimate relationship between writing and politics during the period. Even before Walpole had gained the position of 'prime' minister, Whiggism seemed to pose a threat to national unity; Swift discusses the implications of Whiggish politics while Bolingbroke felt the full force of them when they came into prominence. In the town, crime seemed to rule and it is to Gay and Fielding that one turns for an analysis of the implications. Finally, Pope and others emerge as the men who suggest that a better world was still possible , even though the language of satire suggested that the country ideology had been suppressed for ever and that Walpole and his tactics had triumphed. What emerges most is that both camps were committed to one thing - self-interest

B. W. Last.
August 1984.

v

CHAPTER 1

Introduction: Town and Country

Contemporary historians tend to regard the division of Whig and Tory, with its equivalence of Town and Country, as an over-simplified way in which to view the political parties and their ideologies in the early eighteenth-century. In the broadest sense, however, the division was a preoccupation of eighteenth-century commentators and authors and it is a convenient introduction and starting-point for a study of this kind. One word which certainly unites the two factions is 'money'. The Tories, as landowners, wished to protect their interests which rested in the form of land, while the Whigs, as either aspiring merchants or acquisitive politicians, saw that the outward trappings of success could be bought. Socially, the Whigs were regarded as inferior by the Tories but, financially and politically, the former gradually began to outstrip the latter. The fear amongst the Tories tended to be that moneyed, self-made men were gaining political control by means of a ruthless, selfish and amoral form of behaviour which they found difficult to counter and which seemed to them to be typical of the shift in the attitudes of the time. One man - Robert Walpole - stood as an example of everything which was anti-Tory. He was self-made, without a particular social order or tradition behind him; he ignored title or rank, favouring instead political manoeuvreability; he seemed corrupt and vulgar as well as a rogue and a thief. Moreover, Walpole committed many crimes, but he went unpunished.

The Tories' fears had dated from before Walpole's acquisition of power. During the early years of the eighteenth-century, England was at war in Europe and it was the Whig party which wished to continue the war, while the Tories pressed for peace. The Tories' fears were that the continuation of the war was permitted less for national political reasons than for selfish financial motives on the part of a small number of Whigs. Swift defended the position of the Tories in pursuing peace, and by doing so helped to articulate the attack upon the Whigs. War meant that more money was pouring into the state coffers and several Tory squires were convinced that the Whigs were riding on the back of the war in order to become rich. Sir John Pakington, writing in 1709, argued that there were dangers in allowing 'the moneyed and military men becoming lords of us who have the lands' and Swift pursued much the same line in *The Examiner*[1]

To the Tories, the Whigs were a force bent on destroying the traditions of England and thereby ruining the English way of life; to the Whigs, the Tories represented a force which insisted on preserving

1

power within a small elite and whose motives were therefore as political as their own.

The trend that the Tories also noticed was one towards professionalism. Life seemed to be not only corrupt but also highly organised in its corruption. The towns began to absorb people more rapidly and this encouraged industry among the highest and lowest of the population. By 'town' most people meant London and it was in the town that the merchant and the politician could rub shoulders, where the bookkeeper and the lawyer could exchange ideas and where trade could be established. And it was the connection between all those upon which the Tory opposition to Walpole centred in order to attempt to highlight the ills of his regime. For not everyone regarded the apparently liberal exchange of views as a good thing, nor did they regard the growth of the town as auspicious for the nation. The state seemed to be ruled by book-keepers turned politicians while the traditional rulers were subsumed under a plethora of new ideas. The politician had turned lawyer, serving his own interests; the politician also employed the techniques of the thief in order to become rich.

From a Tory point of view, the nation had degenerated into chaos; from a Whig stance, something more interesting was happening. Property was important and the Whigs saw themselves as the party most committed to protecting it; the position was not just a practical one, but also ideological in the sense that the material possessions of the individual could be seen to benefit the nation as a whole and allow liberty to flourish. 'Liberty' became a word with which the Whigs wished to become associated since it meant that the power of the monarchy and its attendant landed interests would be forced into decline. There was no sense in which the Whigs needed to destroy the hierarchy completely, but by creating a different set of values, a new sort of politician emerged who could force himself into what had seemed an unshiftable scale of values. This new politician regarded private property as being of the highest importance and the Whigs attempted to dedicate themselves first to its acquisition and secondly to its preservation. Of course, as the rule of the Whigs wore on, it became apparent that 'liberty' would have to disappear as a catchword since its over-emphasis would make it impossible to even attempt to gag the intellectual criticism that gathered apace.

Over every issue that has been mentioned above, the Whigs and Tories were divided. England's role in Europe, the power of the monarchy, the re-alignment of power and the rise of the businessman, all forced committed men into one or other of the camps. Certainly after 1714, when the rise of the Whigs really began, the Tories seemed to be a 'country' party, arguing their ideological position from traditional stands and writing along lines which suggested that tradition, judgement, taste and the proper organisation of the state belonged in the hands of those of high birth and wealth.[2]

The remainder of this chapter will be concerned with establishing certain basic assumptions which lay behind the opposition to Walpole and it will examine, too, some of the more positive aspects of the time which were put forward by more Whiggish writers. Many of the points raised here will be examined in further detail as the book progresses.

The Town: Literary Attacks

Although Alexander Pope was intimately connected with the town, he was a critic of its values. For Pope, the town represented a place in which money dominated all values. Pope felt that money had been devalued in the sense that it had taken precedence over morality; in fact, proper standards of self-conduct had virtually disappeared under the influence of the desire for wealth and property:

> Who counsels best? Who whispers, 'Be but Great,
> With Praise or Infamy, leave that to Fate;
> Get Place and Wealth, if possible, with Grace;
> If not, by any means get Wealth and Place.' (ll.101-104)[3]

The feeling is that 'place' is no longer something which can be earned by merit but that it may be bought. The successful man was the one who acquired a position through any means - preferably, it is implied, by amoral ones - and he will be judged solely on the outward appearance. Pope is concerned that the times have elevated the moneyed stockjobber above the rank to which he more properly belongs; the society into which he entered, though, was reduced in stature simply by his inclusion in it:

> For what? to have a Box where Eunuchs sing,
> And foremost in the Circle eye a King.
> Or he, who bids thee face with steady View
> Proud Fortune, and look shallow Greatness thro':
> And, while he bids thee, sets th'Example too? (ll.105-109)[3]
>
> . . . . .
>
> Adieu to Virtue if you're once a Slave:
> Send her to Court, you send her to her Grave. (ll.118/9)[3]

These people are moral eunuchs and they can merely aspire to the office of kingship but they can never properly attain it. Like Bolingbroke, Pope saw the rise of the jobbing, Walpolean, class as a threat to the monarchy and therefore a threat to traditional civilised standards. The Court was being reduced to holding on to the trappings of taste, but 'Virtue' was being eroded by the incursions of the new class into what had been a protected world.

3

This world was being invaded by an enemy whose identity was difficult to determine and which was, at the same time, in a state of rapid change; the identity of this enemy seemed hardly credible. It was, on the surface, insubstantial and yet it held power over so many:

Blest Paper-Credit last and best Supply
That lends Corruption lighter Wings to fly
Gold imp'd by thee, can compass hardest Things,
Can pocket States, can fetch or carry Kings;
A single Leaf shall waft an Army o'er,
Or ship off Senates to a distant Shore. (ll.69-74)[4]

Manipulating the stock market and gaining vast sums by shifting around pieces of paper seemed a strange art to the likes of Pope. 'Paper' had usurped Gold: the latter, tangible and easily identifiable, had been replaced by something flimsy and insubstantial. This seemed to typify what was happening in politics: the once solid Tories were being removed from their position of dominance by a party whose ideals were difficult to pin down and who altered with the times rather than remaining consistent. The fear was that such an attitude, if allowed to operate on a national level, would bring with it ruin and despair; this would happen simply because the Whigs seemed to believe only in money and paper credit:

National Credit can never be supported by lending Money without Security, or by drawing in other People to do so; by raising Stocks and Commodities, by Artifice and Fraud, to unnatural and imaginary Values; and consequently delivering up helpless Women and Orphans, and the ignorant and unwary, but industrious, Subject, to be devour'd by Pickpockets and Stock-jobbers: a sort of Vermin that are bred and nourish'd in the Corruption of the State.[5]

If the Court and politics were corrupt, the town itself offered little or no refuge; it had grown and it had encouraged the worst excesses of human nature. Nothing and no-one was safe to walk around the streets, and poets celebrated the fact:

Nor is thy Flaxen Wigg with Safety worn,
High on the Shoulder; in a Basket born,
Lurks the sly Boy, whose Hand to Rapine bred,
Plucks off the curling Honours of the Head.
Here dives the skulking Thief, with practis'd Slight,
And unfelt Fingers make thy Pocket Light.
Where's now the Watch, with all its Trinkets flown?
And thy late Snuff-Box is no more thy own.[6]

The above may be trivial but it reflects a broader feeling that the times themselves were corrupt and that the corruption was not something that was confined to the Court. Some politicians were mere street

4

thieves, ready and able to knock anyone from their pedestal if advancement was to be gained. The conclusion so often reached was that the critics of the times were a small group, untainted by the movement of the times and that the whole age was immoral and materialistic:

I grant Corruption sways Mankind,
That Int'rest too perverts the Mind, That Bribes have blinded common
    Sense,
Foiled Reason, Truth and Eloquence;
I grant you too, our present Crimes
Can equal those of former Times.
Against plain Facts shall I engage,
To vindicate our righteous Age?
I know, that in a modern Fist,
Bribes in full Energy subsist:
Since then these Arguments prevail,
And itching Palms are still so frail,
Hence Politicians, you suggest,
Should drive the Nail that goes the best;
That it shows Parts and Penetration,
To ply Man with the right Temptation.[7]

England, as Swift had already argued, was bankrupt morally as well as financially and certain writers saw it as their duty to advance that case. Literature was so often at the heart of a political controversy in both general and specific terms: specific when referring to such characters as Walpole and general when discussing the nature of social organisation.

Trade

Not everyone who earned money, rather than inherited it, was regarded as a low, mean fellow. Only those who seemed to gain wealth through invisible earnings on the stock market were considered to be a danger to the nation. Others, notably the merchants, were set aside and generally held up as examples of industry and, consequently, as true patriots. The merchant was, after all, extending the empire of the nation and he was gaining wealth and stature through an honourable profession. He was an outsider, too, in the sense that he could claim to be neither a member of the court nor of the country and so he could establish his own values. At the same time, the merchant could claim to be superior to the country squire, as Steele and Addison show. The merchant was working for the good of the nation and he had personal virtues which served as examples to all:

Sir Roger....has been very severe upon the Merchant. I shall not....at this time remind Sir Roger of the great and noble Monuments of Charity and publick Spirit which have been erected by Merchants since the

Reformation, but at present content myself with what he allows us, Parsimony and Frugality....[8]

The speaker in the above quotation is Sir Andrew Freeport, who is speaking against the view of Sir Roger de Coverly who has argued that 'Frugality and Parsimony be the Virtues of the Merchant' and that he is therefore no gentleman. It is an argument set up for Sir Andrew to knock down and so demonstrate the virtues, economic and social, of the merchant; Sir Andrew continues:

> If to drink so many Hogsheads is to be hospitable, we do not contend for the Fame of the Virtue; but it would be worth while to consider, whether so many Artificers at Work ten Days together by my Appointment, or so many Peasants made merry on Sir Roger's Charge, are the men more obliged: I believe the families of the Artificers will thank me, more than the Households of the Peasants shall Sir Roger. Sir Roger gives to his Men, but I place mine above the Necessity or Obligation of my Bounty.

The argument is heavily weighted in favour of the merchant, Freeport, and yet the writing works on a different level from that of Pope. In their journals, Addison and Steele are establishing that ordinary, reasonable discourse can be entertaining, instructive and relevant. The argument appeals to a broad audience: the journal, unconfined by the walls of the coffee-house or the University, had less of an elitist appeal than many of the satires which followed. Addison and Steele were working in the public sphere.

This is not to say that Addison and Steele were writing some kind of objective account of the nature of the differences between the squire and the merchant. On the contrary, they wished to portray a typical squire in the person of Sir Roger de Coverley and at the same time debunk the values with which he was associated. Sir Roger is likeable but inefficient; he believes in a fixed and traditional hierarchy; he has obtained his peaceful country seat through inheritance and he expects to be able to continue to retain it. Sir Andrew, although never vicious or scathing in his comments upon the life-style of his friend and rival, always maintains an attitude of down-to-earth common sense, which is businesslike and compassionate at the same time:

> This is the Oeconomy of the Merchant, and the Conduct of the Gentleman must be the same, unless by scorning to be the Steward, he resolves the Steward shall be the Gentleman. The Gentleman no more than the Merchant is able without the Help of Numbers to account for the Success of any Action, or the Prudence of any Adventure. If, for Instance, the Chace is his whole Adventure, his only Returns must be the Stag's Horns in the great Hall, and the Fox's Nose upon the Stable Door. Without Doubt Sir Roger knows the full Value of these Returns; and if before-hand he had computed the Charges of the Chace, a

6

Gentleman of his Discretion would certainly have hanged up all his Dogs, he would never have brought back so many fine Horses to the Kennel, he would never have gone so often like a Blast over Fields of Corn. If such too had been the Conduct of all his Ancestors, he might truly have boasted at this Day that the Antiquity of his Family had never been sullied by a Trade; a Merchant had never been permitted with his whole Estate to purchase a Room for his Picture in the Gallery of the Coverleys, or to claim his Descent from the Maid of Honour. But 'tis very happy for Sir Roger that the Merchant paid so dear for his Ambition. 'Tis the Misfortune of many other Gentlemen to turn out of the Seats of their Ancestors, to make Way for such new Masters as have been more exact in their Accompts than themselves; and certainly he deserves the Estate a great deal better who has got it by his Industry, than he who has lost it by his Negligence.[9]

The parting shot is apt and it is designed to sum up the argument: the merchant combines certain ideals and he is able to manage them and himself for the good of everybody.

Several years later, Steele was to confirm that he still believed in the ideals of the merchant. His pamphlets on *The Theatre* include at one point a portrait of an eminent merchant, Mr Sealand:

He is a true Pattern of that kind of third Gentry, which has arose in the World this last Century: I mean the great, and rich families of Merchants, and eminent Traders, who in their Furniture, their Equipage, their Manner of Living, and especially their Oeconomy, are so far from being below the Gentry, that many of them are now the best Representatives of the ancient ones, and deserve the Imitation of the modern Nobility.[10]

Social mobility is all and the merchant is a worthy, dignified and noble person who has created a new class whose distinguishing characteristics are virtue and honesty.

Having stated this, it must be equally indicated that the merchant was, after all, a Whig, and any defence of the position of the merchant was also an attack upon that of the Tory party. By the time Addison came to write *The Freeholder* (1716), he was less concerned with giving a balanced view than with indicating that the Country Party was a reactionary element in society. The Tory squire in *The Freeholder*, no. 22, is a caricature of a fox-hunting gentleman who believes that the mercantile class was ruining the tradition of England and thereby challenging his own way of life. He (the squire) 'expatiated on the Inconveniences of Trade, that carried from us the Commodities of our Country, and made a Parcel of Upstarts as rich as Men of the most ancient Families of England'.[11.] Trade, he believes, will ruin the nation. It is clear, then, from the attitudes expressed in *The Freeholder* that the political climate was changing rapidly. Both groups were suspicious of one another and politicians had to be seen to belong to either one or the other. In a later issue, no. 48, Addison states that 'there is no other Nation which is so equally divided into two opposite Parties, whom it is impossible to please at the same time.'[12] As the Whigs became more and more powerful and as it became evident that they were almost impossible to defeat politically, even after 1720, the Tories were driven more and more into defending and taking sustenance from a way of life that seemed to be disappearing rapidly. The middle men, the 'middle condition or state' were the ones who had control because of their rigorous application of their principles concerning money and trade. Sir Andrew Freeport is a gentleman, but he is also a man who believes in the expansion of the boundaries of trade; the human qualities of Sir Roger, relevant in 1711, were impossible to produce after about 1720 as the political world became more rigidly divided. For Addison, 'Merchants who honorably exercised their Calling' were his heroes, the protagonists of an unfolding success story, while at the same time 'an undue appetite for property and wealth' invites Addison to question their actions and attitudes.'[13] It was this last propensity that became more prevalent, at least according to the critics of Walpole and the Whigs. The former quality was taken as accepted, and the latter as an inevitable and unfortunate consequence of it. The commercial element became much more conspicuous and the Tory tradition was pushed further and further away from the realities of political life. As Walpole argued 'it can never be conceived but that a Gentleman of liberal Fortune and tolerable Education is fitter to serve his Country in Parliament than a Man bred to Trade and brought up in a Shop.'[14]

The Country

The Tories had no intention of bowing to the kind of shift in political power that the above quotation suggests. Instead, they employed the greatest mind of the age - Swift's - in order to defend their traditional position. Swift's rhetoric is impressive and powerful and it is the most forcefully expressed of the Tory ideological statements, but its message seemed almost to wear itself out and, by 1714 or so, Swift seemed to be commentating on events which had passed. He was structuring his prose on the lines of a comment on an historical event rather than on a relevant contemporary issue. However, the Tories' arguments did not die out with Swift's withdrawal from political pamphleteering, and their ideological position remained the same.

More than anything, the Tories feared that the Whigs would bring a kind of anarchy to the nation: not, of course, in the modern sense, but more in the sense of sudden changes in values without consultation. The Whigs seemed to be capable of forming alliances as and when it suited them and words like 'tradition' and 'landed gentry' carried no force or value for them. The effects would be far-reaching. The Tories believed that political authority should rest with those who were charged to hold it by virtue of their estate:

> In their view, only men of substantial property possessed the qualities necessary to sit in Parliament or to act as magistrates: namely, leisure, education, independence and a sense of duty and responsibility. The overwhelming majority of subjects lacked all of these qualities, while even merchants and financiers were too preoccupied with the business of making money to have sufficient leisure to devote to public responsibilities.[15]

The argument was convenient for the landed gentry, but it was hardly likely to win the support of those who aspired to public office and yet did not have sufficient acreage to allow them to reach it.

Moreover, the Tories feared that the admission of others into the network of power would involve a change of values: they guessed, probably correctly, that the Whigs would be more free with money in order to secure election and that bribery, used in order to gain power, would become a political rule. Walpole did not disappoint them in their fears; he also protected those who allied themselves to him and he used the public purse for private ends.[16] One consequence of this could be the gradual erosion of the power of the gentry and their ally, the monarch.

The Tories looked upon the Whigs with contempt because, not only were they professional politicians, stockjobbers and of low breeding, but also because they were anti-nationalistic and anti-monarchy. The appeal in so many Tory tracts is to a nationalism that is ill-defined but is nevertheless emotional and is connected with a desire to be superior to the rest of Europe - to such an extent as to be isolationist. The parody of the Tory squire written by Addison may not be so far from a true portrait in that there is in it an underlying naive assumption that trading meant draining the nation's wealth rather than enhancing it. But this is not to denigrate the attempt by the Tories to establish an ideology for their party; they had intelligent, politically astute men working for them and their members were determined to attack Walpole's power-base and expose it for what it was, crude and materialistic. Their failure was a result of the narrowness of the appeal rather than of political ineptitude: after all, not all Tories were like Sir Roger.

Many were more like Bolingbroke: and that, in turn, is to say clever but outdated; it is also to say distant and removed. Bolingbroke believed that liberty was being eroded and that it could only be preserved by taking the state back to the principles upon which it was founded:

> This Change, or Renewal of the State, hath been sometimes wrought by external Causes, as it happened at Rome, upon the Invasion of the Gauls. The Romans had departed from their ancient Observances. The Ceremonies of Religion and the Laws of Justice were neglected by them.

An Enemy whom they despised and provoked, conquered them. The Impression made by this dreadful Calamity brought them back to their first Institutions and to their primitive Spirit. They sprang up from this second Original, as Livy calls it, with new Vigour, and rose to greater Fame, Power and Dignity than ever.[17]

This belief in the power of tradition - reinforced by an intellectual, historical parallel - is typical of Bolingbroke and of the Tory philosophers in general. The return to tradition contains the answer to the threat which Walpole posed; after all, the Tories represented all that was best in England:

> But whatever Ministers may govern, whatever Factions may arise, let the Friends of Liberty lay aside the groundless Distinctions, which are employed to amuse and betray them; let them continue to coalite; let them hold fast their Integrity, and support with Spirit and Perseverance the Cause of their Country, and they will confine the good, reclaim the bad, vanquish the incorrigible, and make the British Constitution triumph, even over Corruption.[18]

Bolingbroke, like Swift before him, was concerned about the lack of consistency that characterised the new regime. Only through consistency could liberty and the 'true spirit' of Britain be preserved. Swift had maintained that the English Gentry should keep a firm grip on the Old Principles in Church and State and so preserve the standard. The Whigs were too much of a hotch-potch of Dissenters, Presbyterians and Atheists and were thus too disparate in nature to be the proper governing party of England:

> On the other side; I take a State to be truly in Danger, both as to its Religion and Government, when a Set of ambitious Politicians, bred up in a Hatred to the Constitution, and a Contempt for all Religion, are forced upon exerting these Qualities in order to keep or encrease their Power, by widening their Bottom, and taking in (like Mahomet) some Principles from every Party that is in any way discontented at the present Faith and Settlement; which was manifestly our Case. Upon this Occasion, I remember to have asked some considerable Whigs, whether it did not bring a Disreputation upon their Body, to have the whole Herd of Presbyterians, Independents, Atheists, Anabaptists, Deists, Quakers and Socinians, openly and universally Listed under their Banners? They answered, That all this was absolutely necessary, in order to make a Ballance against the Tories; and all little enough: For indeed, it was as much as they could possibly do, although assisted with the absolute Power of disposing every Employment, while the Bulk of English Gentry kept firm to their old Principles in Church and State.

> But, notwithstanding whatever I have hitherto said, I am informed, several among the Whigs continue still so refractory, that they will hardly allow the Heads of their Party to have entertained any Designs of ruining the Constitution; or that they would have endeavoured it, if they

had continued in Power. I beg their Pardon if I have discovered a Secret; but who could imagine they ever intended it should be One, after those Overt-Acts with which they thought fit to conclude their Farce? But perhaps they now find it convenient to deny vigorously; that the Question may remain; Why was the old Ministry changed? Which they urge on without ceasing, as if no Occasion in the least had been given; but that all were owing to the Insinuations of crafty Men, practising upon the Weakness of an easy Prince. I shall therefore offer, among a hundred, one Reason for this Change, which I think would justify any Monarch who ever reigned, for the like Proceeding.[19]

A Whig might argue that his party was therefore more representative of the nation and more fit to govern it, but the ideological position of the Tories remained unshakeable even though their power was being removed from them. They continued to maintain that certain people were naturally endowed with the ability to govern and they were charged with upholding standards which were associated with the protection of the land. The politician should be a landowner, removed from the world of the court and thus better able to be close to 'his' people and so make them happy:

> Are you not Lord of these Arcadian Plains? Where, like the Substitute of Heav'nly Power, You dole the Blessings you from thence receive, And make a People, by your Bounty, happy. Yet not more blest by Bounty, than Example: Your Life has taught those Virtues, you reward. And is not his a Cause for general Joy?[20]

In conclusion, one may argue that the fears of the Tories stemmed from one or more of the arguments outlined above; England's pastoral innocence, although a part of a myth, was recreated by many in order to try and show exactly what the Whigs were doing to the land and how the moral base that had been established in the country was being swept away by the new philosophy of the town and of Walpole. Walpole was *the* threat. Having survived a Tory onslaught upon him in 1712, when he was imprisoned, he emerged as the man who could manipulate the public purse for his own ends and as the man who was typical of the new age of corruption. The world may be full of merchants, but they were so close to stockjobbers in character as to make the Tories feel uncomfortable in their presence. Jobbers, too, were close to a world which the Tories failed to understand, that of ledgers and bookkeeping. The 'business of government' was taking over from the tradition of government: simplicity, patriotism and, above all, honesty, were disappearing

NOTES

1. Geoffrey Holmes, 'The achievement of stability,' in *The Whig Ascendancy*, edited by John Cannon (London, 1981), p.18.

2. See W. A. Speck, *Stability and Strife, England 1714-1760* (London, 1977), pp. 7-21 *passim*.

3. Alexander Pope, *The First Epistle of the First Book of Horace Imitated*, in *Poems*, edited by John Butt (London, 1963), p. 628.

4. idem., *Epistle to Bathurst*, ibid., p. 574.

5. Trenchard and Gordan, *Cato's Letters*, 4 vols. (London, 1724), I, p. 17.

6. John Gay, *Trivia*, pt III, ll.55-62, in *Poetry and Prose*, edited by Vinton A. Dearing, 2 vols. (Oxford, 1974), pp. 161/2.

7. idem., *Fables,1738, Fable IX: To a Modern Politician,*, ll. 1-16, ibid., pp. 410-411.

8. Richard Steele, *The Spectator*, no. 174, 19 Sept.1711, in *Selections from The Tatler and The Spectator*, edited by Angus Ross (Harmondsworth, 1982), p.448.

9. idem., ibid., p.450.

10. idem.,*The Theatre, 1720*, edited by John Loftis (Oxford, 1962), p. 12.

11. Joseph Addison, *The Freeholder*, no. 22, 5 Mar.1716, in *The Freeholder*, edited by James Leheny (Oxford, 1979), p. 133.

12. idem., ibid., no. 48, 4 Jun.1716, p. 245.

13. Edward A. and Lillian D. Bloom, *Joseph Addison's Sociable Animal*, (Brown University Press, Providence, 1971), pp .26-7.

14. Quoted by J. C. Beasley, 'Portraits of a Monster: Robert Walpole and Early English Prose Fiction', in *Eighteenth-Century Studies*, no 4, 1981, pp. 413-4.

15. H. T. Dickinson, *Liberty and Property. Political Ideology in Eighteenth-Century Britain*, (London, 1977), p. 51.

16. See, for example, H. T. Dickinson, *Walpole and the Whig Supremacy*, (London, 1973), pp. 78 & 142.

17. Bolingbroke (Henry St John), *Remarks on the History of England*, in *Historical Writings*, edited by Isaac Kramnick (Chicago, 1972), p. 165.

18. idem., *A Dissertation Upon Parties*, letter XIX in *Works*, 4 vols., (London, 1841), II, p. 171.

19. Jonathan Swift. *The Examiner*, no. 29, 22 Feb.1710 in *The Examiner and Other Pieces Written in 1710-11*, edited by Herbert Davis (Oxford, 1941), pp. 92-3. (*Complete Prose*, 14 vols., Oxford, 1939-59, vol. III).

20. Colley Cibber, *Love in a Riddle,*, 1729 in *Classical Subjects II: Pastoral and Comedy,*. edited by Walter Howard Rubsamen (New York, 1974), p. 2.

CHAPTER 2

Swift

Swift is always around the next corner; he is forever waiting to challenge our assumptions and firmly-held beliefs; our positions of strength are made to seem weak when faced with the onslaught of argument, irony and sheer determined self-righteousness which Swift employs when called upon to perform an ideological battle. All writers on Swift are convinced that they have discovered something new about him: the shifting force of language removes him from a seemingly fixed position and places him in another. Swift can be seen to be on the reader's 'side' one moment - provided that the struggle is seen as a 'two-sided' affair - but he is capable of pulling the ground away by linguistic manoeuvres which suggest that he was all the time manipulating a response in order to destroy it. That is why there will be no end to writing about Swift, and it should also be the reason why there will be few claims to categorize him either: "If the reader is entering into a discourse with the writer, the former had better beware, for his travelling companion is not a static being: he is, like language itself, moving onward, acting and performing".[1]

If one is aware of the pitfalls in writing about Swift, then several issues have to be confronted. Is it possible to limit the discussion to a certain number of apparently consistently argued documents in order to arrive at definite conclusions? If so, does this mean that a distortion of the man and his writings will arise? Should one, then, attempt to complete a 'review' of Swift's career, balancing and checking arguments against the shifting sands of language and against the gradual realisation of one's own probable inadequacy to perform any absolute judgement upon the text? Even by entitling a chapter 'Swift', a writer should be aware that it cannot be a total evaluation: it must be a gathering-together of certain information in order to clarify a particular position. This present chapter will confine itself to Swift's earlier political prose in an attempt to define more precisely the nature of the interests of the 'country' community; in doing so it links with the previous general examination of the issue, and stresses too that the Whig cause, far from being lost, was only just beginning.

1. Politics

In 1710 the Whig party seemed to be in a state of decline. The Harley ministry, although receiving the satiric attentions of Steele, was in a strong position and it quickly enlisted the support of Swift to bolster its position. Swift, seeing that the Tories would be more likely to support his own views with regard to the Church, set about defending the ideological position of the Tories and vindicating their political policies from this standpoint. Any brief description of the ideology must, of necesssity, fall short of adequacy, but Swift's position in the early pamphlets and essays remained consistent with the kind of aristocratic ideal that was prevalent after 1688; he saw too that the 'New Whiggery' rode counter to his own proposals, so he allied himself firmly to the Tory camp which seemed to offer so much more in both ideological and practical terms.

The assumption behind *The Examiner*, written 1710-11, is that 'England' must be preserved; it must recognise that tradesmen, although potentially honest people, are but new upon the scene of government and unfit - indeed, unable - to control the country. 'England' should not be a land of shifting ideologies and loyalties, but a steadfast country of character and integrity. All reasonable men must recognise this, and the voice of the reasonable man must prevail against that of narrowness or selfishness:

> It is Practice I have generally followed, to converse in equal Freedom with the deserving Men of both Parties; and it was never without some Contempt, that I have observed Persons wholly out of Employment, affect to do otherwise: I doubted whether any Man could owe so much to the Side he was of, altho' he were retained by it; but without some great point of Interest, either in Possession or Prospect, I thought it was the Mark of a low and narrow Spirit. It is hard, that for some Weeks past, I have been forced, in my own Defence, to follow a Proceeding that have so much condemned in others. But several of my Acquaintance, among the declining Party, are grown so insufferably Peevish and Splenatick, profess such violent Apprehensions for the Publick, and represent the State of Things in such formidable Ideas, that I find myself disposed to share in their Afflictions, although I know them to be groundless and imaginary; or, which is worse, purely affected. To offer them Comfort one by one, would be not only an endless, but a disobliging Task. Some of them, I am convinced, would be less melancholy, if there were more Occasion. I shall therefore, instead of hearkening to further Complaints, employ some Part of this Paper for the future, in letting such men see, that their natural or acquired Fears are ill-grounded, and their artificial ones as ill-intended. That all our present Inconveniences are the Consequence of the very Counsels they so much admire, which would still have encreased, if those had continued: And that neither our Constitution in Church or State, could probably have been long preserved, without such Methods as have been already taken. (no. 13; 2 Nov.1710)[2]

In these, the opening paragraphs of Swift's contribution to the journal, an appropriate stance is adopted in which the author is represented as open-minded and partisan at the same time. The trick is one of rhetoric, as Swift moves from a general observation on mankind at the end of the first paragraph, to a concern with the nature of the Opposition who 'are grown so insufferably Peevish and Splenatick'; the central intelligent 'I' of the argument is retained. These paragraphs are significant since they perform all this and more, for the reader is drawn into the argument and also into the nature of the argument: that is, he believes in Swift, the author, and in doing so he must more readily accept the incipient judgement upon the Opposition. The reader must be convinced by the patriotic nature of the argument that will follow, and the purpose of the last sentence is to introduce the Constitution, the State and the Church in order to envelop their interests with the concerns of the Tory party. If the Harley ministry can be seen to be active in the support of these, and the Whigs active in their destruction, then Swift's rhetoric will have achieved its aim. The aim is the representation of the Tory party as the traditional ruling party of England and also the ideal party to rule since its ideological framework is the structure to which the Englishman may relate and which should be preserved. The symbol of all these is the Monarch.

The references to the Queen are made, in general, not to glorify one person but to use her as a representative of the glorious institution, the alternative to which is too awful to contemplate. Swift must announce himself as firmly opposed to a Commonwealth form of government: that would be pre-1688; it would be anarchistic and it would be dedicated to its own ends rather than to those of the nation at large. In general, the present system of government is good; Swift argues against all those things which the present government does *not* contain and by doing so shifts them onto the Opposition:

> The Evils we must fence against are, on the one side Fanaticism and Infidelity in Religion; and Anarchy, under the name of a Commonwealth, in Government... (no.15; 16 Nov.1710)[2]

In the following extract, Swift claims to overhear that the Tories wish to introduce the country to 'Popery, Arbitrary Power and the Pretender':

> I defy our Adversaries to produce one single Reason for suspecting such Designs in the Persons now at the Helm; whereas I can upon Demand produce twenty to show that some late men had strong Views towards a *Commonwealth*, and the Alteration of the Church... (no.25: 25 Jan.1711)[2]

By the following April, Swift was declaring that 'they (the Whigs) prefer a Commonwealth before a Monarchy'. The Whigs will, therefore, overthrow much of what is 'Common Sense', since Swift remains the reasonable man, willing to introduce concrete evidence to support his case. The Whigs have no veneration for the crowned heads, nor do they see any necessity for a National Faith. Here, a transference takes place: the 'crowned head' becomes 'representative of all that is good in the State' and, indeed, is implicit in the contradistinction of 'Queen' and 'Commonwealth'. This idea may be approached by examining a quotation from Bolingbroke. In a *Letter to the Examiner*, he writes on the attempts by the Whigs to lower the stature of the monarch:

> Notwithstanding all the Pains which have been taken to lessen her Character in the World, by the Wits of the *Kit-Kat* and the sages of the *Cellar*;

mankind remains convinc'd that a Queen possess'd of all the Virtues requisite to bless a Nation, or to make a private Family Happy, sits on the Throne.[3]

The metonymy, although not complete here, moves forcefully onwards as Bolingbroke states that the Queen is 'the Nation', the protector and the microcosm of all that is immediately recognisable as good. The difference between the two parties is the difference between self-love and social, for, according to Swift, they are not the same. In Swift, the Whig party is one which deals solely with money; the Tories deal with the principles and interests of a Nation. If the desire for money is not immoral in itself, it becomes so when the implications of such a view are taken into account, for it suggests shiftiness and easy alliances instead of steadfastness and cohesion. But Swift refuses to simplify matters in exactly this manner; the opposing parties may be enemies now, but they emerged from the same historical circumstances and only recently have the Whigs become the opposition to the tradition and reason of the Tories. The Whigs came from an honest institution but they appear to have changed:

> Some Time after the Revolution, the Distinction of High and Low-Church came in; which was raised by the Dissenters, in order to break the Church Party, by dividing the Members into High and Low; and the Opinion raised, That the High joined with the Papists, inclined the Low to fall in with the Dissenters.

> And here I shall take Leave to produce some Principles, which in the several Periods of the late Reign, served to denote a Man of one or the other Party. To be against a Standing Army in Time of Peace, was all High-Church, Tory and Tantivy. To differ from a Majority of Bishops was the same. To raise the Prerogative above Law for serving a Turn, was Low-Church and Whig. The Opinion of the Majority in the House of Commons, especially of the Country-Party or Landed Interest, was High-flying and rank Tory. To exalt the King's Supremacy beyond all Precedent, was Low-Church, Whiggish and Moderate. To make the least Doubt of the pretended Prince being Supposititious and a Tyler's Son, was, in their Phrase, Top and Top-gallant, and perfect Jacobitism. To resume the most exorbitant Grants that were ever given to a Set of profligate Favourites, and apply them to the Publick, was the very Quintescence of Toryism; notwithstanding those Grants were known to be acquitten, by sacrificing the Honour and the Wealth of England. (no. 43; 31 May 1711)[2]

The tone of the passage is interesting, for it is closely bound up with the rhetoric and the intention. Under the freedom of the Constitution, Swift argues, there was room for parties who could remain loyal to the interests of the nation, yet it seemed that the Tories sacrificed 'the Honour and Wealth of *England*'. Swift is the objective historian, eager to uncover the facts and eager to share those facts with his readers even if they appear to reveal his party in a bad light. But by mentioning the history of the parties, Swift can, by way of contrast, introduce the present-day concerns of each party and show that the Whigs are now less concerned with the nation than with their own selfish interests. In a sense, it does not matter that the Tories made mistakes in the past, for it is only the present to which his readers can relate and it is the reversal of the moral and political standards upon which Swift concentrates in order to sharpen his focus upon the contemporary state of the parties and of the nation.

The Whigs have changed; they have become men of few principles, intent upon political opportunism for financial gain:

> Since that Time, the Bulk of the Whigs appeareth rather to be linked to a certain Set of Persons, than any certain Set of Principles: so that if I were to define a Member of the Party, I would say, he was one who believed in the late Ministry. And therefore, whatever I have affirmed of Whigs in any of these Papers, or objected against them, ought to be understood either of those who were Partisans of the late Men in Power, and Privy to their Designs; or such who joined with them, from a Hatred to our Monarchy and Church; as Unbelievers and Dissenters of all Sizes: or Men in Office, who had been guilty of much Corruption, and dreaded a Change; which would not only put a Stop to further Abuses for the Future, but might perhaps introduce Examinations of what was past: or those who had been too highly obliged, to quit their Supporters with any common Decency. Or lastly, the Money-Traders, who could never hope to make their Markets so well of Praemiums and Exorbitant Interest and high Remittances, by any other Administration...

> Under these Heads, may be reduced the whole Body of those whom I have all along understood for Whigs. For I do not include within this Number, any of those, who have been misled by Ignorance, or seduced by plausible Pretences, to think better of that Sort of Men than they deserve, and to apprehend mighty Dangers from their Disgrace. Because, I believe, the greatest Part of such well-meaning People, are now thoroughly converted. (no.43; 31 May 1711)[2]

Swift asserts that the past is not actually irrelevant, but an examination of it may be an evasion of contemporary corruption, an avoidance of the truth rather than a revelation of the whole of it. The Whigs believe in what the 'late Ministry' contained within it; they pursued no principle and sought nothing but power and money. The Monarch, and therefore, the Nation, far from being protected by the Whigs was actually in danger of being destroyed by them. The Whigs were ideologically resourceless.

At this point, it is worth pausing in order to consider the nature of *The Examiner* and the political circumstances which caused its birth. These facts help to explain Swift's invective in this and other pamphlets and political tracts.

Swift had agreed to write for *The Examiner* after a request from Harley who was attempting to consolidate the position of the Tory party. The Tories had clearly gained the upper hand during the October elections; Harley however was concerned to show the electorate that he was not prepared to withdraw completely from the War of the Spanish Succession and that England should have peace, but not at any price. Although the Tory press (and *The Examiner* in particular) argued that England had footed most of the bill for the war while gaining least from it, Harley's policy was not to withdraw unilaterally from the war without the compensation of dignity. Nor did he seem to regard the Whig/Tory division as being an absolute one, for Whigs were incorporated into his new government. But there was no sense in which the Tory journals could be in any way objective. The arguments had to be subtle enough to persuade the reader that the previous Ministry had been unfit to govern without the invective becoming so vitriolic as to persuade the reader that the present administration was simply fighting from the opposite stance merely for the sake of it. Swift's position now becomes an interesting one. There is no doubt that, previous to 1709/1710, he had decidedly Whiggish inclinations: he had written for *The Tatler* and he had met Addison and Steele who had admired the *Bickerstaff Papers*. Swift was 'a nominal Whig, at least as far as his personal associations were concerned'[4.] Two factors begin to emerge which changed Swift into a 'nominal Tory'. First, Swift's major concern was to gain as much as he could for the advancement of the Church of Ireland and it was becoming clear that a ministry controlled by Harley would be more supportive than any Whig-dominated government. Secondly, a new breed of Whig appeared to be emerging: a 'Town' Whig, more concerned with the laws of the market place than with those of the country. Swift's sympathies were with a 'Country' party - whether called 'Tory' or 'Old Whig' - and he rejected the ideas of New Whiggery. The Whig administration had failed Swift in that he had not gained any personal preferments from it, nor had he gained anything for the Irish Church. Swift began to realise that the New Whigs did not see things the way he did; they were not landed gentry and so did not share the ideals of that class. Swift had to ask himself, and then communicate, what the exact principles were of this new breed.

Swift was the ideal man for Harley to employ for his cause. Swift had the mastery of style and fluency of language that was required to manipulate public opinion. He would enjoy the politics of the challenge in which he was bound up. The arguments that Swift put forward in *The Examiner* turn upon the fact that there were once two reasonable parties, and that it is not reasonableness that has changed, but the ideology of one of the parties involved. This is Swift's theme in the last part of the essay of May 31, 1711:

> Whoever formerly professed himself to approve the Revolution, to be against the Pretender, to justify the Succession in the House of Hanover, to think the British Monarchy not absolute, but limited by Laws, which the Executive Power could not dispense with; and to allow an Indulgence to scrupulous Consciences; such a Man was content to be called a 'Whig'. On the other side, whoever asserted the QUEEN's Hereditary Right; that the Persons of Princes were Sacred; their lawful Authority not to be resisted on any

Pretence; not even their Usurpations, without the most extreme Necessity: that, Breaches in the Succession were highly dangerous; that, Schism was a great Evil, both in itself and its Consequences; that, the Ruin of the Church would probably be attended with that of the State; that, no Power should be trusted with those who are not of the established Religion, such a Man was usually called a Tory. Now, although the Opinions of both these are very consistent, and I really think are maintained at present by a great Majority of the Kingdom; yet, according as Men apprehend the Danger greater, either from the Pretender and his Party, or from the Violence and Cunning of other Enemies to the Constitution; so, their common Discourses and Reasonings turn either to the first or second Set of these Opinions I have mentioned; and are consequently styled either Whigs or Tories. Which is, as if two Brothers apprehended their House would be set upon, but disagreed about the Place from whence they thought the Robbers would come; and therefore would go on different Sides to defend it; they must needs weaken and expose themselves by such a Separation; and so did we, only our Case was worse: For in order to keep off a weak, remote Enemy, from whom we could not suddenly apprehend any Danger, we took a nearer and a stronger one into the House. I make no Comparison at all between the two Enemies: Popery and Slavery are without doubt the greatest and most dreadful of any; buy I may venture to affirm, that the Fear of these, have not, at least since the Revolution, been so close and pressing upon us, as that from another Faction; excepting only one short Period, when the Leaders of that very Faction, invited the abdicating King to return; of which I have formerly taken Notice.

Having thus declared what Sort of Persons I have always meant, under the Denomination of Whigs, it will be easy to shew whom I understand by Tories. Such whose Principles in Church and State, are what I have above related; whose Actions are derived from thence, and who have no Attachment to any Set of Ministers, further than as these are Friends to the Constitution in all its Parts; but will do their utmost to save their Prince and Country whoever be at the Helm. (no. 43; 31 May 1711)[2]

Swift argues that it is not the Tories who have weakened the nation, but the Whigs. They have allowed faction, encouraged England's natural enemies, and by doing so they have opened up a schism in political life that is clearly to the detriment of the nation. Swift's nationalistic cause is apparent, and it is related to the ideology of the ruling party: Harley had to convince the nation that peace would mean prosperity for many but that continuation of the war would mean prosperity for only a few. Swift avoids outright jingoism, but he enters into a dialogue, the outcome of which is predetermined and which is designed to clarify the Tory cause. The metaphor of the Brothers, Biblical in its implications, is a familiar one to readers of Swift, and it is one which is not only concerned with the broad aspects of Church and State, nor is he content to argue on a purely political level. The metaphor is deliberately homely in order to emphasise the domestic security and harmony that one brother offers and the anarchy and disruption offered by the other. Peace and security in the home is linked with peace and security in the nation and the associated opposites of faction, schism and war are shown as a threat to both. The Whigs, quite simply, are the ones who encourage faction within the nation and even within the boundaries of their own party.

If Swift was to claim that the character of the Whig party had changed, and was therefore no longer worthy of support, generalisations about the character of the party and metaphors relating to the implications of its ideology could only go so far. The question would continue to arise about the necessity of proving the case on more specific grounds and of the nature of the veracity of the evidence. Swift tackles these problems by putting forward arguments that are firmly rooted in recent history and of which any intelligent reader would be aware, while reserving his wrath for a representative of the New Whig cause - Wharton - in order to blacken further the name of the party. The issue of *The Examiner* of November 2, 1710 tackles those questions. It is one of the most significant since Swift is establishing himself as the fair-minded commentator:

> It is odd, that among a free trading People, as we call ourselves, there should so many be found to close in with those Counsels, who have been ever averse from all Overtures towards Peace. But yet there is no great Mystery in the Matter. Let any man observe the Equipage in this Town; he shall find the greater Number of those who make a Figure, to be a Species of Men quite different from any that were ever known before the Revolution; consisting either of Generals and Colonels, or of such whose whole Fortunes lie in Funds and Stocks: so that Power, which, according to the old Maxim, was used to follow Land, is now gone over to Money; and the Country Gentleman is in the Condition of a young Heir, out of whose Estate a Scrivener receives half the Rents for Interest, and hath a Mortgage on the Whole; and is therefore always ready to feed his Vices and Extravagancies while there is any Thing left. So that if the War continue some Years longer, a Land Man will be little better than a Farmer at a rack Rent, to the Army, and to the publick Funds. (no. 13; 2 Nov. 1710).[2]

Within this paragraph are many of the arguments that Swift was to develop in later issues of the journal. The emphasis at first is on England, which is and which must continue to be a 'free trading' nation and whose people should be free to continue their vocation of trading. But the ordinary man, set apart from those who 'make a Figure' in the town, is threatened by the 'Figure', for his motives are not trade for the protection and advancement of the State, but trade for self-aggrandisement; this may mean robbing the State's coffers in order to achieve his objectives. The principles which governed England before the Revolution are being challenged and eroded by a new breed who ignore tradition - and therefore all that is valuable - and exploit one of the main principles of trading (acquisition of money) for their own ends. Swift's argument turns upon several contrasts: first, the historical one of pre- and post- 1688; secondly, the value-based one of traditional as opposed to modern and lastly the contemporary, observable phenomenon of the new breed versus the landed gentry. Each of these has its corresponding values and Swift makes the reader judge one against another. Swift pushes his audience into seeing that the inevitable consequence of allowing power to this 'Species of Men' would be the dissolution of observably good, traditional landed interests, to be replaced by an unknown factor, but one which could be demonstrated to be bad. If money is earned without merit, the consequences will be the destruction of all national values.

He continues by arguing that the War of the Spanish Succession has been prolonged for only one reason: the increase in taxes has devalued the worth of England, and only one class of men has gained:

> By this means the Wealth of the Nation, that used to be reckoned by the Value of Land, is now computed by the Rise and Fall of Stocks: And although the Foundation of Credit be still the same, and upon a Bottom that can never be shaken; and although all Interest be duly paid by the Publick, yet through the Contrivance and Cunning of *Stock-Jobbers*, there hath been brought in such a Complication of Knavery and Couzenage, such a Mystery of Iniquity, and such an unintelligible Jargon of Terms to involve it in, as were never known in any other Age or Country of the World. (no.13; 2 Nov. 1710)[2]

The ordinary man, the honest trader, is not to blame, for he is in the hands of a minority of men who hold different values: those of jobbing. The closed world of the stock market stands in contrast to the openness of the Country. The social, political and moral implications are evident: what would be the value of the nation if such men were to control it; how could one even communicate with such people?

After having allied himself to the Tory cause, Swift found he could extend his arguments into different areas. Harley was determined to withdraw from the war, and it was Swift's task to justify the withdrawal as the time for it came closer. So, from a position which had overtones of reasonableness and objectivity, Swift moved further towards a hard-line form of argument. In 1711, Swift published *The Conduct of the Allies*, an open denunciation of England's war leader, Marlborough, and of the previous Whig administration. There was no room in the document for an historical perspective, nor could Swift devote any time to nice distinctions between the Old and the New Whigs. The arguments are polemical in the sense that they are confined to the present issue usually without deviation and often expressed in poignant, direct language:

> The great Traders in Mony were wholly devoted to the Whigs, who had first raised them. The Army, the Court, and the Treasury continued under the old Despotick Administration: The Whigs were received into Employment, left to manage the Parliament, cry down the Landed Interest, and worry the Church. Mean time, our Allies, who were not ignorant, that all this artificial Structure had no true Foundation in the Hearts of the

People, resolved to make their best use of it, as long as it should last. And the General's Credit being raised to a great height at home, by our success in Flanders, the Dutch began their gradual Impositions; lessening their Quotas, breaking their Stipulations, Garrisoning the Towns we took for them, without supplying their Troops; with many other Infringements: All which we were forced to submit to because the General was made easie; because the Monied Men at home were fond of the War; because the Whigs were not yet firmly settled; and because that exorbitant degree of Power, which was built upon a supposed Necessity of employing particular Persons, would go off in a Peace. It is needless to add, that the Emperor, and other Princes, followed the Example of the Dutch, and succeeded as well, for the same Reasons.

I have here imputed the Continuance of the War to the mutual Indulgence between our General and Allies, wherein they both so well found their Accounts; to the Fears of the Mony-changers, lest their Tables should be overthrown; to the Designs of the Whigs, who apprehended the Loss of their Credit and Employments in a Peace; and to those at home, who held their immoderate Engrossments of Power and Favour, by no other Tenure, than their own Presumption upon the Necessity of Affairs. The Truth of this will appear indisputable, by considering with what Unanimity and Concert these several Parties acted towards that great End. (pp.42-43).[5]

The themes that were introduced in *The Examiner* are here pursued with vigour: the 'Landed Interest' and the 'Church' had been subject to a campaign of subordination by the Whigs, who had been determined to ally themselves to a cause which was anti-nationalistic. It was also a drain on the resources of the state and a benefit only to those who were both 'Monied' and who were 'at home': the attack, then, is on those who were successful in the Stock Market. Swift is careful to structure his argument, so that it becomes an attack upon a certain minority while at the same time it can be seen as a defence of the ordinary, decent citizen and of traditional civilised values. Swift does not call into question the bravery of the men who are called upon to fight battles, nor does he underestimate the insight of 'the People' into the real nature of the doctrines which are being forced upon them. Instead, he writes of them as victims of a conspiracy of a minority of politicians - the 'General' and the 'Monied Men' - whose self-interests revolved around a continuation of the war. Swift's prolonged argument in *The Examiner* which centred around the historical facts and ideological struggles between the different parties are here narrowed down to focus upon a particular contemporary concern. Swift has already made his general point, and he now moves onto the case in question. He never loses sight of the power position, for he writes of the 'Designs of the Whigs' and that 'immoderate Engrossments of Power and Favour' as reminders of what the Whigs' position really is. The specific example of the War is used to indicate how they would achieve their aims.

24

Swift's language is persuasive and the majority of his readers would relate to it, while it is clearly designed to illustrate the enormity of the consequences of prolonging the war. Not only will 'Monied Men' gain control of England, but they may also sell the Island and its people:

> Now, to give the most ignorant Reader some Idea of our present Circumstances, without troubling him or my self with Computations in form: Every body knows, that our Land and Malt Tax amount annually to about Two Millions and an half. All other branches of the Revenue are mortgaged to pay Interest, for what we have already borrowed. The yearly Charge of the War is usually about Six Millions; to make up which Sum, we are forced to take up, on the Credit of new Funds, about Three Millions and an half. This last Year the computed Charge of the War came to above a Million more, than all the Funds the Parliament could contrive would pay Interest for; and so we have been forced to divide a Deficiency of Twelve hundred thousand Pounds among the several Branches of our Expence. This is a Demonstration, that if the War lasts another Campaign, it will be impossible to find Funds for supplying it, without mortgaging the Malt Tax, or by some other Method equally desperate.

> If the Peace be made this Winter, we are then to consider, what Circumstances we shall be in towards paying a Debt of about Fifty Millions, which is a fourth Part of the Purchase of the whole Island, if it were to be Sold. (p.54).[5]

The Whigs are clearly interested in nothing but Money, while Swift's emphasis on money is designed to have the opposite effect: that is, although money is vital to the economy of the nation, the war is a plot through which the nation's resources are channelled into providing sustenance for one group. Moreover, the computation of the figures would suggest that England is so much in debt that one solution to the problem would be to sell a substantial proportion of the island. The rhetorical trick that Swift employs is a typical device: he introduces figures and he draws what on the surface is a reasonable conclusion, but which on close examination turns out to be outrageous. By the time the reader has untangled the inconsistencies in the argument, the damage has been done, for implanted in his mind is the suggestion that the basis for England's existence is under threat. Many readers, too, might neglect to analyse the passage in close detail, and this is one way in which the argument works. Swift is hoping, not for close analysis, but for a generally effective argument based on a specific instance, the outcome of which would be sympathy for Tory policy. The purpose, as a perceptive contemporary of Swift observed, is to deceive.[6]

It is a mistake to dismiss *The Conduct of the Allies* as mere deceit, for its flourishes are provoking, immediate and entertaining. They indicate too how Swift managed his prose in order to communicate to as wide an audience as possible:

> It is the Folly of too many, to mistake the Echo of a *London* Coffee-House for the Voice of the Kingdom. The City Coffee-Houses have been for some

25

years filled with People, whose Fortunes depend upon the *Bank, East India,* or some other Stock: Every new Fund to these, is like a new Mortgage to an Usurer, whose Compassion for a young Heir is exactly the same with that of a Stockjobber to the Landed Gentry. (p.53).[5]

The images are immediate and striking and relate to everyday experience, while the observant reader would have no trouble in discovering the people to whom Swift refers. If the intention is to deceive, then the deceit is achieved by forcing the reader to recognise the concrete world around him for what it signifies and then forcing him to recognise that the significance extends into political ideology from which there is no escape and inside which everyone is enveloped. Swift's major theme is survival; he insists that one party should be supreme in order to safe-guard the nation.

From these observations on the nature of contemporary politics emerges a set of principles to which any minister must adhere and which define the nature of good government. In the essay *Some Free Thoughts upon the present State of Affairs*, Swift outlines these principles, many of which read as prophecies on the nature of the arguments which were to arise with the advent of Walpole onto the political scene:

I know no Station of Life, where Virtues of all Kinds are more highly necessary, and where the want of any is so quickly or universally felt. A great Minister has no Virtue for which the Publick may not be the better, nor any Vice by which the Publick may not be a Sufferer..... It is not always sufficient for the Person at the Helm, that he is disinterested in his Nature, free from any Tincture of Avarice or Corruption, that he hath great naturall and acquired Abilities, that he loves his Prince and Country, and the Constitution in Church and State. (p.80).[7]

Here, the argument has moved completely away from the particular. Swift's concern in the essay is to establish the general principles that must underlie the taking of office. The design behind Swift's argument is the re-establishment of the moral nature of public office, but his arguments have a curiously outmoded aspect to them; only a few years afterwards Walpole was skilfully manoeuvring himself away from direct involvement with the South Sea Bubble affair, while the charges of 'Avarice and Corruption' were soon to be levelled at the nature of government itself. Walpole transformed not only the nature of government, but also the nature of speaking and writing about government too, for writers after Swift were aware that words like 'great' or 'naturall and acquired Abilities' or even 'loves his Prince and Country' could only be used ironically. Walpole was to become 'Prime' Minister and it is this acquisition of personal wealth and power that Swift goes on to condemn:

... too great an affectation of Secrecy, is usually thought to be attended with those little Intrigues and Refinements which among the vulgar denominate a Man a great Politician, but among others is apt ... to acquire the Opinion of Cunning ... Neither indeed am I altogether convinced, that this Habit of

multiplying Secrets may not be carried on so far as to stop that Communi-
cation which is necessary in some degree among all who have any considerable Part in the management of Publick Affairs ... I suppose, when a
Building is to be erected, the Model may be the Contrivance only of one
Head; and it is sufficient that the under-workers be ordered to cut Stones
into certain Shapes, and place them in certain Positions; but the several
Master-Builders must have some general Knowledge of the Design, without
which they can give no Orders at all. (p.81)[7]

Once again, this may be read as a prophetic passage, for Walpole carved
out a new state from the politics of the old and he seemed to support the
state while at the same time he remained at the head of it. Whereas Swift
argues that no one person is above the State, and that no one person should
control the Constitution, Walpole's domestic policies ensured that he
followed precisely the opposite. There is, according to Swift, a common
enemy against which the Crown stands as a symbol of all that which
means unity and forbearance:

The generall Wishes and Desires of a People are perhaps more obvious to
other Men than to Ministers of State. There are two points of the highest
Importance, wherein a very great Majority of the Kingdom appear perfectly
hearty and unanimous. First, that the Church of England should be preserved
entire in all her Rights, Powers and Priviledges; All Doctrines relating to
Government discouraged which She condemns (sic); All Schisms, Sects and
Heresies discountenanced and kept under due Subjection, as far as consists
with the Lenity of our Constitution. Her open Enemies (among whom I
include at least Dissenters of all Denominations) not trusted with the
smallest Degree of Civil or Military Power; and Her secret Adversaries
under the Names of Whigs, Low-Church, Republicans, Moderation-Men,
and the like, receive no Marks of Favour from the Crown, but what they
should deserve by a sincere Reformation. (p.88)[7]

From the general argument arises the solution to the country's problems;
Swift has here departed from his stance in *The Examiner* and *The Conduct
of the Allies* for he is now openly contemptuous of every ideology which
does not conform to his own: in fact, he hardly recognises them as ideologies
at all. The invective is an inevitable consequence of the earlier pieces, for
Swift was never the 'reasonable man': he adopts a mask of reasonableness
in order to speak to the general reader, but his prose is designed to appeal
in the first instance to the landed gentlemen in order to confirm their
beliefs. After *The Conduct of the Allies* there was no doubt that Swift was
a Tory hireling - to his enemies - or, to his friends, a defender of tradition.
The seriousness of Swift's cause is perhaps best summed up by the
following quotation:

he became convinced that the whole complex of his old enemies - the Deists,
the Dissenters, the Grub Street hacks, and all the infinitely presumptuous
corrupters of religion and learning - had become too dangerous to laugh
away; they had grown in insolence and power to the point where, unless

vigorously checked, they could carry out what Swift saw as their all but avowed intention to destroy society.[8]

The pamphlets of 1710 - 1714 confirm that Swift's line had indeed hardened: he had become a writer whose intention was not simply to satirise certain harmless traits, for he regarded the New Whiggery as an ideological threat. Contemporary opinion was often less charitable however:

> One abandon'd Wretch, from a Despair of raising his Figure in his *Profession* among the men of Distinction of one Side, fraught with Revenge and the Gleanings of Politicks which he pick'd up in exchange for his constant Buffoonery, and rehearsing merry *Tales of a Tub*, can best tell what glorious Fruits he has reap'd from Apostacy, and brandishing his *Pen*, in Defence of his new Allies, against the D-ke of M-h: it must be a melancholy Reflection to one who has nothing in View but the present Charm of Profit, to drudge on in *Renegade's Pay* without Murmuring, and from being *Buffoon* of one *Party*, become the *Setting Dog* of Another.[9]

But Swift was a greater master of prose than the above quotation would suggest, and his satiric attacks upon individuals achieve a greater subtlety.

2. Satire

Swift had a job to do, and one which appeared simple on the surface: to support and justify the policies of the new administration while denigrating the policies of the previous one. But the task created other problems, for Swift was keenly aware of the passions that were aroused during the war; it would be no use simply attacking the moct men and supporting the landed, for then the accusation in the *Protestant Post-Boy*, quoted above, could be seen to be true. Instead, Swift turned his satiric talents towards the Whig policies and he isolated several individuals who might be viewed as representatives of the party. The individuals were so chosen as to represent foreign affairs, domestic policy and the new Whig position.

Any writer who chose to attack the Duke of Marlborough had to be careful, for the General had achieved notable victories and he appeared to confirm England's superiority in the military field and his victories up until the year 1709 were greeted with acclamation in the country. But Swift had little choice: if he wished to represent the last ministry as a failure he had to show that the people who were associated with it were failures also. Marlborough was a Whig and therefore the enemy, and since he was connected with the politicians of the day, he had to be attacked in a similar manner. However, Swift was too astute a political commentator to begin an attack by any overt blackening of character; instead, he indicated that histrionic attacks serve no purpose for they may convince the reader that an unreasonable campaign was being conducted against an individual. His discussion about recent persons and events will be conducted, he insists, in a reasonable manner.

> If a Stranger should hear these furious Out-cries of Ingratitude against our General, without knowing the Particulars, he would be apt to enquire where was his Tomb, or whether he were allowed Christian Burial? Not doubting but we had put him to some ignominious Death. Or, hath he been tried for his Life, and very narrowly escaped? Hath he been accused of high Crimes and Misdemeanours? Has the Prince seized on his Estate, and left him to starve? Hath he been hooted at as he passed the Streets, by an ungrateful Rabble? Have neither Honours, Offices nor Grants, been conferred on him or his Family? Have not he and they been barbarously stript of them all? Have not he and his Force been ill payed abroad?
>
> And doth not the Prince, by a scanty, limited Commission, hinder him from pursuing his own Methods in the Conduct of the War? Hath he no Power at all of disposing Commissions as he pleaseth? Is he not severely used by the Ministry of Parliament, who yearly call him to a strict account? Has the Senate ever thanked him for good Success; and have they not always publickly censured him for the least Miscarriage? Will the Accusers of the Nation join Issue upon any of these Particulars; or, tell us in what Point our damnable Sin of Ingratitude lies? (no.16. 23 Nov 1710)[2]

The General has been ignobly dealt with, for the arguments against him have been extreme and to little effect. He was carrying out government policy; he was an agent and representative of the government and, as such, he must be criticised on the same level as the government. The danger with extreme vitriol is that the acerbity leads merely to sympathy for the supposed target; Swift is more concerned to show that Marlborough must be a target because of his association with the government and because, like any politician, he could not be above the Constitution; his success should not guarantee timeless acclamation:

> Why, it is plain and clear; for while he is commanding abroad, the Queen dissolveth her Parliament, and changeth her Ministry at home: in which universal Calamity, no less than two Persons allied by Marriage to the General, have lost their Places. Whence came this wonderful Sympathy between the Civil and Military Powers? Will the Troops in Flanders refuse to fight, unless they can have their own Lord Keepers; their own Lord President of the Council; their own chief Governor of Ireland; and their own Parliament? In a Kingdom where the People are free, how came they to be so fond of having their Counsels under the Influence of their Army, or those that lead it? Who in all well-instituted States, had no Commerce with the Civil Power; further than to receive their Orders, and obey them without Reserve.
>
> When a General is not so popular, either in his Army, or at Home, as one might expect from a long Course of Success; it may perhaps be ascribed to his Wisdom, or perhaps to his Complection. The Possession of some one Quality, or a Defect in some other, will extremely damp the People's Favour, as well as the Love of the Soldiers. Besides, this is not an Age to

produce Favourites of the People, while we live under a Queen who engrosseth all our Love, and all our Veneration; and where the only Way for a great General or Minister to acquire any Degree of subordinate Affection from the Publick must be by all Marks of the most entire Submission and Respect to her sacred Person and Commands; otherwise, no pretence of great Services, either in the Field or the Cabinet, will be able to skreen them from universal Hatred. (no.16. 23 Nov.1710: p.20)[2]

The embodiment of the ideal of the State resides in the person of the Queen. No other person but the monarch could represent the State Order or the State Ideal and any man can find that his popularity can change, and find too that his own brand of politics is no longer required. Swift's objective here is to begin to de-mystify or de-mythologize Marlborough while preserving the symbol of the monarch. Swift will not undermine a national ideal; he will instead insist that circumstances can and must change. Marlborough's policies, although glorious at the time of their undertaking when a Whig administration was in power, must be viewed now from a clearer perspective. They were an attempt to ensure that a new system of power would prevail. No sensible race, which the English certainly are, would allow itself to adopt a *new* hero quite so easily.

The principle begins to emerge; but the character of the man himself remains, as does the possibility that new political leaders would clear away the memories of the past glory without acknowledging their gratitude. Swift reminds his readers that Marlborough has been well rewarded:

Those are the most valuable Rewards which are given to us from the certain Knowledge of the Donor, that they fit our Temper best: I shall therefore say nothing of the Title of Duke, or the Garter, which the Queen bestowed on the General in the beginning of her Reign: But I shall come to more substantial Instances, and mention nothing which hath not been given in the Face of the World. The Lands of Woodstock, may, I believe, be reckoned worth 40,000*l*.. On the building of Blenheim Castle, 100,000*l* have been already expended, although it be not yet near finished. The Grant of 5,000*l* per Annum on the Post Office is richly worth 100,000*l*. His Principality in Germany may be computed at 30,000*l*. Pictures, Jewels and other Gifts from foreign Princes 60,000*l*. The Grant at the Pall Mall, the Rangership, etc., for want of more certain Knowledge, may be called 10,000*l*. His own, and his Dutchess's, Employments at five years Value reckoning only the known AND AVOWED Salaries, are very low rated at 100,000*l*. Here is a good deal above half a Million of Money; and I dare say, those who are loudest with the Clamour of Ingratitude, will readily own, that all this is but a Trifle, in Comparison of what is untold. (no.16. 23 Nov. 1710: pp.21-2)[2]

The primary object is not to build up resentment against a rich man, but to inform the reader that sympathy for him would be misplaced: he was not misused, only abused. He may have been the victim of political expediency but he had no cause to blame anything other than politics or those who control policies. The people of the island are not ingrates who are content to ride with the tide of politics without looking over their shoulders: they reward their heroes properly, but they recognise too that policies may change for the better and that traditional values may re-assert themselves.

The above quotation also serves as an example of Swift's method where financial matters are concerned: the reader is swamped with facts, and he emerges at the other side of the argument convinced that Marlborough has little to complain about after all, and that the nation has rewarded him in a proper manner. The financial specifications are followed by a story which is a moral fable and which concludes the paper:

> A Lady of my Acquaintance, appropriated twenty six Pounds a Year out of her own Allowance, for certain Uses, which her Woman received, and was to pay to the Lady or her Order, as it was called for. But after eight Years, it appeared upon the strictest Calculation, that the Woman had paid but four Pounds a Year, and sunk two and twenty for her own Pocket: It is but supposing instead of twenty six Pounds, twenty six thousand; and by that you may judge what the Pretensions of modern Merit are, where it happens to be its own Paymaster. (no.16, 23 Nov.1710:p.24)[2]

If the 'Lady' is the Queen and 'her Woman' is the Duchess of Marlborough, then no further comment is necessary: Swift has once more manipulated his readers into a position from which they have little chance of escape, except to agree with the author.

The charge of greed is one which Swift pursues in a later paper. He has already shown that Marlborough is a wealthy man and he has hinted at the method by which he has acquired his wealth. In the second prolonged attack upon Marlborough, Swift begins with observations upon human avarice. They are observations written with one aim in mind, destroying the credibility of one man:

> I am ready to conclude from hence, that a Vice which keeps so firm a Hold upon human Nature, and governs it with so unlimited a Tyranny, since it cannot be wholly eradicated, ought at least to be confined to particular Objects; to Thrift and Penury, to private Fraud and Extortion, and never suffered to prey upon the Publick; and should certainly be rejected as the most unqualifying Circumstance for any Employment, where Bribery and Corruption can possibly enter.

> If the Mischiefs of this Vice, in a Publick Station, were confined to enriching only those particular Persons employed, the Evil would be more supportable; But it is usually quite otherwise. When a Steward defrauds his Lord, he must connive at the rest of the Servants, while they are following the same Practice in their several Spheres; so that in some Families you may observe a Subordination of Knaves in a Link downwards to the very Helper in the Stables, all cheating by Concert, and with Impunity. And, even if this were all, perhaps the Master could bear it without being undone; but it so happens, that for every Shilling the Servant gets by his Iniquity, the Master

loseth twenty; the Perquisites of Servants being but small Compositions for suffering Shopkeepers to bring in what Bills they please. It is exactly the same Thing in a State: An avaricious Man in Office is in Confederacy with the whole Clan of his District or Dependance, which in modern Terms of Art is called, To Live, and let Live; and yet their Gains are the smallest Part of the Publick's Loss. Give a Guinea to a knavish Land-Waiter, and he shall connive at the Merchant for cheating the QUEEN of an Hundred. A Brewer gives a Bribe to have the Privilege of selling Drink to the Navy; but the Fraud is a hundred Times greater than the Bribe; and the Publick is at the whole Loss. (no.27; 8 Feb. 1710: pp.81/2).[2]

Marlborough - or any other officer elected to serve the public - is in the same position as a Steward serving a Lord, for he is in a position to cheat, yet he is expected to behave honestly and with dignity. The enormity of the crime of robbing the state can only be imagined, for the trust that is broken in doing so represents a complete breakdown of any recognisable moral code. The homely metaphors of Stewards and Shopkeepers are designed to bring about the maximum impact, for they are immediate and they signify so much more than their surface meaning. Their underlying message is concerned with the preservation of the state, of the wealth of the nation and of the ideals of the country. If fraud is practised on a large scale by people in high office, then the fabric of society must inevitably wear thin and eventually disappear. If the guardians of England act selfishly, then the public as a whole will suffer.

Having established the general principle, Swift continues by giving the specific example of a man who was in office in order to accumulate personal wealth and who remained there in spite of the disapproval of the public. The story of 'Marcus Crassus' is a thinly disguised fable on the activities of Marlborough. Swift addresses an open letter to him:

To Marcus Crassus, Health:

If you apply as you ought, what I now write, you will be more obliged to me than to all the World, hardly excepting your Parents, or your Country. I intend to tell you, without Disguise or Prejudice, the Opinion which the World hath entertained of you. And, to let you see I write this without any Sort of ill Will, you shall first hear the Sentiments they have to your Advantage. No Man disputes the Gracefulness of your Person; you are allowed to have a good and clear Understanding, cultivated by the Knowledge of Men and Manners, although not by Literature. You are no ill Orator in the Senate; you are said to excel in the Art of bridling and subduing your Anger, and stifling or concealing your Resentments; you have been a most successful General, of long Experience, great Conduct, and much Personal Courage; you have gained many important Victories for the Commonwealth, and forced the strongest Towns in Mesopotamia to surrender; for which, frequent Supplications have been decreed by the Senate. Yet with all these Qualities, and this Merit, give me Leave to say, you are neither beloved by the Patricians or Plebeians at home, nor by the Officers or private Soldiers of your own Army abroad. And, do you know, Crassus, that this is owing

32

to a Fault, of which you may cure yourself by one Minute's Reflection? What shall I say? You are the richest Person in the Commonwealth; you have no male Child, your Daughters are all married to wealthy Patricians; you are far in the Decline of Life; and yet you are deeply stained with that odious and ignoble Vice of Covetousness. It is affirmed, that you descend even to the meanest and most scandalous Degrees of it; and while you possess so many Million; while you are acquiring so many more, you are solicitous how to save a single Sesterce, of which a hundred ignominious Instances are produced, and in all Mens' Mouths. I will only mention that Passage of the Buskins, which after abundance of Persuasion, you would hardly suffer to be cut from your Legs, when they were so wet and cold, that to have kept them on, would have endangered your Life. (no.27: 8 Feb.1710: p.83)[2]

Crassus is, on one level, a self-centred buffoon, but he is too wise politically to be dismissed simply as a fool. He has acquired profit at the expense of others and he has acquired glory by relying upon the experience of others:

When your Adversaries reflect how far you are gone in this Vice, they are tempted to talk as if we owed our Successes not to your Courage or Conduct, but to those Veteran Troops you command; who are able to conquer under any General, with so many brave and experienced Officers to lead them. Besides, we know the Consequences your Avarice hath often occasioned. The Soldier hath been starving for Bread, surrounded with Plenty, and in an Enemies Country, but all under Safeguards and Contributions; which, if you had sometimes pleased to have exchanged for Provisions, might at the Expence of a few Talents in a Campaign, have so endeared you to the Army, that they would have desired you to lead them to the utmost Limits of Asia. But you rather chose to confine your Conquests within the fruitful Country of Mesopotamia, where Plenty of Money might be raised. How far that fatal Greediness of Gold may have influenced you, in breaking off the Treaty with the old Parthian King Orodes, you best can tell; your Enemies charge you with it; your Friends offer nothing material in your Defence; and all agree, there is nothing so pernicious, which the Extreams of Avarice may not be able to inspire. (no.27: 8 Feb.1710: pp.83/4)[2]

The tale of the Buskins is an amusing one, but it tells only a part of the story. Crassus is a fool, but he is a fool who knows how to manipulate people and events for his own ends. Swift's point returns to the general one of the 'State of England' and the underlying causes of the present war. He insists, once more, that a small group of men rely on the fortitude of others and that they see events in terms of personal gain rather that in terms of benefit for the nation as a whole. The specific point is also made that such men must be identified, that their motives must be exposed and that a return to peace through the good offices of the present administration is the only way forward. The satire against one man is also a satire against an institution and the language is designed to denigrate both while affirming the worth of opposite, Tory, values. The demystification of the man is completed by exposing him as human in the sense that he is motivated by grossly selfish acts.[10]

If Marlborough represented a form of Whiggery that deserved attack, then Wharton, Governor of Ireland, came under more severe censure for being a representative not only of Whiggism, but also of anti-Irish Whiggism. The two most sustained attacks are to be found in *The Examiner* of November 30, 1710, and in the pamphlet *A Short Character of Thomas, Earl of Wharton*. Wharton had gained Swift's enmity since he had refused to help the Irish Church or the Irish cause and it seemed that he was content to allow the sufferings of the Irish people to continue while using the office to become wealthy. In *The Examiner* attack, Swift concentrates on the idea of a fable from the past in order to illustrate a general point about bad government and the necessity of ridding the country of those who perpetuate it. Swift claims to draw on Tully's 'Harangus' against Verres, who was expelled by Cicero from the Roman Senate after mismanaging the affairs of Sicily for the three years of his governorship of the island. Cicero made several speeches on the nature and character of Verres and Swift translates them:

> I have brought here a Man before you, my Lords, who is a Robber of the Publick Treasure; an Overturner of Law and Justice; and the Disgrace, as well as Destruction of the Sicilian Province: Of whom, if you shall determine with Equity and due Severity, your Authority will remain entire, and upon such an Establishment as it ought to be: But if his great Riches will be able to force their Way through that Religious Reverence and Truth, which become so awful an Assembly, I shall, however, obtain thus much, That the Defect will be laid where it ought; and that it shall not be objected, the Criminal was not produced, or that there wanted an Orator to accuse him. This Man, my Lords, hath publickly said, That those ought to be afraid of Accusations who have only robbed enough for their own Support and Maintenance; but that he hath plundered sufficient to bribe Numbers; and that nothing is High or Holy which Money cannot corrupt. (no.17. 30 Nov. 1710)[2]

The themes are by now familiar; the method, too, is one which Swift employs in much of *The Examiner*: he makes general reference to the character of the man, all of which may be related to specific instances and then removed from the one man and applied to the Whig movement in general. The man and the party are amoral, only interested in exploiting the 'Sicilian Province' (Ireland) for their own ends; the man asserts that everything may be subverted by money, with the suggestion that even those who are highest in the state hierarchy are capable of being corrupted. Swift has already argued, and he will continue to argue, that the Head of State must remain 'untouchable' and that there are certain fixed principles upon which one must act if one is to be an effective agent of the government. The principles by which Verres acts are established and the examples of his behaviour in Sicily confirm that he sticks closely to those principles:

He hath left of late such Monuments of his Villainies in Sicily; made such Havock and Confusion there, during his Government, that the Province cannot by any Means be restored to its former State, and hardly recover it self at all under many Years, and by a long Succession of good Governors. While this Man governed in that Island, the Sicilians had neither the Benefit of our Laws, nor their own, nor even of common Right. In Sicily no Man possesseth more than what the Governor's Lust and Avarice have overlooked; or what he was forced to neglect out of meer Weariness and Satiety of Oppression. Everything where he presided, was determined by his arbitrary Will; and the best Subjects he treated as Enemies. To recount his abominable Debaucheries, would offend any modest Ear, since so many could not preserve their Daughters and Wives from his Lust. I believe, there is no Man who ever heard his Name, that cannot relate his Enormities. We bring before you in Judgment, my Lords, a publick Robber, an Adulterer, a Defiler of Altars, an Enemy of Religion, and of all that is sacred; in Sicily he sold all Employments of Judicature, Magistracy, and Trust, Places in the Council, and the Priesthood it self, to the highest Bidder; and hath plundered that Island of forty Millions of Sesterces. (no.17: 30 Nov.1710:p.28)[2]

Verres is the Seven Deadly Sins rolled into one - with the possible exception of Sloth. In order to press home his point, the speaker lists his timetable:

And here I cannot but observe to your Lordships, in what manner Verres passed the Day: The Morning was spent in taking Bribes, and selling Employments; the rest of it in Drunkenness and Lust. His Discourse at Table was scandalously unbecoming the Dignity of his Station; Noise, Brutality, and Obsceneness. One Particular I cannot omit, that in the high Character of Governor of Sicily, upon a solemn Day, a Day set a-part for Publick Prayer for the Safety of the Commonwealth, he stole at evening, in a Chair, to a married Woman of infamous Character, against all Decency and Prudence, as well as against all Laws both Human and Divine. Didst thou think, O Verres, the Government of Sicily was given thee with so large a Commission, only by the Power of That to break all the Barrs of Law, Modesty, and Duty, to suppose all Mens Fortunes thine, and leave no House free from thy Rapine, or Lust, etc. (no.17: 30 Nov.1710:pp.28/29)[2]

So the oration ends; the character of the man is complete. We are invited to laugh at him, and to denounce him, for he is not just an over-indulgent harmless eccentric.

In the above extracts, Swift does not draw a clear parallel between the behaviour of the man and the encouragement of that behaviour by the party he supports, but the credibility of both can be undermined by condemnation of the one or the other. In a different *Examiner*, which is concerned with lying, Swift pulls these two ideas very close together; if a man lies, then so may the party to which he is affiliated:

There is one essential Point wherein a Political Lyar differs from others of the Faculty; That he ought to have but a short Memory, which is necessary according to the various Occasions he meets with every Hour, of differing from himself, and swearing to both Sides of a Contradiction, as he finds the Persons disposed, with whom he hath to deal. In describing the Virtues and Vices of Mankind, it is convenient, upon every Article, to have some eminent Person in our Eye, from whence we copy our Description. I have strictly observed this Rule; and my Imagination this Minute represents before me a certain Great Man famous for this Talent, to the constant practice of which he owes his twenty Years Reputation of the most skilful Head in England, for the Management of nice Affairs. The Superiority of his Genius consists in nothing else but an inexhaustible Fund of Political Lyes, which he plentifully distributes every Minute he speaks, and by an unparallelled Generosity forgets, and consequently contradicts the next half Hour. He never yet considered whether any Proposition were True or False, but whether it were convenient for the present Minute or Company to affirm or deny it; so that if you think to refine upon him, by interpreting every Thing he says, as we do Dreams by the contrary, you are still to seek, and you will find yourself equally deceived, whether you believe or no: The only Remedy is to suppose that you have heard some inarticulate Sounds, without any Meaning at all. And besides, that will take off the Horror you might be apt to conceive at the Oaths wherewith he perpetually Tags both ends of every Proposition: Although at the same Time, I think, he cannot with any Justice be taxed for Perjury, when he invokes God and Christ; because he hath often fairly given publick Notice to the World, that he believes in neither. (no.14; 9 Nov. 1710)[2]

Any integrity that the man or the party may have possessed before has now vanished completely. Any suggestion of honesty is renounced and any loyalty to any cause is rejected, for Wharton may side with God or with the Devil, depending on which one espouses the cause closest to his own interests. The language is heavily ironic, embracing notions of 'skilful management of nice Affairs' and 'Genius' which are normally reserved for those who have made a positive contribution to the advancement of the State. Wharton has turned the general, positive, aspects of mankind into specifically selfish ones; Swift turns around the associations which are present in the vocabulary in order to make his satiric point. Gay was to follow this practice in *The Beggar's Opera* in which words like 'honest' are employed to mean precisely the opposite of their normal associations. Swift uses the same technique and he anticipates too the ironic phrase 'Great Man': although it is here used to refer to Wharton, the phrase became associated with Walpole.

Wharton's propensity to lying is no unusual thing for a Whig; an earlier commentator had remarked that "We modern Whigs are for Lying, tho' the Lye will last but three Hours" because "we modern Whigs have no aim but to do our own Business".[11] This aspect of Wharton's character is something which Swift dwells upon a paper written in August 1710 and which is devoted to exposing the heart of the man. From the outset, the author appears to be a mild-mannered individual, with no one line to pursue:

> In the same manner, his Excellency is one whom I neither personally love
> nor hate. I see him at Court, at his own House, and sometimes at mine (for
> I have the Honour of his Visits) and when these Papers are public, it is
> Odds but he will tell me, as he once did upon a like Occasion, that he is
> damnably mauled; and then with the easiest Transition in the World, ask
> about the Weather, or Time of the Day? So that I enter on the Work with
> more Chearfulness, because I am sure, neither to make him angry, nor any
> Way hurt his Reputation; a Pitch of Happinesss and Security to which his
> Excellency hath arrived, which no Philosopher before him could reach.[12.]

The mask is one which Swift has worn during the writing of *The
Examiner*. The reasonable, dispassionate individual is concerned with
observing and describing the proclivities of a person who has done him
the 'Honour' of paying him visits. But the rhetoric here is not a trap for
the reader, nor is it a pretence that the writer will be objective. It is more
of a game which Swift plays; he is aware of the expectations of the reader
and he decides to delay the expected invective in order to allow both the
reader and himself the pleasure of indulgence in argument for argument's
sake and not for the revelation of some truth. Swift has commented upon
Wharton; he then launches into a diatribe that extends beyond the attacks
in *The Examiner*. There is personal animosity here - it is not an argument
which is perpetrated by political expediency:

> Thomas, Earl of Wharton, Lord Lieutenant of Ireland, by the Force of a
> wonderful Constitution hath some Years passed his Grand Climacteric,
> without any visible Effects of old Age, either on his Body or his Mind, and
> in Spight of a continual Prostitution to those Vices which usually wear out
> both. His Behaviour is in all the Forms of a young Man at five and twenty.
> Whether he walketh or whistleth, or sweareth, or talketh Bawdy, or calleth
> Names, he acquitteth himself in each beyond a Templar of three Years
> standing. With the same Grace, and in the same Style he will rattle his
> Coachman in the Middle of the Street, where he is Governor of the Kingdom;
> and, all this is without Consequence, because it is in his Character, and
> what every Body expecteth. He seemeth to be but an ill Dissembler, and
> an ill Liar, although they are the two Talents he most practiseth, and most
> valueth himself upon. The Ends he hath gained by Lying appear to be more
> owing to the Frequency, than the Art of them: His Lies being sometimes
> detected in an Hour, often in a Day, and always in a Week. (p.179).[12]

Wharton is hardly capable of controlling his own behaviour. To lie is a
part of his nature and to dissemble defines his whole being:

> He tells them freely in mixed Companies, although he knows half of those
> that hear him to be his Enemies, and is sure they will discover them the
> Moment they leave him. He sweareth solemnly he loveth, and will serve
> you; and your Back is no sooner turned, but he tells those about him you
> are a Dog and a Rascal. He goeth constantly to Prayers in the Forms of
> his Place, and will talk Bawdy and Blasphemy at the Chapel Door. He is

a Presbyterian in Politics, and an Atheist in Religion; but he chuseth at present to whore with a Papist. In his Commerce with mankind his general Rule is, to endeavour to impose' on their Understanding, for which he hath but one Receipt, a Composition of Lies and Oaths: And this he applieth indifferently, to a Freeholder of forty Shillings and a Privy-Counsellor; by which the Easy and the Honest are often either deceived or amused, and either Way he gaineth his Point. He will openly take away your Employment To-day, because you are not of his Party; Tomorrow he will meet or send for you, as if nothing at all had passed, lay his Hands with much Friendship on your Shoulders, and with the greatest Ease and Familiarity, tell you that the Faction are driving at something in the House; that you must be sure to attend, and to speak. (p.179)[12]

Wharton is totally depraved, totally dishonest and totally corrupt; he exists only for himself and any policy which ensures the furtherance of his own self-interests is the one which he will adopt.

In passages which follow the ones quoted above, Swift is entirely honest about his motives for the attack. Wharton's crime has been against a section of humanity with whom Swift was closely involved:

He has three predominant Passions, which you will seldom find united in the same Man, as arising from different Dispositions of Mind, and naturally thwarting each other: These are Love of Power, love of Money, and love of Pleasure; they ride him sometimes by Turns, and sometimes all together: Since he went into *Ireland*, he seemeth most disposed to the second, and hath met with great Success, having gained by his Government, of under two Years, five and forty thousand Pounds by the most favourable Computation, half in the regular way, and half in the prudential. (pp.180-181).[12]

The portrait is a critique of the nature of one man, beginning with a disavowal of any personal antagonism, followed by a stringent personal attack on Wharton's lying and his general attitudes towards those close to him. It ends with a statement of fact about the acquisition of a personal fortune. The last section confirms Swift's original statement, while at the same time providing evidence that the invective has not been without foundation. As with the portrait of Marlborough, Swift destroys the man with facts, although he is here much more outspoken in his attack since it originates from the abuse of something even closer to him than Toryism - the love of Ireland.

3. Steele and Swift

It is a pity that Swift did not have an equivalent commentator for the Whig cause; several tried but they usually ended up by merely abusing Swift or by producing tracts which were easily pulled apart and denounced. One serious advocate of the Whig Cause, Richard Steele, did attempt to place the previous Whig administration into its proper ideological perspective and to indicate the follies and dangers inherent in the politics of the present government. However, his pamphlet *The Crisis*, in which he attempts to do all this, is dull and it displays none of the efficacy of style and awareness of technique that is evident in Swift's reply, *The Publick Spirit of the Whigs*.

Steele's *The Crisis* was published in January 1714; his purpose was to look back into recent history in order to relate the religious issues and the questions of civil rights which had arisen after the Glorious Revolution of 1688. The method is not an exciting one: Steele relates facts, reciting laws which had been passed during the previous twenty-five years and which had been designed "to extirpate the Arbitrary Power of a Popish Prince". He lists and discusses such Acts as the Declaration of Right and the Bill of Rights (1688 and 1689, the purpose of which was to debar Catholics from the throne); the Act of Settlement (1701); the Abjuration Act (1702), which denied the concept of 'Divine Right', the Union Treaty (1707) and many others.[13] It is not difficult to see Steele's intention: by discussing at length the Whig policies that contributed to the unification of the nation and, indeed, to any national cause, he could assert that the Whig party had the interests of the country at heart. The Whigs could be seen to be the ones who acted according to tradition, and one which was designed to benefit a large number of people rather than a small clique. Steele could also deny the charge of faction, for the laws that he cites were designed to promote unity rather than diversity. His arguments are dry and factual and so lack the rhetorical flourishes that characterise Swift's prose; they do, however, represent a significant rejoinder to Toryism, for they attempt to show that the Whigs have a firm and honourable ideological base from which to work, while the Tory policies make very little sense logically. Steele indicates that Marlborough had been responsible for the routing of the French at both Blenheim and Ramillies and he rebukes the Tories for changing the nation's general, pointing out that while the French changed their general in defeat, the English did the same in victory. He continues:

> The Minds of the People, against all Common Sense, are debauch'd with Impressions of the Duke's Affectation of prolonging the War for his own Glory; and his adversaries attack a reputation which could not well be impaired without sullying the Glory of *Great Britain* it self ...
> ... there can be no Crime in affirming, (if it be a Truth) that the House of *Bourbon* is at this Juncture become more formidable, and bids fairer for an Universal Monarchy, and to engross the whole Trade of Europe, than it did before the War. (pp.172-4)[13]

Although Steele is at his best when dealing with contemporary issues, it takes the reader a long time to reach these stages and the rhetorical point is blunted by the previous prolonged effort of reading the inventory of recent political decisions.

Swift had a challenge before him: here was a pamphlet by an eminent author which argued the Whig case from a factual basis. Swift could not allow the challenge to pass, and he published *The Public Spirit of the Whigs* a few months after *The Crisis* had appeared. Swift's pamphlet is both an indirect and a direct comment on Steele's: it is indirect because it includes so much in the way of style that Steele omits, and direct since it meets head-on the arguments that Steele puts forward. The first tactic that Swift employs is to turn, not to the arguments themselves, but to the properties of Steele's pamphlet and what this may imply about the arguments:

> It was proposed to be printed by Subscription, Price a Shilling. This was a little out of Form; because Subscriptions are usually begged only for Books of great Price, and such as are not likely to have a general Sale. Notice was likewise given of what this Pamphlet should contain; only an Extract from Certain Acts of Parliament relating to the Succession, which at least must sink ninepence in the Shilling, and leave by three Pence for the Author's political Reflections; so that nothing very wonderful or decisive could be reasonably expected from this Performance. (The Publick Spirit of the Whigs. (p.32)[14]

A pamphlet, Swift implies, is not simply an argument, nor is it simply a series of words to be taken in and digested. A pamphlet is in many ways an event, a kind of showpiece for the doctrines which it contains. 'The whole thing' is the argument, and that includes the physical appearance, the cost, what the words mean and what the combination of all these may imply about the veracity of the argument. Steele has forgotten that a pamphlet is an opportunity to display oneself as a virtuoso of both doctrine and of language. A pamphlet is not the product solely of one man, but it is a combined effort; this effort may, however be turned against the author who remains responsible for the pamphlet as a whole:

> I am told by those who are expert in the Trade, that the Author and Bookseller of this Twelve-Penny Treatise, will be greater Gainers, than from one Edition of any Folio that hath been published these twenty Years. What needy Writer would not sollicite to work under such Masters, who will pay us before-hand, take off as much of our Ware as we please at our own Rates, and trouble not themselves to examine either before or after they have bought it, whether it be staple or no? (p.33)[14]

Having partially dismissed the background to *The Crisis*, yet at the same time affirming that it is not merely background, Swift begins to examine the document in detail. Swift's analysis indicates that Steele's arguments are in no sense original, that they contribute little to learning or advancement and that they are constituted of clichés disguised as proper arguments:

> We come now to the Crisis: Where we meet with two Pages by Way of Introduction to those Extracts from Acts of Parliament that constitute the Body of his Pamphlet. This Introduction begins with a Definition of Liberty, and then proceeds in a Panegyrick upon that great Blessing; his Panegyrick

40

is made up of half a dozen Shreds, like a school-boy's Theme, beaten, general Topicks, where any other Man alive might wander securely; but this Politician by venturing to vary the good old Phrases, and give them a new Turn, commits an hundred Solecisms and Absurdities. The weighty Truths which he endeavours to press upon his Reader are such as these. That, Liberty is a very good Thing; that, without Liberty we cannot be free; that, Health is good, and Strength is good, but Liberty is better than either; that, no Man can be happy, without the Liberty of doing whatever his own Mind tells him is best; that, Men of Quality love Liberty, and common People love Liberty; even Women and Children love Liberty; and you cannot please them better than by letting them do what they please. (pp.45-6)[14]

But this is not all; Steele is not just an unoriginal thinker, he is also a hack whose facility with the English language leaves much to be desired:

But, let us hear some of these Axioms as he hath involved them. We cannot possess our Souls with Pleasure and Satisfaction except we preserve to our selves that inestimable Blessing which we call Liberty: By Liberty, I desire to be understood, to mean the Happiness of Men's living, etc. - The true Life of Man consists in conducting it according to his own just Sentiments and innocent Inclinations - Man's Being is degraded below that of a free Agent, when his Affections and Passions are no longer governed by the Dictates of his own Mind - Without Liberty, our Health (among other Things) may be at the Will of a Tyrant, employed to our own Ruin and that of our Fellow Creatures. If there be any of these Maxims, which is not grossly defective in Truth, in Sense, or in Grammar, I will allow them to pass for uncontroulable. By the first, omitting the Pedantry of the whole Expression, there are not above one or two Nations in the World, where any one Man can possess his Soul with Pleasure and Satisfaction. In the second, He desires to be understood to mean, that is, he desires to be meant to mean, or to be understood to understand. In the Third, The Life of Man consists in conducting his Life. In the Fourth, he affirms, That Men's Beings are degraded when their Passions are no longer governed by the Dictates of their own Mind; directly contrary to the Lessons of all Moralists and Legislators; who agree unanimously, that the Passions of Men must be under the Government of Reason and Law, neither are Laws of any other Use than to correct the Irregularity of our Affections. By the last, Our Health is ruinous to our selves and other Men, when a Tyrant pleases; which I leave him to make out. (pp.46-7)[14]

By placing his prose next to that of Steele, Swift brings out the deficiencies in the latter and so undermines the intelligence of the man and of the arguments that are put forward. Steele cannot control his prose: he therefore cannot control the response of the reader, nor then can he expect agreement from the reader. A political debate is not a matter of outlining certain facts or of establishing a kind of historical precedence; it involves flourishes of rhetoric, irony, recognition of an audience and general interest and entertainment. Swift can defeat Steele in all of these; even

Steele's facts could be questioned. Steele had argued that the Act of Union showed the nationalistic inclinations of the Whigs and that they had the well-being of the whole of Britain in mind when they had negotiated the Act. Swift disputes this:

> But towards the End of the late King's Reign, upon Apprehension of the Want of Issue from him or the Princess Anne, a Proposition for uniting both Kingdoms was begun, because Scotland had not settled their Crown upon the House of Hanover, but left themselves at large, in hopes to make their Advantage: And, it was thought highly dangerous to leave that Part of the Island inhabited by a poor, fierce Northern People, at Liberty to put themselves under a different King. However, the Opposition to this Work was so great, that it could not be overcome until some Time after her present Majesty came to the Crown; when by the Weakness or Corruption of a certain Minister since dead, an Act of Parliament was obtained for the Scots, which gave them leave to arm themselves; and so the Union became necessary, not for any actual Good it could possibly do us, but to avoid a probable Evil; and, at the same Time, save an obnoxious Minister's Head, who was so wise, as to take the first Opportunity of procuring a general Pardon by Act of Parliament, because he could not with so much Decency or Safety desire a particular one for himself. (p.49)[14]

The Union came from no political ideology but from political expediency which was engendered in order to avoid a negative outcome rather than ensure a positive one. All Whig actions are like this, Swift implies: the party acts according to immediate necessity rather than formulating policies which arise from traditional values. Steele attempts to disguise old arguments in a new dress; Swift's readers will not be taken in so easily. Swift appeals to the reader's intelligence, his sense of humour, his insight and his general understanding of political events. Steele argues from a position which may be challenged and he puts forward an interpretation of history which may be debunked as dubious and occasionally as plain wrong. Swift really wants to ask what all the fuss is about, since the arguments are well-rehearsed and everyone knows the political implications of the death of childless Anne. The Tories are in a good position to govern, while the Whigs excite needless discord. In the poem 'The First Ode of the Second Book of Horace', Swift writes:

> Dick, thou'rt resolved, as I am told, Some strange *Arcana* to unfold, And with the help of *Buckley*'s pen To vamp the *good old Cause* again, Which thou (such *Burnet*'s shrewd advice is) Must furbish up and Nickname CRISIS Thou pompously wilt let us know What all the World knew long ago... That we a German Prince must own When ANN for Heav'n resigns Her Throne.[15]

If Swift was an agent for the Tory government, then he was one who, in addition to his political duties, also attended to the duty of rhetoric, of control of language and of exposing the deficiencies in the language of a Whig opponent. Swift satisfied his masters, himself, and his audience.

4. The Audience

In *The Examiner* of November 9, 1710, Swift asserts that "we have
seen a great Part of the Nation's Money got into the Hands of those, who
by their Birth, Education and Merit, could pretend no higher than to wear
our Liveries". The statement identifies the aim, and it identifies the social
inclinations that Swift had and to which group he wished to appeal. There
is an overt identification of author and audience, a bonding which Swift
was intent upon making firmer as *The Examiner* continued to be published.
Swift was aware than an enunciation of arguments in prose was no
substitute for a proper campaign which would include timing, an active,
appealing vocabulary and a play on words and arguments which would
delight his readers and which would enable them to enjoy the merits of
good prose style. At the same time, the readers' beliefs and ideals would
be confirmed as correct. Swift's task is not to repeat arguments, but it is
to embroider them and so make them more attractive and, therefore,
somehow truer. In confirming them he was aware that he had to appeal
to the holders of the opinions, who were the educated landed gentry; nor
could he appear to be merely brash in his denunciation of the Whig
opposition, for it was a strong force and one which did have an ideology.
What he had to do was to decorate the denunciation with rhetorical
flourishes which, at the same time, could be seen to be an active part of
Toryism; he was appealing to the intelligent reader, asking him to
participate in the analysis. Swift must have known too that he was writing
for posterity as well as for the moment:

> The *Whigs*, according to Custom, may chuckle and solace themselves with
> the visionary Hopes of coming Mischief, and imagine they are grown
> formidable, because they are to be humour'd in their Extravagancies, and
> to be paid for their Perverseness. Let them go on to Glory in their projected
> Schemes of Government, and the blessed Effects they have produced in the
> World. Twas not enough for them to make *Obedience* the Duty of the
> Sovereign, but this *Obedience* must at length be made *Passive*; and that
> *Non-resistance* may not wholly vanish from among the Virtues, since the
> Subject is weary of it, they would fairly make it over to their Monarch. The
> *Compact* between Prince and People is suppos'd to be mutual: but Grand
> Alliances are, it seems, of another nature: a failure in one party does not
> disengage the rest; they are tied up and entangled, so long as any one
> Confederate adheres to the *Negative*; whilst we are not allow'd to make use
> of the *Polish* argument, and plead *Non Loquitur*. But these Artifices are too
> thin to hold: They are the Cobwebs which the *Faction* have spun out of the
> last Dregs of their Poison, made to be swept away with the unnecessary
> Animals who contrived them. Their Tyranny is at an end, and their Ruin
> very near: I can only advise them to become their Fall, like *Caesar*, and *die
> with Decency*. (p.169).[14]

Precedents have been set in the past; contemporary politics should not
be different from those of other times in the sense that the 'compact'

43

between 'Prince and People' should be honoured by both. Recognition of the rights and status of the two is an integral part of the preservation of honour.

Status and honour are the very things which Swift denies that the Whigs possess. He appeals to his audience's sense of tradition, social priority, and to its sense of political merit. The aim of the Whigs is to destroy this accepted hierarchy:

> a perpetual War encreases their Money, breaks and beggars their *Landed Enemies*. The Ruin of the Church would please the Dissenters, Deists and Socinians, whereof the Body of their Party consists. A *Commonwealth*, or a *Protector*, would gratify the *Republican Principles* of some, and the Ambition of others among them.

The above quotation is taken from Swift's *Letter to the October Club*. The Letter is overt in its thesis that the Whigs are intent upon creating wealth for themselves at the expense of their country. Swift is an anti-Dissenter, an advocate of the High Church and, accordingly, intensely pro-monarchy. All of these ideas are contained within the quotation and it shows the pithiness with which Swift wrote when the audience consisted of an easily identifiable body of men, but one which needed their prejudices confirmed without the disguise of a factual analysis. There is no persuasion involved; there is simply confirmation of prejudice.

The writing of *The Examiner* presented a different challenge, for Swift's audience had to be assumed to be unknown: that is, although the arguments had to confirm the Tory position, they had to do so in a manner which would persuade the relatively uncommitted reader that the stance was a worthwhile one and that the previous ministry's actions suggested a lack of ideological commitment. Swift invites the reader to participate in an interpretation of a text:

> Liberty, the Daughter of Oppression, after having brought forth several fair Children, as Riches, Arts, Learning, Trade, and many others; was at last delivered of her youngest Daughter, called Faction, whom Juno doing the Office of Midwife, distorted in its Birth, out of Envy to the Mother; from whence it derived its Peevishness and Sickly Constitution. However, as it is often the Nature of Parents to grow most fond of their youngest and dis-agreeablest Children, so it happened with Liberty, who doated on this Daughter to such a Degree, that by her good will she would never suffer the Girl to be out of her Sight. As Miss Faction grew up, she became so termagant and froward, that there was no enduring her any longer in Heaven. Jupiter gave her warning to be gone; and her Mother, rather than forsake her, took the whole Family down to Earth. She landed at first in Greece, was expelled by degrees through all the Cities by her Daughter's ill Conduct; she fled afterwards to Italy, and being banished thence, took Shelter among the Goths, with whom she passed into most parts of Europe; but being driven out everywhere, she began to lose Esteem; and her Daughter's Faults were imputed to her self: So that at this Time she had hardly a Place in the World to retire to. One would wonder what strange

Qualities this Daughter must possess, sufficient to blast the Influence of so divine a Mother, and the rest of her Children: She always affected to keep mean and scandalous Company; valuing no Body, but just as they agreed with her in every capricious Opinion she thought fit to take up; and rigorously exacting Compliance, although she changed her Sentiments ever so often. Her great Employment was to breed Discord among Friends and Relations; and make up monstrous Alliances between those whose Dispositions least resembled each other. Whoever offered to contradict her, although in the most insignificant Trifle, she would be sure to distinguish by some ingnominious Appellation, and allow them to have neither Honour, Wit, Beauty, Learning, Honesty or common Sense. She intruded into all Companies at the most unseasonable Times; mixt at Balls, Assemblies, and other Parties of Pleasure; haunted every Coffee-house and Bookseller's Shop; and by her perpetual Talking filled all Places with Disturbance and Confusion. She buzzed about the Merchant in the Exchange, the Divine in his Pulpit, and the Shopkeeper behind his Counter. Above all, she frequented Publick Assemblies, where she sate in the shape of an obscene, ominous Bird, ready to prompt her Friends as they spoke. (no. 31: 8 Mar. 1710).[2]

The political implications cannot be extracted from the fable; but the fable must be allowed to exist in its own right. In other words, the narrative remains a narrative; it relies for its effect upon the reader's knowledge of myth and the tradition of disguised narration, and it shows too the company that the factions keep. This company is low and therefore unfit for the reader. The social prejudices are confirmed and the sense of deserved merit is established. Swift is not avoiding the centre of political discussion, but aiming at the heart of it through narrative and through the subsequent exegesis:

The Heads of a Faction, are usually a Set of Upstarts, or Men ruined in their Fortunes, whom some great Change in a Government, did at first, out of their Obscurity, produce upon the Stage. They associate themselves with those who dislike the old Establishment, Religious and Civil. They are full of new Schemes in Politicks and Divinity; they have an incurable Hatred against the old Nobility, and strengthen their Party by Dependents raised from the lowest of the People; they have several Ways of working themselves into Power; but they are sure to be called when a corrupt Administration wants to be supported, against those who are endeavoring at a Reformation: and they firmly observe that celebrated Maxim of preserving Power by the same Arts it is attained. They act with the Spirit of those who believe their Time is but short; and their first Care is to heap up immense Riches at the Publick Expence; in which they have two Ends, beside that common one of insatiable Avarice; which are to make themselves necessary, and to keep the common Wealth in Dependance: Thus they hope to compass their Design, which is, instead of fitting their Principles to the Constitution, to alter and adjust the Constitution to their own pernicious Principles. (no.31: 8 Mar.1710).[2]

The struggle is one between good and evil, between those with social consciences and those with none at all. The power of the adversary, like the power of the Devil, is not to be underestimated. The lust for power is a result of intense self-seeking at the expense of the majority and the more dangerous since it is not always manifest in everyday life. The messages within the narrative are many: they include confirmation of received opinion and an acknowledgement that there is a class fit for power, while at the same time Swift admits that the activities of the new Whigs pose a real threat. Although the traditional, natural right to govern may rest with the Tories, the Whigs do not respect tradition and therefore they represent a new sort of opposition. Swift's argument calls for action: passivity would result in defeat and a retreat to the country would leave the way open for the town.

The pamphlets are, then, important as 'events': Swift tackles contemporary questions with verve and skill, insisting that 'the pamphlet' is a work within itself, which then extends beyond itself to an assumed, often previously defined, audience. After 1714, when Walpole's ascendancy began, the pamphlets are almost negative judgements passed on themselves; but the technique - and therefore the appeal - remains firm, detached from power-struggles.[16] This is why we may read *The Examiner* today while *The Crisis* remains fixed in an historical moment. Perhaps the essential difference may be summed up in a quotation in which Swift addresses an altogether different audience - Stella. This, too, is on the art of lying and the exposure of those who lie:

> I heard at Court, that Walpole (a great Whig member) said, that I and my Whimsical Club writ it at one of our Meetings, (it = a Grub Street Speech of Lord Nottingham) and that I should pay for it. He will find he lies; and I shall let him know by a third Hand my Thoughts of him. He is to be Secretary of State, if the Ministry changes: but he has lately had a Bribe proved against him in Parliament, while he was Secretary at War. He is one of the Whigs chief Speakers.[17]

In an earlier letter to Stella, he had referred to the Whigs as 'malicious toads.'[18] Here are examples of Swift the honest, open-hearted letter-writer, not Swift as narrator or politician. It is Swift's versatility which makes him so interesting.

NOTES

1. See Henry W. Sams, 'An End to Writing about Swift.' in *Essays in Criticism*, xxiv, 1974, pp. 275-285

2. Jonathan Swift, *The Examiner*, Quotations are from *The Examiner and other Pieces written in 1710-11*, edited by Herbert Davis. (Oxford, 1941, reprinted 1966).

3. ibid., pp. 224/5.

4. Bernard A. Goldgar. *The Curse of Party. Swift's Relations with Addison and Steele*. (Univ. of Nebraska Press, Lincoln, Nebraska, 1961), p.48.

5. Jonathan Swift, *The Conduct of the Allies*, in *Political Tracts 1711-1713*, edited by Herbert Davis, (Oxford, 1951, reprinted 1964),pp.42/3.

6. Hare, Marlborough's chaplain, wrote *The Allies and the late Ministry defended* (London, 1712), in which the confused nature of the arguments is considered. See Davis, op. cit., introduction, pp.x/xi.

7. Jonathan Swift, *Some free Thoughts upon the present State of Affairs* in *Political Tracts 1713-1719* edited by Herbert Davis and Irvin Ehrenpreis, (Oxford, 1953), pp.73-98.

8. Richard I. Cook, *Jonathan Swift as a Tory Pamphleteer*, (Washington, 1967), p.17.

9. *Protestant Post-Boy*, 19 Jan.1711, quoted in *Political Tracts 1711-1713* ed. Davis, p.x.

10. Swift's attacks on his opponents were often less subtle. See his poem *The Fable of Midas*, in *Poetical Works*, edited by Herbert Davis (London, 1967), p.100.

11. Charles Davenant, *Tom Double Return'd out of the Country: or, the True Picture of a Modern Whig* (1702), quoted in *The History of John Bull*, edited by Alan W. Bower and Robert E. Erickson, (Oxford, 1976), p.lxxiii

12. Jonathan Swift, *A short Character of his Excellency THOMAS Earl of WHARTON, Lord Lieutenant of IRELAND*, in ref. 2 above, p.178.

13. See Richard Steele, *The Crisis*, in *Tracts and Pamphlets by Richard Steele*, edited by Rae Blanchard (Baltimore, Md, 1944), p.125 et seq.

14. Jonathan Swift, *The Publick Spirit of the Whigs*, in ref. 7 above, p.32

15. Jonathan Swift, *Poetical Works*, pp.139-140.

16. See Edward W. Said, 'Swift's Tory Anarchy', in *Eighteenth Century Studies*, vol 1. 1969, p. 48-66

17. Jonathan Swift, *Journal to Stella*, edited by Harold Williams, 2 vols., (Oxford, 1948), II,p.442, letter xxxviii, 15 Dec.1711.

18. idem., ibid., I,159, letter xiii, 4 Jan.1710.

CHAPTER 3

Bolingbroke

By the time Bolingbroke had written his philosophical treatises on the nature of government, their form and content must have seemed curiously outmoded. Bolingbroke had experienced the new age at first hand: he had been flung into exile by Walpole, a man vilified and abused in satire, and he witnessed from France the continuing acquisition of power and wealth by self-made men such as Walpole and, at the same time, he saw the gradual ebbing away of his own social power base as the landed gentry became less and less important in national decision making.

Or so it must have seemed to Bolingbroke. Swift, during the years 1710 to 1714, had attempted to establish that the Tory ideal was continuing and that it would continue, but events proved him wrong. Political writing after that date in England took on a new form and a new language, as it became clear that revelations through the medium of satire and direct abuse were the only means to attack an enemy who appeared to embody Machiavellian principles. Bolingbroke, although intimately associated with Walpole's accusers, seemed strangely remote from the language that they employed, and insisted in his prose that the landed ideal had not disappeared, that the present age was an aberration upon history and that the true England would re-emerge after the age of Walpole had passed. His prose works, written in the 1730s, have an optimistic note to them but they seem almost naive as well as stylistically outmoded. Many passages seem to assume that conservatism and the golden age, being the natural order of things, will triumph through the inherent and inherited good sense of such as he:

> History is our ancient Author: Experience in the modern Language. We form our Taste on the first, we translate the Sense and Reason, we transfuse the Spirit and Force; but we imitate them according to the Idiom of our own Tongue, that is, we substitute often Equivalents in lieu of themselves and are far from affecting to copy them servilely. To conclude, as Experience is conversant about the past, and by knowing the Things that have been, we become better able to judge the Things that are. (p.29).[1]

The prose is a call for the re-establishment of past ideals. The style and the choice of words reveal an attitude that takes little notice of current political vicissitudes, but seeks a resurgence of past hopes and of a past social order. He is looking for sense and reason, he believes in a perfect world in which certain 'graces' may be copied and in which the ideal lessons of past actions may be translated into terms that are relevant for the future. The present age, Bolingbroke hopes, has nothing to do with reality; it must pass, so that the old order may re-establish itself.

Bolingbroke had entered parliament (as a Tory) in 1700 and in 1711 after another Tory victory, he was made Secretary of State under Queen Anne. In 1713 the Treaty of Utrecht brought an end to the War of the Spanish Succession: Swift had been successfully brought into the Tory ranks and it was his propaganda that had established the ideological base for attacking Whig policy and defending Toryism. Only one year later however, in 1714, the Whigs took control again and between 1715 and 1725, Bolingbroke was in exile in France. He was able to observe from afar the rise of Walpole, from Paymaster General to Prime Minister, and observe the political machinations over such incidents as the South Sea Bubble. He saw that a new kind of politician seemed to be emerging in England: one who, in Bolingbroke's terms, looked back to Machiavelli for inspiration rather than to the ideals of the country gentlemen of England.

Bolingbroke lived through another, connected, change: the change in the method of attack. The language of politics seemed to be changing; Pope, Swift and Gay were reflecting this movement in literary attacks upon the Walpole regime. *The Beggar's Opera* (1720), for example, reverses the normal associations of language and of political morality in order to show the dramatic change in the organisation of society. Politicians had become thieves; the ordinary citizen was a man to be duped. In spite of all this, Bolingbroke persisted in arguing that the Tory ideal was not dead and that traditional morality would re-appear after the downfall of Walpole. The fact that his most important political tracts appear in the 1730s, after Walpole had been in power for over a decade, reflect his belief that conservativism was the natural form of government for England and that a continuing assertion of the ideals of conservatism would ensure its safe return.

1. A Dissertation upon Parties (1734)

A Dissertation Upon Parties was written in exile, as were most of Bolingbroke's attacks on Walpole. It attempts to establish that the party system was founded upon sound principles and that those principles will survive even if attacked by such people as Walpole and the present regime. Walpole is dangerous because he may force people to believe that the new order is the accepted way of behaving in political circles; it is the task of political commentators to ensure that the ideals of the past are kept alive. The danger of allowing Walpole to continue unchallenged is at least twofold - he is preventing Bolingbroke and his party from gaining power, and he is challenging something which Bolingbroke sees as fundamental to the English way of life. In the *Dedication*, Bolingbroke writes of parties whose 'contests brought even the fundamental principles of our constitution into question, and whose excesses brought liberty to the very brink of ruin'. Walpole is exploiting the right of liberty in order to destroy it, and at the same time he is ignoring the political fact that, although the *king* may do no wrong, a *minister* may. Bolingbroke argues that:

(Ministers) are answerable for the Administration of the Government, each for his particular Part, and the prime, or sole, Minister, when there happens to be one, for the Whole. He is so the more, and the more justly, if he hath affected to render himself so, by usurping on his Fellows; by wriggling, intriguing, whispering, and bargaining himself into his dangerous Post, to which he was not called by the general Suffrage, nor perhaps by the deliberate Choice of his Master himself. It follows, then, that Ministers are answerable for everything done to the Prejudice of the Constitution... (II, pp. 3-7).[2]

The stance is, not surprisingly, pro-monarchy, but it implies that Walpole is seeking to usurp the rights of the monarch and replace them by his own philosophy of government, a philosophy which depends upon intrigue and the market forces of bargaining rather than an acknowledgement that the traditional hierarchical structure is the one which must be adhered to and obeyed without challenge. Walpole is dangerous because he confuses the office of 'prime' minister with that of 'king': whereas one may be removed by the free vote of the people, the other operates through natural law.

After the ironic 'Dedication' Bolingbroke continues the *Dissertation Upon Parties* by writing a series of Letters which examine the conduct of political leaders and the nature of government. The letters are written with an eye on Walpole, since Bolingbroke is aware that he represents something different in English politics, and the nation needs to be reminded of his immorality. Superficially, Walpole could be seen to be successful: he was, after all, rich and powerful, but Bolingbroke insists that it is not the possession of riches and power that counts, but the use to which a deserved possession of them is put. 'Greatness' means nothing if it is gained through corruption:

Every busy, ambitious Child of Fortune, who hath himself a corrupt Heart, and becomes Master of a large Purse, hath all that is necessary to employ the Expedient of Corruption with Success. A Bribe, in the Hand of the most blundering Coxcomb that ever disgraced Honor and Wealth and Power, will prevail as much as in the Hand of a Man of Sense, and go farther too, if it weigh more. An intriguing chamber-maid may slip a bank Note into a griping Paw, as well as the most subtle Demon of Hell. (II, p.22)[2]

The structure of the arguments can be confusing, but the general sense is clear. The prose suggests that Bolingbroke's anger has bubbled over, leaving an analogy as the most satisfactory means of expressing the way in which he feels about the degraded manner of Walpole's behaviour.

Bolingbroke feared that the landed gentry had become extinct as a species, that the emphasis was now overtly on money. The Tories distrusted jobbing. It had too much of the corrupt about it, too much of the idea that large corporations were now in power, rather than a small elite. Speculation on the stock market was an intangible thing, full of risks and the market was changeable in its nature; land was secure and visible. The latter suggested honesty and security for he who protected his own property also protected the nation. The man who dedicated himself to the stock market could not be trusted to place the interests of the nation first:

> The Bank, the East India Company, and in general the moneyed Interest... enjoyed Advantages so much greater than the Rest of their fellow Subjects. The mischievous Consequence which had been foreseen and foretold too, at the Establishment of those Corporations, appeared visibly. The country Gentlemen were vexed, put to great Expenses and even baffled by them in their Elections: and among the Members of every Parliament Numbers were immediately or indirectly under their Influence... But that which touched sensibly, even those who were but little affected by other Consider-ations, was the prodigious Inequality between the Condition of the moneyed Men and the Rest of the Nation. The Proprietor of the Land, and the Merchant who brought Riches home by the Returns of foreign Trade, had during two Wars borne the whole immense Load of the national Expenses; whilst the Lender of Money, who added nothing to the common Stock, throve by the public Calamity, and contributed not a Mite to the public Charge.[3]

The contrast is between a man who believes in his country and the man whose actions emanate from selfish motives. Tradition has shown that the landed gentry put the nation first, while the new order appeals to the baser side of man. The nation is controlled by an amoral clique, dedicated to the preservation of power and ruled by corruption. The monarch, symbol of liberty and honour and the representative of tradition, must be challenged and threatened by Walpole because he instinctively reacts against anything which is an opposite force; corruption can, in fact, ensure that power is maintained:

> To argue from this supposed Deficiency of Power in the Crown, in favour of a Scheme of Government repugnant to all Laws divine and human, is such an Instance of abandoned villanous Prostitution, as the most corrupt Ages never saw, and as well place the present Age, with infamous Pre-eminence, at the Head of them, unless the Nation do itself Justice and give the Brand on those who ought alone to bear it. (II, p.95)[2]

Bolingbroke not only insists that corruption is the mainstay of the present government, but he persists with the idea too, repeating his charge that there are 'enemies of the constitution' who abound and who are headed by Walpole. The prose is once more somewhat heavy in style: Bolingbroke maintains a front which is one of general ideology and which attempts to steer away from personal invective towards considerations about the nature of the age and notions about the crown and divine laws. It is worth placing such passages by the side of others which are on the same subject, but in which Bolingbroke allows his venom to escape:

> Whilst a wicked and corrupt Minister is weighing out Panegyrics and Dedications against just Satires and Invectives; or, perhaps, is numbering his Creatures, and teaching them their implicit Monosyllables; whilst he is

drawing out his Screen, and providing for a safe and decent Elopement; or, it may be, comforts himself with the Hopes that the public Job, at his Removal, will drown all future Enquiries; or that he shall keep sweet a good while longer, till the Worm seizes the Carcass, and Prosperity preys upon his Memory; it may not be improper to turn your Thoughts upon the Reverse of his Character, and to inquire by what Marks a good Minister may be found out.[4]

The emphasis in this extract is on the characters of those who hold office: the ideal, although implicit in the argument, never seizes hold of it and the prose exhibits a clarity of purpose that much of the previous quotations lack. The behaviour of an individual has angered Bolingbroke because he has detracted from the absolute in behaviour of a minister, while the prose has more of an immediacy because of the personal nature of the conflict. This tendency in Bolingbroke's prose finds parallel in the *Dissertation Upon Parties*: occasionally, Bolingbroke is aware that the age, although totally unsatisfactory, may be a reflection of the corruption of mankind. He shows himself capable of producing prose the vocabulary of which matches much of that produced by the Scriblerus Club; its invective is a result of deliberations over current politics and the implications for human nature contained within it:

In order to become Slaves, we of this Nation must be beforehand what other People have been rendered by a long Course of Servitude, we must become the most corrupt, the most profligate, the most senseless, the most servile Nation of Wretches, that ever disgraced Humanity: for a Force sufficient to ravish Liberty from us, such as a great standing Army is in time of Peace, cannot be continued, unless we continue it; nor can the Means necessary to steal Liberty from us, be long enough employed with Effect, unless we give a Sanction to their Iniquity, and call Good Evil, and Evil Good. (II, p. 111)[2]

What Bolingbroke is complaining about is that Britannia no longer rules the waves - in fact, she rules little at all. The general survey of contemporary events offers Bolingbroke little satisfaction: only by a return to the past and only by remembering the tradition of English liberty and of an English golden age (intimately bound up with the tradition of the landed gentry) can liberty in the future be preserved. Factionalism, Bolingbroke hopes, is merely a temporary setback and nationalism will triumph:

But whatever Ministers may govern, whatever Factions may arise, let the Friends of Liberty lay aside the groundless Distinctions, which are employed to amuse and betray them; let them continue to coalite; let them hold fast their Integrity, and support with Spirit and Perseverance the Cause of their Country, and they will confirm the good, reclaim the bad, vanquish the incorrigible, and make the British Constitution triumph, even over Corruption. (II, p.171)[2]

The struggle is one between good and evil; Toryism, inherently good because of its traditions, must triumph over the devilish impulses of the

Walpoles of the world, since the future of the nation as an upright, moral and free country is at stake. One may also comment that the future of such people as Bolingbroke is also under threat if Walpole continues to triumph. The liberties achieved after 1688 may perish unless the nation unites against new Whiggery - and unites, presumably, to form a government which will combine tradition with liberty and which will consist of good ministers whose fitness to govern has been tried and tested by their background.

2. The Idea of a Patriot King

If ministers govern they do not do so by right: they do so through the good offices of the people but, more that that, they are surveyed from above by an absolute, by an ideal which is untouched by the sullied nature of politics. That ideal is the monarch, the embodiment of liberty, honour and justice. No politician can protect the nation in such a manner; Walpole has abandoned men, morals and his country:

> The Principles I have reasoned upon in my Letter to my Lord **** and those I shall reason upon here, are the same. They are laid in the same System of human Nature. They are drawn from that Source from whence all the Duties of public and private Morality must be derived, or they will be often falsely, and always precariously, established. Up to this Source there are few Men who take the Pains to go: and, open as it lies, there are not many who can find their Way to it. By such as do, I shall be understood and approved: and, far from fearing the Censure, or the Ridicule, I should reproach myself with the Applause, of men who measure their Interest by their Passions, and their Duty by the Examples of a corrupt Age; that is, by the Examples they afford to one another.

> Such, I think, are the greatest Part of the present Generation; not of the vulgar alone, but of those who stand foremost, and are raised highest in our Nation. Such we may justly apprehend too that the next will be; since they who are to compose it will set out into the World under a Direction that must incline them strongly to the same Course of Self-interest, Profligacy, and Corruption.[5]

If the age is corrupt then ministers should attempt to overcome the corruption and not to live by its strictures. Men must, then, despise the age; the moral responsibility lies with those who are 'highest' in the nation. The general theme of 'self-love' is the familiar insistence upon the profligacy and utter selfishness of the new Whigs, and the damage that they do will live after them, for 'such men sin against posterity...the consequences of their example remain'. Bolingbroke's mood is one of pessimism, for he sees no future elected leader as capable of restoring the tradition of British liberty, once the canker has eaten into the rose:

> Will their Sentiments, which are debased from the Love of Liberty, from Zeal for the Honor and Prosperity of their Country, and from a Desire of

honest Fame, to an absolute Unconcernedness for all these, to an abject Submission, and a rapacious Eagerness after Wealth, that may sate their Avarice, and exceed the Profusion of their Luxury; will these, I say again, be so easily or so soon elevated? In a Word, will the British Spirit, that Spirit which has preserved Liberty hitherto in one Corner of the World at least, be so easily or so soon reinfused into the British Nation? I think not. (II, p. 374)[2]

Bolingbroke, like Swift before him, is careful to tread a politic path. He wishes to attack most vociferously those who follow Walpole and he needs to establish that the age has been corrupted by those people. In order to ensure that he has a basis for future support he appeals to the sense of liberty which, he insists, remains a part of the British spirit or the British character. The two most significant points here are the Britishness of the argument and the insistence upon the tradition of the country's character: the British have really only existed for a matter of twenty years or so and, despite Tory misgivings about the Act of Union, political expediency demanded that he put forward an argument which could include the whole nation and which at the same time would avoid the emphasis on materialism upon which the administration seemed intent. The reasoning behind Bolingbroke's assertions is that tradition and history has shown that Britain can maintain itself in an honourable way; there is an interruption, and one which may have far-reaching consequences, but the character has not been destroyed and the honour and tradition may be re-formed in the future.

Bolingbroke's language is general and his formulations are idealised versions of political and social conduct:

We have been long coming to this Point of Depravation: and the Progress from confirmed Habits of Evil is much more slow that the Progress to them. Virtue is not placed on a rugged Mountain of difficult and dangerous Access, as they who would excuse the Indolence of their Temper, or the Perverseness of their Will, desire to have it believed; but she is seated, however, on an Eminence. We may go up to her with Ease, but we must go up gradually, according to the natural Progression of Reason, who is to lead the way, and to guide our Steps. On the other Hand, if we fall from thence, we are sure to be hurried down the Hill with a blind impetuosity, according to the natural Violence of those Appetites and Passions that caused our Fall at first, and urged it on the faster, the further they are removed from the Control that before constrained them. (II, p.374).[2]

Bolingbroke has decided to inhabit a world of ruling passions in order to prove his point, and, indeed, the world is an intellectually respectable one to inhabit: it places his argument in an Augustan context, it emphasises his Toryism and it allows for his belief that Britain is redeemable from perdition. But Bolingbroke has, potentially, created a problem for himself; namely, he mentions virtue and it must be incumbent upon him to identify wherein virtue resides. Before this, however, he must correlate vice with specific characters:

> The Minister preaches Corruption aloud and constantly, like an impudent Missionary of Vice; and some there are who not only insinuate, but teach the same occasionally. I say, some; because I am as far from thinking, that all those who join with him, as that any of those who oppose him, wait only to be more authorised, that they may propagate it with greater Success, and apply it to their own Use, in their Turn.[4]

These sentiments would not be unfamiliar to a contemporary reader, already acquainted with the attacks on Walpole's character. Bolingbroke is really more concerned with establishing an ideal towards which one may look for an example of totally correct, gentlemanly and undefiled behaviour. No supporter and follower of Bolingbroke would be surprised to find that the example is enshrined in the British constitution in the personage of the monarchy. The office of the monarch is, as he had already hinted in *A Dissertation Upon Parties*, endowed by Divine Right (II, p. 379-80).[2] A patriot king may survey his realm and, since he is there eternally - through the continuation of the office - his subjects may, if they choose, turn to him for guidance:

> A Patriot King will see all this in a far different and much truer Light. The Constitution will be considered by him as one Law, consisting of two Tables, containing the Rule of his Government, and the Measure of his Subjects' Obedience; or as one System, composed of different Parts and Powers, but all duly proportioned to one another, and conspiring by their Harmony to the Perfection of the Whole. (II, p. 391).[2]

Within the Patriot King is harmony; within the monarch is a unity of national purpose and a belief in the righteousness of the cause of one's country; one should recognise that the interplay between vice and virtue is a perennial one, limited only by the selfishness of certain citizens (Walpole and his gang) who should exalt the king rather than attempt to usurp his authority. Bolingbroke associates the ideal of kingship with the King so intimately as to make them indistinguishable. The King will remove corruption and his subjects 'will not only cease to do evil, but learn to do well' (II. p. 396). Later, towards the end of the tract, the vocabulary reflects the nature of the essay as a hymn in praise of kingship and as a warning against the vicissitudes of human nature:

> To sum up the Whole and draw to a Conclusion: this Decency, this Grace, this Propriety of Manners to Character, is so essential to Princes in particular, that whenever it is neglected their Virtues lose a great Degree of Lustre, and their Defects acquire much Aggravation. Nay more, by neglecting this Decency and this Grace, and for want of a sufficient Regard to Appearances, even their Virtue may betray them into Failings, their

failing into Vices, and their Vices into Habits unworthy of Princes and unworthy of Men. (II, p. 423).[2]

Normally, the King is in a state of grace, but he may fall; these assertions surely lead Bolingbroke into more contradictions. In his almost desperate attempt to include the whole of British history and contemporary politics, he argues that the King operates by Divine Right and yet may be, at the same time, fallible. Despite his belief that 'I am a Briton still' (II, p. 395),[4] Bolingbroke seems much more French. The King, ruling by Divine Right, must - or, in Bolingbroke's terms should - control the political (and therefore, moral) affairs of the nation. His Britishness is revealed in the contradiction which is inherent in the argument, since he also wishes to say that the king, after the turmoil of the late seventeenth-century and after the Glorious Revolution, is the equal of his subjects and so is fallible.

An answer to the contradiction may be posited by a further consideration of Bolingbroke's position and of the sort of ideological stance he was taking. He saw clearly that the Old Toryism was fast disappearing, together with his own power-base, the landed gentry. He saw too that a new kind of politician was being formed out of a broadened, yet corrupt, electoral system and that the adjective 'Machiavellian' was generally applicable to the characters who now controlled the fiscal (and political) resources of the nation. The ideal of grace for which Bolingbroke longs is, then, an attempt to counter one political theorist - Machiavelli - with another - himself - in the hope that the theory could be changed into practical terms. Therein lies the problem: for at no stage during his arguments does Bolingbroke suggest a pragmatic solution, and that is where Machiavelli (and, presumably, Walpole) gains the upper hand. An amoral approach, coupled with practical advice, scores time and time again over theories which belong to the past.

His stance, with its appeal to virtue, to an unswerving loyalty to the nation and to morality as a fundamental answer to the needs of a corrupt state, is an honourable one but it contains contradictions and it seems curiously out of touch with contemporary anti-Walpole propaganda.[6] The last comment may not really matter, of course, since Bolingbroke's appeal is to a wider ideology, but it is also bound up with his personal position as an exile who is watching, as he sees it, the whole of his power disappear. He is not simply an exponent of Augustanism, for his arguments are more recondite than many in that age would allow: he looks back further than that to a 'Chain of Being' on which the King, the state, the church and man all have their fixed positions and not one of them can be allowed to transgress the power of the other. Any reasonable man - and Bolingbroke is the prime example - would see the justice of this scheme. If only a few are designed to govern, then their superior knowledge may be passed along in order to ensure that the others remain firmly set in their own position. Liberty grows from a kind of self-love but certainly not from the kind displayed by Walpole. Bolingbroke is so involved with Toryism, the land and the reinforcement of the old order, that he longs for the golden age once more: the age when there were no such things as Parties to bother him, or Pamphlets attacking him. An age very much like the actual one he experienced in France in fact:

> The hoarse Voice of Party was never heard in this quiet Place; Gazettes and Pamphlets are banished from it .... When I am there, I forget I was ever of any Party myself; nay, I am often so happily absorbed by the abstracted Reason of Things, that I am ready to imagine that never was any such Monster as Party.[7]

3. *The Use of History* and *On the Policy of the Athenians*

Letters on the Study and Use of History were written in exile between 1735 and 1738. The title reveals much about the ideas, for it indicates Bolingbroke's turn of mind and his ideological concerns. Not only are the present times corrupt, but only in history will correct behaviour, manners and morals be found, and only in the study of the lessons of History and in the direct application of those lessons will man be ensured a better future. Bolingbroke's concerns are with the past; his backward look is a steadfast stare at more glorious, stable and - for him - happier times. Bolingbroke is both general and particular in his arguments, and the general nature of them turns on certain familiar words and phrases:

> The Tone and proper Object of this Application is a constant Improvement in private and in public Virtue. An Application to any Study that tends neither directly nor indirectly to make us better Men and better Citizens, is at best but a specious and ingenious sort of Idleness.... and the Knowledge we acquire by it is a creditable kind of Ignorance, nothing more. (p.8)[1]

Bolingbroke's views on the nature of history and politics are clear: he sees the study of them as a 'Use' since they would provide a kind of linear progression which would lead eventually to the attainment of virtue. The struggle is not one which centres around the acquisition of power but one which concerns the continual struggle between good and evil; goodness is something which may be acquired through proper study and application, and of which all men - especially those close enough to the seat of power to benefit from it - are capable.

In the same Letter he is more precise about the identities of those involved in the struggle:

> I am not so uncharitable, however, as to believe that they intended to bring upon their Country all the Mischiefs that we, who came after them, experience and apprehend. No, they saw the Measures they took singly, and unrelatively, or relatively alone to some immediate Object. The Notion of attaching men to the new Government, by tempting them to embark their

fortunes on the same Bottom, was a Reason of State to some: the Notion of creating a new, that is, a moneyed Interest, in opposition to the landed Interest or as a Balance to it, and of acquiring a superior Influence in the City of London at least by the establishment of great Corporations, was a Reason of Party to others: and I make no doubt that the Opportunity of amassing immense Estates by the Management of Funds, by trafficking in Paper, and by all the Arts of jobbing, was a Reason of private Interest to those who supported and improved this Scheme of Iniquity, if not to those who devised it. They looked no farther. (p. 21)[1]

The landed interest must be involved in the struggle against the jobbers. The latter have acquired wealth through manipulation not merit and, although not necessarily inherently bad, their tactics work against what is traditional, stable, and in Bolingbroke's terms 'right'. Those of Bolingbroke's persuasion remained totally suspicious of the new men, for their wealth had nothing tangible as a foundation. Paper was the only means whereby they gained their property and, surely, that commodity could disappear as quickly as it had appeared. The only solid means of support and therefore basis for judgment is land. For the gentry who owned it, land had acquired a significance beyond wealth for it seemed to be involved in a symbolic struggle against paper. As he had written in the previous paragraph, he wishes to develop and support 'all the wise, honest, and salutary precepts' which history may be seen to possess.

If history possesses those precepts, it may also contain examples of the opposite; if history may be seen in terms of significant struggles, then the struggle needs to be identified at each stage. Recent history provided examples of deviousness and of selfishness. In Letter 8, Bolingbroke turns to the subject of the War of the Spanish Succession and the reasons for the prolongation of it. The events, however, are hardly immediate, and one interesting point about the following passage is its sterility of argument when compared with the prose of Swift:

I called the Necessity of reducing the whole Spanish Monarchy to the Obedience of the House of Austria, a pretended Necessity: and pretended it was, not real, without doubt. But I am apt to think your Lordship may go further, and find some Reasons to suspect, that the Opinion itself of this Necessity was not very real, in the Minds of those who urged it; in the Minds I would say of the able Men among them; for that it was real in some of our zealous British Politicians, I do them the Justice to believe. Your Lordship may find reasons to suspect perhaps, that this Opinion was set up rather to occasion a Diversion of the Forces of France and to furnish Pretences for prolonging the war for other Ends. (p.116)[1.]

Bolingbroke seems stuck in the year 1710 or thereabouts; he is ready to do battle with those who wish to continue the war for their own profit. True, Bolingbroke writes in the past tense, but a reader who was unaware of the date of the Letters could easily mistake the passage as belonging to a contemporary debate about the conduct of the war rather than a later reflection of its historical significance. Bolingbroke's arguments have already been made, won and destroyed in turn. His main contention seems lost amidst the verbiage of historical significances; but this point is one with which Swift would have agreed and his observations upon the change in the balance of power are truly Tory:

> In the Administrations that preceded the Revolution, Trade had flourished, and our Nation had grown opulent: but the general Interest of Europe had been too much neglected by us; and Slavery, under the Umbrage of Prerogative, had been well-nigh established among us. In those that have followed, Taxes upon Taxes, and Debts upon Debts, have been perpetually accumulated, till a small Number of Families have grown into immense Wealth, and national Beggary has been brought upon us. (p.125)[1]

The appeal is meant to be to the traditional, almost proverbial, belief in the freedom of the Englishman to conduct his own affairs. It seems to Bolingbroke that an increasingly centralised administration demanded tax from its citizens and at the same time used the money ('paper' in the previous extract) to establish its own power-base. The reflection on the times ('a small number of families') is an example of the Tory mind refusing to see itself from an historical perspective, despite the title of the study. What has happened is that one small group - Bolingbroke and his circle - was being replaced by another whose basis for power - money - was replacing the more traditional one of land. In Tory terms, Walpole is performing a rape upon the land in order to translate it into terms which he understands. The British are being governed by 'a Set of Ministers ... too intent upon their own Interest to have any serious Regard for the Welfare of the Public.' (p.499)[8]

Bolingbroke's portrait of Walpole and his government has the advantage over his other writings of being within the satiric tradition of his time. It is forceful and direct, both general and particular in its attacks while avoiding the high mindedness of the *Use of History*. In a sense, *On the Policy of the Athenians* is a satiric starting point for the ideology which Bolingbroke was to formulate later and it sums up the frustrations and fears of his class. In the tract, Bolingbroke employs the technique of an historian by claiming to be studying the flourishing state of Greece, and her victory over the Persians. He then follows the decline of the country under Pericles. They are, of course, thinly disguised studies of England and Walpole. Pericles is a Machiavellian figure, opportunistic and lacking in scruple or principle:

> As he was Master of great Volubility of Tongue, with a Knack of speaking plausibly in public, and had joined to this a very daring and consummate Assurance; so he knew perfectly well how to improve them to his own Advantage in supporting any Proposition, right or wrong, as it best suited his present Purpose; for nothing was more common than to see him in one Assembly with great Zeal confecting his own Arguments in a former one; and he never scrupled to contradict the most certain Truths, or to assert the

most notorious Falsehoods in order to carry his Point, though sure to be discovered a few Hours afterwards, having always an Evasion ready at hand. (p. 501).[8]

Unlike many of the previous passages quoted from other works, this one requires little commentary for it has a directness that is only rarely found amongst Bolingbroke's writings. There is, of course, a vast difference: in *On the Policy of the Athenians*, Bolingbroke has no need to establish an ideological base from which to work; for the object is to attack, to deflate, to satirize. Like any contemporary opponent of Walpole, the base for the attack is understood; the establishment of a base is irrelevant to the main point which is to unfold the workings of the evil mind which is behind the policies of a once-great nation. As in *The Beggar's Opera* the image is one of a nation now corrupted by a pestilence that was once working craftily against the public but which by now has so inveigled itself into the way of life that it seems natural:

> This extravagant and unnatural Flow of the public Money by degrees introduced that Spirit of Expense and Luxury amongst all Ranks of Men, under the mistaken Notion of Politeness, which consumed the Estates of the best Families in Athens, and soon made them so necessitous, that forgetting their ancient Honors and the Dignity of their Birth, they were not ashamed to become the known Pensioners of Pericles, living in as abject a Dependence upon him as the meanest of the People.

> Thus was universal Corruption spread over the whole State; and, to complete their Misfortune, the very Money which was reserved for the Necessities of War only, was spent in debauching the Minds of the People, and what was designed for their Preservation, turned to their Destruction. (p.502).[8]

Whereas in previous arguments Bolingbroke had mentioned a specific war, and by doing so detracted from his main point, here he emphasises the corruption and debauching of the people which came about as a result of the corrupt policies, of which war-taxation for personal and political gain is the major example. By avoiding a reasoned argument, and by aligning his prose style to the method adopted by his contemporaries, Bolingbroke is able to force his point home with an immediacy that is not apparent in other works. The underlying message may be similar, as indeed are the underlying assumptions, but the method is different. In other arguments, Bolingbroke insisted on waving the Tory flag; on this occasion he allows the waving to be done by emphasising what the opposite of Toryism means in real terms:

> As Pericles was not qualified by his Rank to be of the Assembly of the Areopagus (the great and supreme Judicature of Athens) so to remove every Obstacle to his Ambition, he employed all his Art to undermine their Authority, and by degrees drew all public Business of consequence to the popular Assemblies; where, by the Assistance of Bribes, Pensions and

Employments, which were all at his Disposal, he was secure of carrying every Thing almost without Opposition.

This, together with the scandalous Disrespect with which Pericles affected to treat them upon all Occasions, and their slavish Submission at the same Time, to all his Orders, falling in with the general Depravation of the Times, soon brought them into the lowest Contempt with the People, and destroyed all Regard for that ancient and august Assembly, which had for so many Ages been the Bulwark and Defence of the Constitution.

After this fatal Blow to a State which made the proudest Boast of its Liberties, and had ever showed the greatest Jealousy of any Encroachments upon them, Pericles obtained almost as absolute and uncontrolled a Power as the Tyrant Pisistratus himself; which gave Occasion to the Calling him and his Creatures the new Pisistratides; (p.502).[8]

Liberty is something which Bolingbroke feels he must defend as it is something which the new Whigs are destroying. In foreign affairs, Pericles is an incompetent opportunist who assumes all rulers are as corrupt as he:

Pericles, to remedy these growing Mischiefs, endeavoured to gain over to his Interest some of the neighboring Powers, by the Proposition of certain wild and impracticable Projects; such as joining the Forces of Athens to theirs, and making new Accessions to their Dominions, by altering the Dependencies of some of the lesser Principalities of Greece; but his Scheme gained him nothing but Shame and Contempt; so that after much Time and Labor had been spent in these fruitless Negotiations, he had Recourse to the same Methods abroad which he had found so very successful at Home, and backed all his foreign Transactions with the Offers of a round Sum of Money; by which Means he engaged many of the lesser States of Greece to lend their Names, at least, to his new Alliance and kept some of the favorite Ones in constant Pay, under the Pretence of making good their Expenses, in keeping Troops to assist Athens upon Occasion, though they never raised one Man more for their Service. (p. 504).[8]

Some twentieth-century historians have been equally scathing in their references to Walpole's knowledge of foreign affairs and of his attitude to foreign powers, but they may reflect Bolingbroke's own bias as they often rely on him as a source.[9] The point here is that these passages are stylistically interesting as the vocabulary reflects exactly the contempt which the author felt for his antagonist and it is also designed with a wide audience in mind. This is not simply grand Tory ideology, but is instead a mixture of politics, rhetoric and language blended in such a manner as to gain the reader's attention and to allow him an immediate unreflected reaction. The style here is designed by the author to have the maximum impact; it is not designed simply to appeal to the contemplative Tory gentleman landowner.

In conclusion, Bolingbroke draws upon the same general stance which was to be adopted in the *Use of History*; in the *Athenians*, however, he confined himself to one paragraph, which is sufficient to make clear his political objective:

> Thus we may see that the overgrown Power, Ambition and Corruption of one Man brought Ruin upon the most flourishing State in the Universe, and there are not wanting Instances of the like kind in History to convince us that the same Conduct will have the same Consequences in all Ages and all Nations. (p. 507)[8]

4. Bolingbroke's Reputation

Despite his own writings, in which he presented himself as something of an upright gentleman defending liberty, and his own background which was solidly aristocratic, Bolingbroke did not enjoy a good reputation among his contemporaries. It is really only during recent years that historians have become more generous towards him, tending towards a more liberal view of a man whose personal habits tended to rakishness in his earlier years and whose philosophical writings were viewed as political opportunism. So Kramnick in *Bolingbroke and His Circle* argues that his subject was intensely aware of the corruption in English society and he wished to dig away until the roots of it were thoroughly exposed. 'The financial revolution of the Augustan years', he argues, 'with its growth and development of banking, credit, and capital facilities, was an indispensable prerequisite for the Industrial Revolution conventionally dated from the middle of the century' and it was Bolingbroke who showed that Walpole and 'Robinocracy' were replacing order with chaos and were using the chaos to provide personal wealth. The aristocratic ideal of order and stability was being left behind.[19] Kramnick, too, sees a continuity in Bolingbroke's arguments which centre around the political and moral implications of the war with France and the need for the Tory government of 1710-1714 to end it. True though this may be, the prose in which it is expressed is not exciting, and Bolingbroke's arguments read so often like an attempt to re-phrase Swift. But Bolingbroke was nevertheless consistent and he conforms to the Tory spirit of the age in that he attacks the jobbers, paper money, lack of tradition and the complexities of high finance.

In Bolingbroke's view, one man was above the rest; in the state it was the King, but the King had to have representatives who were steeped in virtue and who were high-minded and selfless; the hero of Lyttleton's *The Court Secret* is no such character:

> Fond of Fame, but more of Virtue: Loyal, but not for Reward: Free in the Delivery of Truth, but gentle in the Manner: modest in defending himself, resolute in the defence of others: not void of human Frailties, but not too

proud to acknowledge them: Incapable of Flattery, tho' to oblige the Woman he lov'd, or temporize with the Prince he rever'd.[11]

Bolingbroke wished to foist such a reputation upon himself and upon those who agreed with him about the nature of the state. According to his own writings, Bolingbroke wished also to protect the ordinary citizen through good political precepts, knowing that 'unless the Commons do enjoy their Rights, and be indulg'd their Freedom .... the King is destitute'.[12] So Bolingbroke claims to be defending the whole nation and the ideals of the whole nation when he exults the leader, while at the same time lauding the people and trade. Toryism could envelop all and could lead to unity and the prolongation of high ideals.

Despite this high-mindedness, or possibly because of it, Bolingbroke came under ruthless attack, especially in the earlier years. Although Walpole obviously saw him as a real threat, and as a man who deserved to be thrown into exile, Bolingbroke's enemies had little difficulty in drawing attention to the contrast between his view of the ideals of office and the reality of his everyday life. Although a country gentleman, he also enjoyed the reputation of a rake; Swift writes to Stella in 1710:

> When Mr St John was turned out from being Secretary at War, three Years ago, he retired to the Country: there he was talking of something he would have written over his summer House, and a Gentleman gave him these verses:
>> From Business and the noisy World retired
>> Nor versed by Love, nor by Ambition fir'd;
>> Gently I wait the Call of Charon's Boat,
>> Still drinking like a Fish, and ----- like a Stoat.[13]

Bolingbroke claimed to be quite distraught at the attack, but he must have been used to such extremes: not only did he encourage such viciousness through his behaviour but he was subject to many attacks of a similar nature. Walpole dismissed him as an 'anti-Minister', who was licentious and dull and

> who thinks himself a Person of so great and extensive Parts, and of so many eminent Qualifications that he looks upon himself as the only Person in the Kingdom capable to conduct the public Affairs of the Nation ... (a Man) void of all Faith and Honour, and betraying every Master he has ever served ... Can there be imagined a greater Disgrace to human Nature than such a Wretch as this?[14]

The words anticipate those which Bolingbroke himself was to use when he came to attack the Walpole regime.

Contemporary ballads reflect a similar attitude towards Bolingbroke: he had a reputation for leading an immoral personal life, and therefore had no right to call from above for correct behaviour. Immorality in personal life may mean the same in public office:

Tho' Times are turn'd, I'm still the same.
No *changling* as you see, Sir;
For which I'm counted much to blame,
But what's all that to me, Sir:
Two Reigns ago I held a *Place*,
Tho' young, a raw Beginner,
And wanton'd in my Sov'reign's Grace,
When I was a *graceless* Sinner

When good Queen Anne dismiss'd her Friends
And Plac'd her *Foes* about her;
The moment we had gain'd our Ends,
We meant to do without her:
There was a reptile vagrant *Thing*,
That stroll'd in Quest of Dinner,
We purpos'd to have made our K(in)g,
When I was a graceless Sinner

I preach, that *Peace* will ruin *Trade*,
A *War* enrich the *Nation*:
That *Harmony*'s a Tune ill play'd,
And *Order*'s *Desolation*:
That *Laws* will eat up *Liberty*,
And *Freedom* quite *enslave* us;
And that a popish *Tyranny*'s
The only Thing can *save* us.[15]

Bolingbroke was and is a 'graceless sinner' and rhetoric could disguise the facts only briefly. Presumably the 'Commons' to whom Bolingbroke hoped to appeal in his prose understood the ballads equally well if not better.

Bolingbroke's defence of his position and his attack upon Robinocracy were in one sense, posed on a philosophical level and they read so often like nostalgia for the past that it is sometimes difficult to remember that Bolingbroke was a Tory philosopher. The emphasis is deliberate, as it has been throughout the chapter, in order to show where Bolingbroke's sympathies really lay. They lay with the re-establishment and re-affir-mation, in philosophical terms, of the old Tory position, in contrast to the new Whiggery which challenged the power-base of Bolingbroke and his class. Bolingbroke was not expressing an objective view, for he remained totally allied to the Tories and he wanted a Tory victory more than anything else. His writings may be philosophical but they are aligned and committed; they are also philosophical in the broad sense that they deal with high ideals - but without any indication of how those ideals could be put into practice. Bolingbroke may have been superior intellectually to Walpole - and modern historians tend to agree that this is the case - but he remained an enigma to his contemporaries, an easy target of abuse, and easily defeated by the single-mindedness of Walpole.[16]

NOTES

1. Bolingbroke, *Letters on the Study and Use of History*, in *Historical Writings*, edited by Isaac Kramnick (Chicago, 1972),
2. Bolingbroke, *Works*, 4 vols., (Philadelphia, 1841), vol. II, pp.5-7.
3. Bolingbroke, 'Letter to Sir William Wyndham,' quoted by H. T. Dickinson in *Bolingbroke* (London 1970), p.187
4. Bolingbroke, 'On Good and Bad Ministers', *Works*, vol. I, p.292
5. Bolingbroke, *Works*, II, vol. p.373
6. See Jeffrey Hart, *Viscount Bolingbroke, Tory Humanist* (London 1965), pp. 83f
7. Bolingbroke to Swift, August 1723. Quoted from Alexander Pope, *Correspondence*, edited by George Sherburn, 5 vols. (Oxford 1956), vol. II, p. 187. 'La Source' is the name of the place to which he refers.
8. Bolingbroke, 'On the Policy of the Athenians,' *Works*, Vol. I, p. 499.
9. See Jeremy Black, 'An "Ignoramus" in European Affairs?', *British Journal of Eighteenth-Century Studies*, vol 6, no 1, pp 55-65
10. Isaac Kramnick, *Bolingbroke and His Circle* (Cambridge, Mass., 1968),pp.4/5
11. George Lyttleton, *The Court Secret* (London 1742), p.6
12. Ambrose Philips, *Humphrey, Duke of Gloucester* (London 1725), II viii, p. 67
13. Swift, *Journal to Stella*, op. cit., I, letter XIII, p. 164
14. Walpole, quoted in Kramnick, op. cit., p.1
15. M. Percival (editor), *Political Ballads Illustrating the Administration of Sir Robert Walpole* (Oxford, 1916), p.59-61
16. See J. H. Plumb, *Sir Robert Walpole. The King's Minister* (London 1960), p. 310-311; Patrick Reilly, *Jonathan Swift: the brave desponder* (Manchester University Press, 1982), p. 176. For an opposite view of Bolingbroke's philosophical position, see Quentin Skinner, 'The Principles and Practice of Opposition: The Case of Bolingbroke versus Walpole', in *Historical Perspectives*, edited by Neil McKendrick (London 1974), pp. 93-128.

CHAPTER 4

Gay and London Life

The relation between social, political and literary life is so intimate in this period that no study could do justice to one without some consideration of the others. The rapid growth of England as a trading mercantile nation had certain political and social consequences. Dramatists and poets used the parallels between high and low life to establish values and to uncover the lack of values too. The ascendancy after 1719 of both England in general and Walpole in particular was not greeted by a universal cheer; the apparent increase in crime - and certainly the increased fear of crime and criminals, and the increasing exploitation of crime by writers as a metaphor on political life - meant that comments were passed upon the consequences of adherence to the mercantile ideal and social reforms were attempted. These remained linked, albeit vaguely, in the minds of most eighteenth-century writers whose works reflect their differing attitudes towards these issues. It is John Gay who is the pivot of any debate and who, in *The Beggar's Opera*, insisted on exposing and discussing the largest of the issues. The ban on *Polly* also signals the new wave of political attitudes towards the theatre; after Gay, Fielding was to take up the struggle only to find himself, like Gay, both popular and vilified, and at the centre of the most controversial of theatrical and political debates.

(1)

It is a truism to state that England had been growing rapidly as a trading nation ever since the time of Elizabeth I, but it is one which needs re-asserting because of its far-ranging consequences and the paramount importance that mercantilism was to assume in the eighteenth-century. By the beginning of the century, England had emerged as one of the leading nations in the world, with markets in America, Africa and Europe. These trade links meant that the expanding mercantile class had the opportunity to extend its fortunes, and increased wealth could mean increased respectability. As trade grew, so did London's population, but not simply owing to an influx of bourgeois gentlemen. London came to have a population of thieves and rogues, all eager to take their own share of the increased wealth in the capital. The desire for possession meant that people stole in order to obtain as many of the goods as possible. Protection against theft became an issue which no-one could avoid, and the most obvious way of removing the threat to property was to attempt to remove the initial factor: the number of offences punishable by death was between 160 and 220 during the early part of the century; the precise number is difficult to determine due to the Benefit of Clergy. While it would be a nonsensical exaggeration to draw definite conclusions from the number of offences on the statute book, it does reflect the importance that was attached to property and the increasing attempts to maintain it in the hands of the lawful owner.[1]

To the Augustan mind, most aspects of society could be viewed in terms of possession or acquisition of property. One possessed money, stocks, an individual fortune, or political power. The aspiration to become a gentleman or gentlewoman was relevant to everyone, and the quickest way to riches, if one was not born with them, was by astute business deals, by political gambling, or, if none of these possibilities was open, by stealing someone else's. This meant that the cleverness with which the businessman operated had to be matched by the craft of the criminal: the latter had to be a professional. Failure at one's job meant financial or political ruin; it could also mean hanging. So, while much of the crime carried out may well have been of the 'hit and run' type, the most successful criminals promoted crime to the level of a financial art, in which the mercantile practice of book-keeping was the largest part. The most ruthless of these organized criminals, Jonathan Wild, controlled crime as others controlled their businesses - by having an efficient work-force which was answerable only to him; only he controlled the stock. England's pastoral days seemed to be over:

> The birds of the air, the rabbits of the heath, the fish in the streams were ferociously protected for the sport and sustenance of gentlemen. Property acquired the sanctity of life and theft meant death ... hanging as punishment for crime increased ... (power was) also for the class which had come to dominate British life - commercially minded landowners with a sharp eye for profit.[2]

While we may now argue that death did not necessarily ensue after a conviction for theft, the general point remains that the image which dominated the literary and social landscape was one of the merchant in pursuit of the material, a man who no longer required the green world for escape but simply for acquisition of property. Criminals, too, needed a commercial mind, as well as a keen eye for survival in what appeared to have become the opposite of the pastoral which was the great wen of the intricacies of the London streets.

If the underworld on London had to contend with a variety of statutes, it did not have the problem of evasion of the police force. Social histories of London reveal that the town was still administered as though it were a mediaeval village, with the police no more powerful than the parish constables.[3] It was not until the time of Fielding that a real push was made towards the fighting of crime, both in theory and in practice.[4] By 1751, Parliament had come around to the idea, backed up by Fielding's suggestions, that hanging was not a deterrent since it had done nothing to curb the number of convicted thieves. A Committee of the House of Commons in 1751 found that:

> It would be reasonable to exchange the punishment of death, which is now inflicted for some sorts of offences, into some other adequate punishments' - a proposal which resulted in a bill ... to substitute 'confinement and hard labour in his majesty's dockyards' for the death penalty in a number of crimes. - (this) reflected a conviction coming to be widely held that the uncritical harshness of the criminal law had distorted the administration of justice and was itself partly to blame for the increase of crime.[5]

In fact, the Bill was thrown out by the Lords, who seemed then to confirm once more that property must be held as sacrosanct. The concern that Parliament felt was one with which many sympathised; the absence of any effective police force and the increasing emphasis on possessions soon came to mean that criminals did not confine their activities to clandestine robberies:

> In 1731, the author of an anonymous pamphlet related how highwaymen and criminals, no longer content to practice their skills on Hounslow Heath or on the outskirts of the capital, were brazenly moving in to the centre; he instanced cases of stage coaches being robbed in High Holborn, Whitechapel, Pall Mall and Soho, and of citizens being held up in their carriages in Cheapside, St Paul's Churchyard and the Strand.[6]

After a robbery the thief would have little difficulty in secreting himself in the back streets of London; they were 'a confused tangle of courts and alleys (which) afforded endless opportunities to escape, where peace-officers penetrated only rarely and in force, and whence unwary strangers were unlikely to escape unharmed'.[7] Some parts of London became dens of thieves for, as the city spread eastwards, the poor crowded into such areas as Stepney, Ratcliffe, Wapping and Shadwell; they were able to create a kind of substitute for the lost communities whence they came.[8] They learned their new trade very quickly; in the following passage, Ned Ward is guided around a prison by a friend:

> 'In this narrow Part of the Street', said my Friend, 'where we are now passing, many such a Wretch has taken his last Walk, for we are now going towards that famous University of Newgate where if a Man has a Mind to educate a hopeful Child in the daring Science of Paddling, the light-fingered Subtlety of Shoplifting, and the excellent Use of Jack and Craw, in the silently drawing Bolts, and forcing Barricades, and the Knack of sweet'ning, or the most ingenious Dexterity of picking Pockets, let him but enter him in this College on the Common Side, and confine him close to his Study but for three months, and if he does not come out qualified to take any Degree of Villainy he must be the most honest Dunce that ever had the Advantage of such eminent Tutors'.[9]

There is certainly irony present in the above, but the passage also testifies to the need for the acquisition of criminal skills in the eighteenth-century.

69

Crime was a profession like any other, and a knowledge of the intricacies of the profession was necessary for success.

Prostitutes often created a diversion for bullies or thieves; Rosamund Bayne-Powell describes a typical example:

> They create a bustle and try over the pockets of unsuspecting persons; till at length having marked one out, the accomplice shoves him hard up against other persons (usually some of the gang) who naturally repress the intrusion. Thus wedged in they hit him over the head with a stick, when he, to save his hat, or resent the insults, lifts up his arms. A third or fourth still further behind gives one more shove, rams his flat hand against the belly of the person marked out to be done, and pulls out his watch.[10]

The highly planned attack ensures that the victim has little idea as to who was responsible, nor would he have much opportunity to escape.

As the population of London increased, the women had more opportunities for increasing their wealth. They also had a firm tradition in which to work; the following is a piece of advice given from a bawd to a pimp, written in 1660:

> give them Instructions to paint, powder and perfume their Clothes and Carkasses, have fine clean Holland-smocks, kiss with their Mouths open, put their Tongues, as all Wantons do, in his Mouth, and suck it, their left Hand in his Cod-piece, the right Hand in his Pocket, commend his Trapstick, pluck their Coats above their Thighs, their Smocks above their Knees.[11]

This is an example of the professionalism of the women, as they are instructed in the correct way to conduct their business in order to maximise their profit. No doubt Defoe's Roxana would have approved.

(2)

London life seemed to have become transformed from one of relative simplicity to one in which the mob could rule and in which 'the crowd' had become the dominant factor. The individual may be seen to be struggling to assert himself, either through the crowd or by being at odds with it. While it would be dangerous to assert the 'mob rule' idea in an over-simplified way, it has its attractions, for it allows the observer of literature and political life to draw interesting parallels. There is little doubt that the crowd became more dominant and noticeable during the course of the earlier part of the century. The drift into the town too, meant the growth of a new breed of criminal: one associated with the mercantile art of stockjobbing. Crowds meant that the individual had to fight for recognition of his individual identity, while at the same time, communities could be destroyed with the establishment of supremacy of mob rule. As one writer has noted, crowds may mean both that the individual becomes lost in society and at the same time this casting adrift could mean that the destruction of a particular community may be inevitable.[12] A not unconnected observation would be that it would be in the interests of such men as Jonathan Wild to ensure that his own community retained the upper hand against the endeavours of another to overthrow or overcome it. One method would be to create the impression - mythical or otherwise - that a new gang of controllers of property and people were gaining the upper hand and it was to them that one owed allegiance. Contemporary writers noted with disgust the apparent proliferation of crime and the new wave of power which seemed to be sweeping over London; Capt Smith, for example, notes that 'London is more pester'd with low Villainy than any other Place whatever' and that prosecutions are neglected due to 'our shameful Negotiations with Thieves, or their Agents, for the Recovery of *Stolen Goods*, by which, in Reality, we become Aiders and Abettors to them'.[13]

But the struggle for supremacy did not confine itself to the streets, and it would again be an over-simplification to suggest that the crowd or the mob was the only topic of interest. Another new breed had emerged, as a result of a different kind of gathering, for as Defoe notes in the *Tour*, the centre of London had become the market place, and it is to the stockmarket and to stockjobbing that one may turn in order to discover another moving force behind London life and London politics.

As mercantilism and stockjobbing came to be regarded as a part of the vitality of London life, so they came to be celebrated and discussed by contemporary writers. On the stage, a new kind of language seemed to dominate and a different kind of hero emerged. After 1711, when the South Sea Company was established in order to finance the national debt, fortunes could be made or lost without recourse to any kind of visible labour. The jobber, dealing in paper in 'Exchange Alley', had as much chance of gaining or losing a fortune as the merchant, dealing in tangible goods. The rivalry and the difference between the two enabled a different kind of dramatic confrontation to take place, within the framework of a different kind of language.

These confrontations are limited, for after a few scenes the language of bulls and bears becomes repetitive, but the inclusion of such scenes reflects the importance that jobbing held. In *A Bold Stroke for a Wife*, Susan Centlivre introduces negotiations between Tradelove and some Stockjobbers. The following scene takes place in 'Jonathan's Coffee House in Exchange Alley'. There is a crowd of people 'with rolls of paper and parchment in their hands'; Tradelove and Jobbers enter, also holding papers:

First Stockjobber
> South Sea at seven-eighths Who buys?

Second Stockjobber
> South Sea bonds due at Michaelmas, 1718 Class Lottery tickets

Third Stockjobber

East India Bonds?

Fourth Stockjobber

What, all Sellers and no Buyers? Gentlemen, I'll buy a thousand Pounds for Tuesday next at three-fourths.

Coffee Boy

Fresh Coffee, Gentlemen, fresh Coffee?

Tradelove

Hark ye, Gabriel, you'll pay the Difference of that Stock we transacted for t'other day.

Gabriel

Ay, Mr Tradelove, here's a note for the Money, upon the Sword Blade Company. (Gives him a note)

Coffee Boy

Bohea Tea, Gentlemen?

Enter a Man

Man

Is Mr Smuggle here?

Coffee Boy

Mr Smuggle's not here, sir; you'll find him at the Books.

Second Stockjobber

Ho Here comes two Sparks from the other End of the Town; what News bring they?

Enter two Gentlemen

Tradelove

I would fain bite that Spark in the brown Coat; he comes very often into the Alley but never employs a Broker.

Enter Colonel and Freeman

Second Stockjobber

Who does anything in the Civil List Lottery? Zounds, where are all the Jews this Afternoon? (To third Stockjobber) Are you a Bull or a Bear today, Abraham?

Third Stockjobber

A Bull, faith - but I have a good Put for next Week.

Tradelove

Mr Freeman, your Servant. (Points to the Colonel) Who is that Gentleman?

Freeman

A Dutch Merchant, just come to England; but hark ye, Mr Tradelove - I have a Piece of news will get you as much as the French King's death did, if you are expeditious.

72

Tradelove
> Say you so, Sir Pray, what is it?

Freeman (showing him a letter)
> Read there; I received it just now from one that belongs to the Emperor's Minister.

Tradelove (reads aloud)
> "Sir, As I have many Obligations to you, I cannot miss any Opportunity to show my Gratitude; this Moment, my Lord has received a private Express that the Spaniards have raised their Siege from before Cagliari; if this prove any Advantage to you, it will answer both the Ends and Wishes of, Sir, your most obliged humble Servant, Henricus Dusseldorp". "Postscript. In two or three Hours the news will be public". (Aside to Freeman) May one depend upon this, Mr Freeman?

Freeman
> You may - I never knew this Person send me a false Piece of news in my life.

Tradelove (aside to Freeman)
> Sir, I am much obliged to you; egad, 'tis rare news. (Aloud) Who sells South Sea for next Week?

Stockjobbers (all together)
> I sell; I,I,I,I sell.

First Stockjobber
> I'll sell five thousand Pounds for next week at five-eighths.

Second Stockjobber
> I'll sell ten thousand at five-eighths for the same Time.

Tradelove
> Nay, nay, hold, hold, not all together, Gentlemen; I'll be no Bull; I'll buy no more than I can take. Will you sell ten thousand pound at a Half, for any day next Week except Saturday?

First Stockjobber
> I'll sell it you, Tradelove[14]

The 'Sword Blade Company', the 'Civil List Lottery' and the Spanish siege of Cagliari are among the contemporary references in the above passage which, if uninteresting to a modern reader may only be so because he is used to such speculative trading and financial dealings. What the passage does contain, besides its fairly obvious 'taking' by Tradelove of the First Stockjobber and the attempt at humour, is almost a celebration of the language of the market place and an acknowledgement that the world of war, of trading and of finance are intimately linked. Although subtleties of character or form are avoided, the overriding impression is one of novelty - here, on stage, is a different world but one which has its own laws and one which has its own language. The sharp exchanges are part of the portrayal of the quick-witted individual who is ever eager for profit and who is always ready to indulge in the war with the new mob of the market-place - the stockjobbers.

The stockjobber, however, had a poor time of it as far as his contemporaries were concerned. Far from being closely associated in kind or degree with the merchant, the stockjobber was often seen as an antipathy to him; while the merchant boosted both his own and the nation's wealth, the stockjobber was a mere wheeler-dealer in paper. This view may be hinted at in the above quotation, in which the stockjobbers appear motivated only by their own self-interest and it seems that we are expected to approve of Tradelove's victory over them. The stockjobber is a parasite whose aim - the preservation of his own power through the manipulation of those around him - would be closely linked with the desire for personal aggrandisement and fortune, which in turn was protected by their tightly knit rules and their private vocabulary. Maybe we are not far away from the world of crime after all. The Merchant, however, remained a man of some honour:

> When I am giving my Thoughts a Loose in the Contemplation of the Ways of Men, there is no Man whom I so highly honour as the Merchant. This is he who turns all the Disadvantages of our Situation into our Profit and Honour. His Care and Industry ties his Country to the Continent, and the whole Globe pays his Nation a voluntary Tribute due to her from his Merit. His Hand-writing has the Weight of Coin, and his good Character is Riches to the rest of his Countrymen. All other Subjects of our Island, from the highest to the lowest, are as much below the Merchant in political Merit as that ravenous Worm in the Entrails of the State, the Stockjobber.[15]

These points, if less radically expressed than in the above passage, occur frequently during this period. The form is usually of a pattern, and conforms to the one suggested by Centlivre and stated explicitly by Steele. The merchant is the defender of all the state and the individual may, without question, hold dear. That is, luxury and wealth are deserved rewards for those who profess industry and who recognise the value of the buying and selling of goods and possessions rather than the purchase (or 'false purchase' in the case of bears) of pieces of paper. In Colley Cibber's play *The Refusal*, Sir Gilbert Wrangle, though a stockjobber, is primarily a merchant. He cannot really come to terms with the 'fever' of stockjobbing, and has this comment to make on the value of City life:

> You'll find 'tis not your Court, but City-Politicians must do the Nation's Business at last. Why, what did your Courtiers do all the two last Reigns, but borrow Money to make War? and make War to make Peace, and make Peace to make War? And then to be Bullies in one, and Bubbles in t'other? A very pretty Account truly: but we have made Money, Man: Money Money there's the Health and Life-Blood of a Government: And there, for I insist upon't, that we are the wisest Citizens in *Europe*, for we have coin'd more Cash in an Hour, than the Tower of London in twenty Years.[16]

In the above extract, the City is at the centre of all political and economic decisions and it may be seen to be active in all affairs and to bring about those affairs in a positive and orderly manner. Politicians, like Stockjobbers in the Steele quotation, are the antithesis of 'help', 'health' or 'life'; they exist merely as parasites upon a system that would thrive better without them. The view that Cibber was a consistent defender of the mercantile class and critic of the stockjobber is one which should not be given too much credence, for in the same play Wrangle is described as a South Sea Director and associated with the Lord Treasurer. In order to be as generous as possible to Cibber, one could argue that the ambiguity which seems to be present in the play may reflect a general confusion; one may admire the merchant for making money, but should one admire the jobber for achieving the same ends through different means? Whereas Steele has few doubts and Centlivre avoids the issue, Cibber plunges in and leaves us with passages which support either view.

Whatever one's view of the nature of the men engaged in trade at this time, there is no doubt that they controlled and fed upon the desire of the nation to increase its wealth and to gain in material stature. The mercantile mind became the mind of the whole country as the City took over from the Country. The vocabulary of the City became the vocabulary of literature and debate. The association between politics, the treasury of the nation, and the rule of money over the land, provoked a further confrontation between those who sought power and those who saw it being removed from them by the new gangs.

(3)

The idea that London had become corrupt under the influence of 'great men' was a familiar one to readers of opposition pamphlets and newspapers. These prose writings were soon to have a grand ally in their fight against corruption, namely, the theatre and more especially in the plays of John Gay. The *Beggar's Opera* now becomes central to the discussion, for Gay includes so many ideas and so many comparisons and parallels with contemporary London. Attention must focus on the play in order to achieve a clear idea of the nature of the satiric attacks.

But although *The Beggar's Opera* occupies this pivotal position, any student of eighteenth-century satire would recognise that the play has a firm tradition in which to work. An ally to the political pamphlet or the opposition newspaper, the play also draws on the traditions of caricature and ballad-singing which were used as weapons against the government and as a means to expose the corruption and degeneration of London, while Walpole himself was portrayed by his contemporaries as being responsible for the entire system of corrupt financial practices. As Percival notes, many minor plays had satiric references. *The Fate of Villainy* (1730), for example, has Ramirez as its villain. He is a chief minister 'who engrossed and betrayed the King's Favour', while the prologue says of him;

Behold a foreign Statesman, vilely great, Tho' long successful, sacrificed to Fate.[17]

Percival adds that, although this may not be a close parallel, it shows that dramatists were intent upon working within a tradition and of criticising political ambition wherever possible. This particular dramatist was quite clearly anticipating with relish the eventual sacrifice.

If the gangs of politicians, stockjobbers and criminals were controlling the life of London and at the same time transforming its language, they could be seen as an extension of a social evil which had been part of the London scene for several years. It is to gang warfare that Gay turns in the early play *The Mohocks*. Described by Gay as a 'Tragi-Comical Farce' it highlights a particular social phenomenon of the time, while providing some interesting parallels with the idea of 'mob rule'. The 'play' is worth considering since it is part of this documentation of the underworld of the time and part of the author's attempt to reveal the contemptible nature of it.[18]

'Mohocks' were gangs of young men who roamed the streets at night to rob and attack women. Called 'Scourers' in the time of Charles II, they had a reputation of being town rakes and bullies, but they may also have been young Whigs out to bait unfortunate Tory nightwalkers.[19] Gay gives the leader of the gang the mock title of 'Emperor' as a reminder that Machiavellian politicians and street brawlers had much in common. The Mohocks boast over their activities:

CABADDON

Thus far our Riots with Success are crown'd, Have found no Stop, or what they found o'ercame; In vain th'embattled Watch in deep array, Against our Rage oppose their lifted Poles; Through Poles we rush triumphant, Watchman rolls On Watchman: while their Lanthorns kicked aloft Like blazing Stars, illumine all the Air.

Moh. Such Acts as these have made our Game immortal, And wide through all Britannia's distant Towns, The Name of Mohock ev'ry tongue employs;[20]

The characters, such as they are, exist to make a point about contemporary society, and it was one which Gay felt was well worth making. The Mohocks although satirised in this play, were apparently not a force to be treated lightly, and Gay returns to his theme in a passage from *Trivia*:

I pass their desp'rate Deeds and Mischiefs done, Where from *Snow-hill* black sleepy Torrents run; How Matrons, hoop'd within the Hogshead's

76

Womb, Were tumbled furious thence, the rolling Tomb O'er the Stones thunders, bounds from Side to Side, So *Regulus* to save his Country dy'd.[21]

The point is that the lawlessness by which the men existed posed a threat to ordinary citizens. Gay and Fielding came close to one another in their concerns here, for both were moved to write about the latent undercurrent of violence and corruption and its effect upon the common man. The Mohocks revel in the fact that the law is incapable of dealing with them:

Great Potentate who leadst the Mohock Squadrons To nightly Expeditions, whose dread Nod Gives Law to those, lawless to all besides: To thee I come - to serve beneath thy Banner. Mischief has long lain dormant in my Bosom Like smother'd Fire, which now shall blaze abroad In glorious Enterprise.[22]

There is a suggestion here that the Emperor is a Satanic figure who leads the crew not just in nightly revelry but also in an attempt to promote anarchy. In a song which appears later in the play, this idea is expressed once more:

Then a Mohock, a Mohock I'll be, No Law shall restrain Our libertine Reign, We'll riot, drink on, and be free.[23]

The confusion between riot and freedom is one which will lead to a selfish operation of their will with complete neglect of the wishes of the ordinary people who are their victims. The high opinion which they have of themselves is coupled with the contempt they have for the law in a scene which parodies the magistrate's court and in which Gay attempts to expose the nature of the gang. The Mohocks disguise themselves as Constables and Watchmen by forcing the latter to change clothes with them and they proceed to try various innocent people - including the Constables - while the Emperor acts as chief magistrate. The scene is an attempt at a farcical reproduction of their anarchical activities as they show total contempt for the process of the law, and by doing so they threaten the whole framework of society. Gentle is put on trial:

Emp: Harkye, Fellow, you seem very suspicious, you have a downcast, hanging Look
Gent: A languishing Air, you mean Sir
Emp: Give an Account of yourself, Fellow, whence come you? whither are you going? What is your Business abroad at this time of Night - take his Sword from him there, lest he should have some evil Design against the Queen's Officer.
Gent: I am a Gentleman, Sir
Emp: A doubtful, a shuffling Answer we need no farther Proof that he is a Mohock - commit him
Gent: 'Tis a strange Thing that the Vulgar cannot distinguish the Gentleman ... Believe me, Sir, there is a certain *Je ne scai quoi* in my Manner that

shews my Conversation to have lain altogether among the politer Part of
the World.

Emp: Look ye, Sir, your Manners in talking *Latin* before her Majesty's
Officer, shew you to be an ill-designing Person.[24]

The scene as a whole fails for several reasons, not least of which is that
it is too long. Gentle himself seems to belong to the tradition of the fop
and this association tends to detract from the main idea behind the mock
trial. Gay has too many masters to serve; Gentle, as a fop and a figure of
fun may be seen to deserve his treatment, although in this scene he is
supposed to be the innocent victim of the Mohocks' pranks. What Gay is
seeking to communicate is the notion that the law needs respect and
attention. The main idea is expressed by Cloudy, a Constable, before the
farce against them commences:

O Magistrate, thou art, as I may say, So great by Night, as is Queen Anne
by Day, And what greater Power can anywhere be seen? For you do
represent the Person of the Queen.[25]

In the face of the control which the Mohocks have over the citizen and
the law, there seems little that anyone can do to prevent their rise to
power. By binding Gentle and the Constables, the Mohocks bring their
control out into the open and make it a physical reality. There is, however,
one solution offered, and one which links Gay with Fielding. The suggested
solution is spoken by Joan Cloudy:

To be tongue-tied is fit for nothing but Liars and Swearers. I'll speak the
Truth, and shame the Devil. Tho' a Constable be to keep Peace and
Quietness, yet the greatest Constable in England shall not make me hold
my Tongue, when there is Occasion for Speaking.[26]

One way to combat the threats which are posed by the gang - and by
all criminals - is to speak out. Fielding and Gay did so through irony and
satire; the persistent effort was to make their audience aware of the reality
of the contemporary situation. *The Mohocks* may fail as far as this absolute
aim is concerned, but it gives a positive indication that Gay's thoughts
were focussed on society and its problems.

Gay's attack upon society and government finds its most intense
expression in *The Beggar's Opera*. The gang in the play is the most
dominant symbol, for Gay is playing upon the idea that London was, by
1728, becoming overrun by gangs of criminals whose methods paralleled
closely those of Walpole and his government. Unwittingly, Walpole had
added to the intensity of the image, for, through a series of measures such
as the 'Black Act', he had encouraged the idea that crime was a rapidly
expanding business and that the law itself must expand in order to deal
with it. A note of caution must be sounded here but it is one which does
not alter the impact of the play. It is easy to arrive at the conclusion that
crime was on the increase during this period, and indeed, evidence suggests

that this was the case; we may also view the rise of gangs as a significant aspect of eighteenth-century life, but a critic of the period must also recognise that the term 'gang' was also a convenient one for the government to use, as it attempted to impose order upon a country which had so many disparate elements and which proved difficult to govern. That, however, is not the point here, for it is the *image* of the gang which dominates the play. The literal truth of the growth of crime makes no difference to the impact of the play which uses the image and the belief in this growth to satirize contemporary institutions.

In *The Beggar's Opera*, Peachum is both Walpole and Wild; he persistently manipulates criminals and balance sheets for his own ends. One of the dangers in any discussion of the play becomes apparent here and that is an insistence upon an absolute alliance between characters in the play and those in real life. Gay's aims can be seen in more general terms and coincide with the aims of Fielding. 'For petty rogues submit to fate/ That great ones may enjoy their state' is the basic message of the play which 'scores its hits by way of a succession of political parallels, each established briefly and then obscured as different character relationships emerge'.[27] Indeed, further to this, the play may be most illuminatingly seen as structured on a system of oppositions, and ideological oppositions at that. The character of Peachum, as both Walpole and Wild, suggests that the court and the criminal are so close in attitude and behaviour as to be indistinguishable, while Macheath represents a kind of erotic, anarchic alternative to organised crime and would find his parallel in the figure of Sheppard.[28]

Peachum sees that his own self-interest must dominate and as a result, reason and morality - two words which acquire an intensely ironic significance as the play progresses - are ignored or turned upside-down. He is in favour of a stagnant society, in which his own riches are increased at the expense of trust, friendship or honour. He attempts to justify his actions as a seller of stolen goods and a thief-taker by a rationalisation which reduces everyone to his level:

> Through all the Employments of Life Each Neighbour abuses his Brother; Whore and Rogue they call Husband and Wife; All Professions be-rogue one another. The Priest calls the Lawyer a cheat; The Lawyer be-knaves the Divine; And the Statesman, because he's so great, Thinks his Trade as honest as mine.

> A Lawyer is an honest Employment; so is mine. Like me too he acts in a double Capacity, both against Rogues and for 'em; for 'tis but fitting that we should protect and encourage Cheats, since we live by them.[29]

The reasoning here is Machiavellian and is full of self-interest, but at the same time it exposes ironically a major issue of the time, the parallel between the politician and the thief. While Gay provokes amusement and condemnation, Peachum expects reward from his acts which are consistent with the corruption of the times. Peachum completely opposes change and he prefers instead a static society which allows him to promote his financial interests. He represents here the class which saw itself as self-made and therefore self-deserving. Peachum sees everything and everybody in terms of their financial use and therefore renders absurd the sanctity of commodity interest. Polly's love for Macheath is condemned:

> A handsome Wench in our way of Business is as profitable as at the Bar of a Temple Coffeehouse, who looks upon it as her Livelihood to grant any Liberty but one. You see I would indulge the Girl as far as prudently we can - in anything but Marriage After that, my dear, how shall we be safe? Are we not then in her Husband's power? For a Husband hath the absolute Power over all a Wife's Secrets but her own ... Married If the Wench does not know her own Profit, sure she knows her own Pleasure better than to make herself a Property My Daughter to me should be, like a Court Lady to a Minister of State, a Key to the whole Gang.[30]

People may be owned in both marriage and trade and family ties are seen in terms of profit and loss, balance sheets and possession. Polly, as a member of a gang, should not be foolish enough to allow her affections to override business interests.

The Peachums decide that the only solution to their problem is to have Macheath 'peached', i.e. to hand him over to the law with evidence that he is a thief, so that he will hang:

> Peachum : But really, my dear, it grieves one's Heart to take off a great Man. When I consider his personal Bravery, his fine Stratagem, how much we have already got by him, and how much more we may get, methinks I can't find in my Heart to have a hand in his Death. I wish you could have made Polly undertake it.
> Mrs Peachum: But in a case of Necessity - our own Lives are in Danger.
> Peachum : Then, indeed, we must comply with the Customs of the World, and make Gratitude give way to Interest. He shall be taken off.[31]

By showing the inhumanity and absurd logic of Peachum, Gay exposes the mentality of the thief-taker and controller of the gang while at the same time he scores a political hit. By alluding to the politician/thief analogy, Gay clarifies his position as one ideologically opposed to the current regime, without suggesting that any alternative, either in the past or in the present, may be preferable. Walpole felt the hit and riposted by insulting Gay as a 'fat clown', words which, in Gay's hands could no doubt be turned upon Walpole himself while Swift wrote to Gay asking 'Does W------ think you intended an Affront on him in your Opera? Pray God he may, for he has held the longest Hand at Hazard that ever fell to any Sharpers Share and keeps his Run when the Dice are changed'.[32]

By way of contrast to Peachum, Gay introduces the vibrantly erotic figure of Macheath. Although a thief, he shows compassion and subscribes to the belief that there should be honour among thieves; he is, of course, condemned by those very thieves towards whom he feels drawn. He sees, too, that the city is also controlled by the mob who are moved not by friendship but by the movement of people and of funds:

> I am sorry, Gentlemen, the Road was so barren of Money. When my Friends are in Difficulties, I am always glad that my Fortune can be serviceable to them. (Gives them money.) You see, Gentlemen, I am not a mere Court Friend, who professes everything and will do nothing.

AIR XLIV *Lillibulero*

> The Modes of the Court so common are grown,
> That a true Friend can hardly be met;
> Friendship for Interest is but a Loan,
> Which they let out for what they can get.
>   'Tis true, you find
>   Some Friends so kind,
> Who will give you good Counsel themselves to defend
>   In sorrowful Ditty
>   They promise, they pity,
> But shift you for Money, from Friend to Friend.

> But we Gentlemen, have still Honor enough to break through the Corruptions of the world. And while I can serve you, you may command me.[33]

Although he accepts that he can do nothing about the court or the city, he can see that there is an alternative and one to which he subscribes, albeit vaguely. A victim of stockjobbing and sale and exchange he may be, but he in turn ensures that others become his victims.

Macheath refers to himself as 'a man of honor' in his relations with women but this is quite clearly not the case. He expresses an avowal of love to both Lucy and Polly and seems quite prepared to marry both or either, provided that the veneer of respectability that he possesses remains intact. So, from the mouths of the controllers and the controlled, emerge attitudes which are contradictory. Peachum takes at face value the words 'Statesman' and 'honest' in order to support his position when, in fact, the words ought to be substituted for, and are synonymous with, their opposites. Macheath, although sensual and apparently a hero-figure (in the sense that he opposes Peachum) contains within himself a contradiction which implies that his honesty, too, is defined by self-interest of sexuality and passion:

> I love the Sex. And a Man who loves Money might as well be contented with one Guinea as I with one Woman ... What signifies a Promise to a Woman? Does not Man in Marriage itself promise a hundred Things that he never means to perform? Do all we can, Women will believe us, for they look upon a Promise as an Excuse for following their own Inclinations.[34]

If Peachum is a self-made man, Macheath is one who must live by Peachum's power and yet he can also argue that he has retained a certain amount of dignity. But his dignity and honour are hardly credible as he uses his wits to dupe Lucy and Polly just as he is controlled by Peachum. Gay's London is full of hypocrisy masquerading as honour and selfishness disguised as altruism. We are thrust into a city which is dominated by gangs, yet which in turn is controlled by one man.

Polly, Gay's sequel to *The Beggar's Opera*, pursues the idea of honour amongst individual members of the gang. Polly and Macheath appear once more, but Gay changes the emphasis; Macheath (alias Morano) is portrayed as an uncompromisng pirate. His answer to all problems is to plunder and kill in order to provide for himself and anyone who opposes him is despatched quickly:

> Morano: Look'ee, Lieutenant, the trussing up this Prince, in my Opinion, would strike a Terror among the Enemy. Besides, dead Men can do no Mischief. Let a Gibbet be set up, and swing him off between the Armies before the Onset.[35]

Any honour that may have been present in *The Beggar's Opera* has now finally disappeared, for Morano's gang are a bunch of selfish squabblers, intent upon lining their own pockets at the expense of honour and friendship. At several points, speeches in *Polly* act almost as a commentary upon the nature of the reality of the former play; Polly disguised as a man, attempts to join Morano's gang:

> Morano: What are you, Friend?
> Polly: A young Fellow, who hath been robb'd by the World and I come on Purpose to join you, to rob the World by way of Retaliation. An open War with the whole World is brave and honourable. I hate the clandestine pilfering War that is practised among Friends and Neighbours in civil Societies. I would serve, Sir.

AIR XXXIV

The World is always jarring;
    This is pursuing
    T'other Man's Ruin,
Friends with Friends are warring,
In a false cowardly Way ...

Each, returning Hate,
Wounds and robs his Friends.
    In civil Life,
    Even Man and Wife
Squabble for selfish Ends.[35]

The terms 'civil' and 'friendship' therefore take on the same duplicity that their counterparts did in *The Beggar's Opera*, but with the truth of the matter being quite openly stated; 'man and wife' simply 'squabble for selfish ends', as the Peachums have done, while Macheath himself has been betrayed by 'friends'. The 'civil life' meaning the life within the city, is one of cheating, where the Peachums and the Lockets of the world have a superficial alliance which may be torn asunder by any trivial dispute. Loyalty means nothing and it may be bought and sold; two of Morano's group, Laguerre and Capstan, are entrusted with the care of their prisoner, Cawwawkee, a West Indian Prince; Polly bribes them to set him free:

> Laguerre: If we conquer'd and the Booty were to be divided among the Crews, what would it amount to? Perhaps this Way we might get more than would come to our Shares.

> Capstan: Then too, I always lik'd a place at Court. I have a Genius to get, keep in, and make the most of an Employment.

> Laguerre: You will consider, Prince, our own Politicians would have rewarded such meritorious Services.[37]

The parallel between the act of the pirates and those of the politicians is made quite clear, as each side sells its services to the highest bidder. While professing an ideology of comradeship, in fact the crew are motivated only by greed and financial gain. Both groups of robbers remain loyal to the side that employs them.

Gay introduces a contrast in the play, and this time it is a real rather than an apparent one. The West Indian King, Pohetohee, and his son, Cawwawkee, are contemptuous of the actions and general way of life of the Europeans. 'Sure', says Cawwawkee, 'speech can be of no use to you', and so sums up much of what happens beneath the words of the two plays, for it is only by removing the surface meaning and exposing the real one that the motives of the characters become apparent. At one point, Morano attempts to do a deal with Pohetohee:

> Poh: Shall Robbers and Plunderers prescribe Rules to Right and Equity? Insolent Madman! Composition with Knaves is base and ignominious. Tremble at the Sword of Justice, rapacious Brute.[38]

During the ensuing battle, Pohetohee puts Morano to death, justifying his action by 'Tis my Duty, as a King, to cherish and protect Virtue', a sentiment of which Bolingbroke would have approved and one which, taken together with the play as a whole and with *The Beggar's Opera*, proved too much for Walpole. *Polly* was suppressed in December, 1728. Morano's condemnation has an ironic side to it:

> In London and at Court (with special innuendoes cast at Walpole and political life), robbers and plunderers do prescribe the rules. The inference is that those rapacious brutes who nourish themselves on money, swollen as they are with the fat of power and the sweat of lechery, have buried the sword of justice in Fleet Street - and human dignity with it.[39]

Even though goodness and virtue triumph at the end of the play, its suppression ensured that its message would have to be communicated by other means. Its suppression was also an acknowledgement of the potential political power of the theatre and of the ideological values that the government possessed, a point which contemporary writers were quick to note. The following ballad appeared in the *Craftsman* of 28 Dec. 1728:

Ye Poets, take Heed how you trust to the Muse,
What Words to make Choice of, and what to refuse,
If she hint at a Vice of *political* Sort
Application cries out, *That's* a Bob for the C (our)t,
Corruption, Ambition, Pomp, Vanity, Pride,
Are terms, that by Guess-Work are often apply'd;
To quote HORACE is thought meer Derision and Sport;
Application cries out, *That's a* Bob for the C (our)t.
If *Macheath* you should name, in the midst of his *Gang*
They'll say 'tis a Hint you would *Somebody* hang;
For *Macheath* is a Word of such evil Report,
Application cries out, *That's a* Bob for the C (our)t.[40]

Political opposition could not be entirely suppressed, and protest ballads of this sort appeared weekly. There is a further irony embedded in *Polly* however, for the action of the play takes place away from London, and so the capital is unaffected by the defeat of Macheath. The problem of how to remove Macheath and his gang from their empire of control remained just as strong.

NOTES

1. Leon Radzinowicz, *A History of English Criminal Law*, 4 vols, (London 1948), vol. I, p.3.
2. J. H. Plumb, 'Political Man' in *Man Versus Society in Eighteenth-Century Britain*, edited by James L. Clifford (Cambridge 1968), pp. 8-9.
3. Dorothy Marshall, *Eighteenth-Century England* (London, 1962), pp. 36-7.
4. See postscript to chapter 5, below.
5. J. M. Beattie, 'Crime and the Courts in Surrey, 1736-1753' in *Crime in England 1500-1800*, edited by J. S. Cockburn (London, 1977), pp. 155-6.
6. George Rude, *Hanoverian London 1714-1808* (London, 1971), p. 96.
7. J. J. Tobias, *Crime and Industrial Society in the Nineteenth Century* (London, 1967) p. 26.
8. See Rude, op. cit., pp. 11-12.
9. Ned Ward, *The London Spy*, edited by Arthur L. Hayward (London, 1927), p. 96.
10. Quoted by Donald Rumbelow in *I Spy Blue. The Police and Crime in the City of London from Elizabeth I to Victoria* (London, 1971), p. 82.
11. John Garfield, *The Wandering Whore*, numbers 1-5 (London, 1660), p. 12, published by The Rota at the University of Exeter, 1977.
12. Max Byrd, *London Transformed. Images of the City in the Eighteenth Century* (Yale University Press,1978), p.25.

13. Captain Alexander Smith, *Memoirs of the Life and Times of the Famous Jonathan Wild* (London, 1726), pp.iii-iv.

14. Susan Centlivre, *A Bold Stroke for a Wife*, edited by Thalia Stathias (London, 1969), IV. i: pp.54-57.

15. Richard Steele, *The Englishman* (first series, no. 4, 13 Oct.1713): quoted by John Loftis in *Comedy and Society from Congreve to Fielding* (Stanford University Press, California, 1959), p.94-5.

16. Colley Cibber, *The Refusal*: in *Plays* vol. II, edited by Rodney L. Hayley (New York, 1980), III, p. 415, collated as Ggg4r in edition of London 1721.

17. Quoted by Percival (ed), op. cit., p.xix. For further discussion of the emblematic representation of Walpole and his policies during this period, see Paul Langford, *Walpole and the Robinocracy* (Cambridge, 1986); the book reproduces over 100 contemporary prints.

18. The 'play' has never been acted. See William Henry Irving, *John Gay Favourite of the Wits* (North Carolina, 1940), p.66.

19. See Sven M. Armens, *John Gay. Social Critic* (London, 1954), p.240.

20. John Gay, *The Mohocks*, scene I: in *The Poetical, Dramatic and Miscellaneous Works* of John Gay, 6 vols, (London, 1795), vol. V, pp. 75-6.

21. John Gay, *Trivia*, pt III, ll. 329-334: in *Poetry and Prose*, edited by V. A. Dearing, 2 vols, (Oxford, 1974), vol. I, pp. 169-170.

22. John Gay, *The Mohocks*, sc.1, op. cit., vol. I, p.78.

23. Ibid. sc.I: p.78.

24. Ibid. sc.II: p.86.

25. Ibid. sc.II: p.79.

26. Ibid. sc.II, p.88.

27. John Loftis, *The Politics of Drama in Augustan England* (Oxford, 1963), p.4.

28. See Michael Denning, 'Beggars and Thieves' in *Literature and History*, vol 8 no. 1 (Spring 1982), pp.41-55, for an interesting discussion of this aspect of the play.

29. John Gay, *The Beggar's Opera*, I,1, edited by Edgar V. Roberts (London, 1969), p.6.

30. Ibid., I, iv, pp.13-14.

31. Ibid., I, xi, pp.26.

32. See Phoebe Fenwick Gaye, *John Gay. His Place in the Eighteenth Century* (London, 1938), p.328: and Pope, *Correspondence*, op. cit., vol II, p.475 (Swift to Gay, February 26, 1727/28).

33. op. cit., III, iv. p.63.

34. Ibid., II, iii, p.35 and II, viii, p.44: see also P. Lewis, 'The Abuse of Language in the Beggar's Opera' in *The British Journal for Eighteenth-Century Studies* , vol. 4, no. 1, (Spring 1981), 44-53.

35. John Gay, *Polly*, act II in *Works*, etc., op. cit., vol. IV, p.184.

36. Ibid., pp.179-180.

37. Ibid., pp.193-4.
38. Ibid., p.201.
39. Armens, op. cit., p.19.
40. *A Bob for the Court* in Percival (ed), op. cit., pp.20-21.

CHAPTER 5

Crime - Jonathan Wild

The automatic, unchallenged assumption that there was a growth in crime at the beginning of the eighteenth century, which continued as the century progressed, is one which is not surprising, given the increase in the number of laws which were passed in an attempt to combat crime and given the increase in the amount of time expended on discussions regarding the nature of and the reasons for the apparent surge. Newspapers of the period were full of crime reports and advertisements which indicated the whereabouts of stolen goods. The Ordinaries of Newgate found themselves in a position to sell accounts of the lives of criminals who had confessed to them before going to hang; between 1700 and 1760, a period which might be referred to as the heyday of crime, about 237 *Accounts* of the lives of various criminals were written, all coming from the pens of various Ordinaries. They tell of the lives of 58 women and 129 men. An Ordinary could earn about 25 for each *Account* and he would write about five *Accounts* per year.[1] Swift wrote one popular ballad on a criminal - "Clever Tom Clinch going to be Hanged" - while Defoe published pamphlets on the lives of criminals, as well as drawing upon their escapades for use in his novels. For Defoe, it was not only the English street criminals such as Sheppard who became subjects of pamphlets: he wrote about the French highwaymen Bizeau and Cartouche as well as histories of the most notorious pirates of his day. Like many of his contemporaries he also examined the nature of crime and the reasons for its increase and suggested remedies for it.[2]

With so much contemporary evidence, a reader would be forgiven if the assumption went unchallenged; evidence has emerged, however, which complicates the issue and which reveals the nature of the power struggle which was taking place during this period. At the same time, it indicates that contemporary writers used crime and criminals as metaphors in order to make social and political points.

(1)

What, then, is the issue, the point of present debate amongst commentators of the early eighteenth-century social setting? First, was there a real increase in crime and second did this cause the increase in the number of laws passed or did the number of laws passed make it appear that the rate of crime had accelerated? This section will summarise the arguments put forward by both camps - it will then attempt to suggest how the debate helps in a reading of contemporary literature.

Pat Rogers has argued that the 'archetypal Augustan crime was theft'; property having so much importance at the time. The money supply had increased, the trading position of the nation was healthy and entrepreneurs found markets in Europe, America and Africa. Those who were less adventurous found the stockmarket a willing recipient of their money. In short, London was growing at a rapid rate and the influx of people into the capital in order to try to take their share of the wealth meant that material goods and property acquired a new significance. The manipulators of power had changed in appearance, too; they were no longer Tory landowners, but self-made men who were a part of the ruthlessness of the times. The growth of London's wealth, accompanied by its mediaeval police system, meant that crime became more easy to organise; this organisation was of precisely the same sort as could be found in any businessman's office: balance sheets, advertisements and regular hours became significant in both commercial and criminal life. Crime became organised and professional, and literary language reflected this change.[3]

At this stage, the issue becomes more complex and the debate centres around the "Waltham Black Act" of 1723. If contemporary sources are to be believed, then not only London suffered an upsurge in crime during this period. The countryside around London appeared to be full of poachers, who found easy game on the King's land. In general, it was thought that there was a permanent criminal underworld, and the undoubted presence of Wild in London and the Waltham Blacks in the country seemed to confirm this. In 1723 the 'Black Act' was passed, making it a capital offence to poach deer and other animals, to cut down trees or to appear in disguise in the forests. The justification for this was that 'several ill-designing and disorderly persons have of late associated themselves under the name of Blacks, and entered into confederacies to support and assist one another in stealing and destroying of deer, robbing of warrens and fishponds, cutting down plantations of trees, and other illegal practices and have, in great numbers ... unlawfully hunted in forests belonging to his majesty, and in the parks of divers of his majesty's subjects'.[4] It is at this stage, too, that opinions diverge. Rogers sees the Act as a necessary addition to the statutes, since the problem was acute and the tide of crime was reaching flood proportions. The Blacks, he argues, constituted a threat similar to the one posed by Wild and his gang. The vocabulary is significant, for it parallels the idea of the gang stated elsewhere in this study and it reinforces the idea that not only London but the country as a whole was under threat. The Blacks were 'extortionists and protection racketeers' who bore a similarity to Wild in their brutal methods and in their ability to remain uncaptured.[5] Radzinowick has used the Act as an 'ideological index' to the capital laws as a whole, for it had revealed an attitude of mind among the law-makers towards the breaking of the law and the threats which such actions posed.

But what if the attitude of mind was, in fact, something different, and did not stem from a concern with the law but from a concern for property in the first instance and a utilisation of the law towards this end? This line is the one pursued by Speck and Thomson. The former, using E. P. Thompson's findings as his main argument, asserts that to accept the contemporary viewpoint of the danger of the Blacks is to accept a distorted view of the situation. There were, he shows, only a limited number of professional criminals in both London and the provinces, and that 'there were at most ten gangs operating in London during Wild's lifetime, with a total membership of around 150.'[6]

The general, received idea that there were more criminals operating in gangs was reinforced by the publicity that such gangs received. He quotes Thompson, whose thorough investigations revealed that many of the Blacks had respectable occupations: there were a few gentry sympathisers, some substantial farmers, poor foresters from Berkshire, farmers, tradesmen and labourers in Hampshire. Again, only a few of those brought to trial had been accused of any previous crime. Speck also indicates that 'indictments in rural areas fluctuated according to the price of bread' which suggests that the crime rate and poverty had a great deal to do with each other, and hardly suggests that the criminal element was growing *per se*.

By far the most rigorous examination of the truth of contemporary statements about the growth of crime and about the 1723 Act is made by E. P. Thompson. He shows (quite correctly) that it was a severe criminal code, but notes that there was little contemporary mention of it. There was a general feeling that there was an emergency in 1723, thus justifying the Act, but was there a real emergency? Could it have been that the events were exaggerated so that the authorities could assert their power and at the same time protect property which was becoming more and more valuable and more and more symbolic of status as time went on?

The gang image is a tempting one to adopt, especially if it can be substantiated by facts, but Thompson is not sure that it can be. He finds little evidence of a criminal subculture and he wonders how Members of Parliament got 'from the premise that poaching is an affray ... to the view that a man could be killed if he hacked down a tree?' The explanation for the passing of the Act lies, according to Thompson, not in the supposed increase in crime, but in the mentality of the legislators:

> We must explain, not an emergency alone, but an emergency acting upon the sensibility of such men, for whom property and the privileged status of the propertied were assuming, each year, a greater weight in the scales of justice, until justice itself was seen as no more than the outworks and defences of property and its attendant status.[7]

What Thompson is trying to achieve is a more global view of the 1723 Act, by placing it in its political camp. Just as Walpole was consolidating his power, a series of fortunate circumstances arose which allowed him to pass Acts in his favour and to ensure his survival whilst being surrounded by opponents. He had survived the South Sea Crisis and during 1722 and 1723 he was able to reveal numerous Jacobite plots against the state. Sunderland, his chief rival, was dead by 1723, but Walpole still needed a common enemy to distract attention from his own activities. By revealing Jacobite conspiracies he created an external enemy; he imposed a tax upon Catholics and the need to swear allegiance was thus renewed; he had, in the Blacks, a ready-made and indisputable internal enemy against whom only he could fight - for to change government at such a time would surely plunge the country into civil war once more.

Modern historical research has tended to move towards Thompson's view of the Act and to draw some general conclusions about the nature of crime at this time. In the Preface to *Albion's Fatal Tree*, one reads that crime seemed to be increasing, but that it may also have been the result of:

> a property-conscious oligarchy redefining, through its legislative power, activities, use-rights in common or woods, perquisites in industry or thefts as offences. For as offences appear to multiply so also do statutes - often imposing the sanction of death - which define hitherto innocent or venial activities (such as some forms of poaching, wood-theft, anonymous letter-writing) as crimes. And the ideology of the ruling oligarchy, which places a supreme value upon property, finds its visible and material embodiment above all in the practice of the law.[8]

The law becomes not a reflection of the state of the nation but a symbolic enactment of the power structure within it, and how those in power maintained their position. In his essay 'Property, Authority and the Criminal Law' Hay makes the point that the law, made by the 'ruling class', was therefore made by about 3% of the population through the institutions of monarchy, aristocracy and gentry.[9]

The assemblage of evidence on the side of the historians who wish to see the law as reflecting the power-structure of the country seems impressive but additional facts have emerged which serve to undermine this position somewhat. There are several loose ends which remain untied and which refuse to be parcelled together in the neat explanation that Hay and Thompson offer. The problem is most succinctly summarised by G. R. Elton, who asks:

> If the ruling classes really wanted more frightful laws against thieves and robbers, why did they not secure a higher percentage of convictions and why did they suffer - indeed, in the persons of judges, encourage - contrived acquittals and the substitution of penalties well short of what the law could exact?[10]

One of the answers may be that the judges themselves were less than honest - as Gay would argue - and that in itself provided an ironic comment on the nature of those in power. The danger, of course, lies in asserting a case for one side which may be undermined by other facts. One must admit, too, that there are too many imponderables for a watertight case, but that also may leave a commentator without any base upon which to structure an argument.

Before that base may be established a fundamental question has to be posed, and that is the relevance of all this methodical research to an interpretation of the literature. Perhaps the answer is obvious but it seems necessary to argue the case once more. Certainly Defoe, Gay and Fielding believed that there was an increase in crime. Over twenty years after the Act, Fielding had the evidence brought before him, while earlier each writer had merely to open a pamphlet or newspaper to read of the growth of gangs in London and of the need for greater protection of property in the face of increased numbers of criminals. Combined with this were the polarities of political ideology, and relatively new ones at that, which asserted business methods as necessary to good government on the one hand, and tradition and land ownership on the other. Gay began by using the idea of the gang to make a social point, and extended the whole thing into the political arena, while Defoe used his own insight to reflect upon the nature of the times and, in turn, to use his business acumen to cash in on the new market of criminal biographies. Fielding was able to use both in the theatre. All writers, then, seemed to agree on this point, but, more importantly, they agreed that the metaphor of the gang and the psychology of the criminal mind could be applied with satiric force to their political opponents. The transference of the metaphor across the imaginary dividing line is the most significant aspect of the period. This, coupled with the new language that was becoming available - the language of business, of stockjobbing and of trade in general which was in contrast to the language of the pastoral - meant that the attack (or defence) of the government and its representatives could take place on many levels at the same time. The combination of efficiency - business - power - organisation - property - crime meant that a new way of looking at things was being acquired and, consequently, a new way of attacking one's ideological enemies was now appropriate. Further, one must add that modern historians have uncovered facts and have applied the theory but contradictions still remain; contemporary writers did not have the benefit of such assiduity and relied instead on the feel of the time. The feel supplied a convenient and lasting image of the *nature* of the times. England was a part of the financial movement which was affecting the whole of Western Europe and this meant that politics and business fused at many levels. It suggested that a profound change was approaching in the structure of the social and political organisation of England and that the politics of 'Robinocracy' would be intimately bound up with the new social order. Jonathan Wild became the symbol of the age and brought out the nature of the political and social scene.

(2)

Jonathan Wild was an expert businessman and he supplied the organisation that ensured his prominence among the London gangs. Not only did he control the members of his gang, but he also realised how much of an asset advertisements in newspapers could be in refurbishing the victims of his own robbers' thievery - at a price. Many scanned newspapers for reports of the latest hanging; others had less exciting motives:

> Jonathan Wild shaped the age, and the age shaped him ... Hangings at Tyburn proved for the victims gala days of applauded heroism, and for pickpockets who plied in the throng occasions of golden harvest. The newspapers, then in their youth, were already devoted to accounts of robberies, rogueries, and executions, as well as to advertisements of articles lost, but to be returned at a price and no questions asked.[11]

Wild presented himself as a finder of stolen goods, but, of course, it was his own gang that had taken the things in the first place. Wild had the controlling hands as long as he remained inside the law. Typical of the sort of advertisement that would appear in newspapers is the following from the *Daily Courant*, May 26, 1714:

> Lost of Friday Evening 19th March last, out of a compting House in Denham Court in Great Trinity Lane, near Bread Street, a Cash Book and a Day Book; they are of no use to any one but the Owner, being posted into a Ledger to the Day they were Lost. Whoever will bring them to Mr Jonathan Wild over-against Cripplegate-Church shall have a Guinea Reward and no Questions asked.[12]

Wild kept his word: the rightful owner would produce his money and the goods would be returned; Wild could then tick off a successful sale in his own ledger, noting the names of the thieves who were 'producing' the most. Wild also presented himself at houses which had recently been robbed, informing the occupants that he had an idea where the goods might be: on production of the correct fee, Wild would direct the victims to the place. Alternatively, the owner would pay for the goods on receipt. Wild never made the mistake of being in possession of stolen goods; by directing the owner to the place of storage he acted as the middle man, always within the law.[13] In fact, he was so concerned with his outward image that he was also active as a thief-taker as well as receiver. Criminals could be arrested if they stepped out of line, as he would denounce them to the authorities. He killed several; one report from the *Weekly Journal or Saturday's Post* of June 20, 1719, reads 'the Highwayman shot by Jonathan Wild, near Oxford, is since dead of his Wound, and Jonathan Wild is still continued in his Recognizances for that Fact, it having been thought not reasonable to imprison an Honest Man for killing a Rogue.'[14] The message was clear to all the thieves under Wild's wing: step out of line and this will happen to you. The authorities were not quite so naive as this brief account may suggest. Hampered by a totally inadequate judicial system, acts of Parliament which attempted to curb the activities of such people as Wild proved ineffectual. One of the most drastic measures, the Transportation Act of 1719, which made it illegal to receive stolen goods or to inform people of their whereabouts, only stemmed the growth in Wild's trade temporarily. By omitting his name from the advertisements, and covering his tracks more carefully, Wild's business expanded after 1719. Also with the collusion of the public, Wild could continue; most people, it seems, were willing to pay and keep quiet. Wild's 'Lost Property Office' kept going despite the attempts of some of the more public-spirited and hard-working magistrates.

Contemporary accounts of Wild confirm this picture of Wild's dictator status amongst thieves. Defoe provides details of Wild's life and methods in several pamphlets, in which he examines Wild's dominance of the underworld and the reasons for it:

> When the late Act was made, which gives a Pardon to one Felon for convicting another, he became absolute over them all; for if any of them disobliged him, or as he call'd it Rebel'd, he took them up, and thereby got the Reward appointed by Act of Parliament for taking Highwaymen: On the contrary, when any of his own People were taken, which he had a Mind to save, then he endeavour'd to take some other; then his own Men by claiming the Benefit of the Act became an Evidence.[15]

The 'late Act' confused matters rather than clarifying them. In effect, it helped Wild to control his men; by contracting out of Wild's union, the danger of arrest and death increased considerably. By joining the gang, the chances were that you could save your own neck by condemning someone else. By depositing stolen goods at a Brokers, he also avoided receiving stolen goods. The risk he ran was when he informed the owners of the whereabouts. By craft and organisation he was not only able to escape punishment for many years, but also present an image of the hardworking public servant:

> It must be confess'd Jonathan play'd a sure Game in all this, and therefore it is not to be wonder'd at that he went on for so many Years without any Disaster: Nay, he acquir'd a strange, and indeed, unusual Reputation, for a mighty honest Man, till his Success hardened him to put on a Face of

public Service in it: and for that Purpose, to profess an open and bare Correspondence among the Gang of Thieves; by which his House became an Office of Intelligence for Enquiries of that Kind; as if all stolen Goods had been deposited with him, in order to be restor'd.[16]

The Newgate Calendar supplies some details of his background; imprisoned for debt in his early years, he used his imprisonment to gain information about criminals and their methods. 'It was impossible', writes the author, 'but he must in some measure be let into the secrets of the criminals there under confinement'.[17] In prison he met Mary Milliner, and struck up a friendship; she was useful as she knew many notorious characters. By getting to know inside information about the lives and activities of the various felons, he was able to control them by blackmail and expand his business. At least he never went to prison again because of debt.

The Newgate Calendar also adds to our perception of Wild's craft. We know from Defoe that Wild used a Broker to deposit the stolen goods, but 'Wild received no gratuity from the owners of stolen goods, but deducted his profit from the money which was paid to the broker: thus did he amass considerable sums without danger of prosecution; for his offences came under the description of no law then existing.'[18]

'Organisation' is a word which often occurs in discussions of Wild's methods, and it is to Defoe that a reader can look to confirm the profundity of this organisation. After his prison sentence he set up the 'Lost Property Office' and his power grew:

> But as the Thieves first set him up only as their Factor, he by degrees made himself their Master and their Tyrant; he divided the City and Suburbs into Wards, or Divisions, and appointed the Persons who were to attend each Ward, and kept them strictly to their Duty. He also call'd them to a very exact Account, and made them produce what they had got, and tho' it were Money he would have his Dividend; and it was not less than Death to sink upon him, as he term'd it.[19]

Defoe is concerned with maintaining the interest of his audience and so the political parallels are pushed into the background; Defoe's purpose is to excite and to entertain, as the following quotation indicates. In this passage, Wild has pursued one Cheesemonger, who has betrayed him; his action on catching him provides an interesting insight into the real Wild:

> *Jonathan*, having a Pistol in his Hand, under his Great Coat, which the other could not see, still continued his Wheedling, and approached nearer and nearer, that he might have a sure Mark, he of a sudden drew forth his desperate Hand, and let fly a Brace of Bullets in the Face of the valiant Cheesemonger, and drawing forth a sharp Hanger at the same Instant flew upon him like a Tyger, and with one Blow fell'd him to his Horse's Feet, all weltering in his Gore - So have I seen, and with as little Mercy, a gallant Ox fell'd to the Ground by some fierce Butcher; and so, like Jonathan, have I seen him Bestride the mighty Beast, and strip him of his Skin ... (Wild

94

then proceeds to rob the man) ... I presume this Story may suffice to let the Reader know by what kind of Policy this *Machiavel* of Thieves supply'd his Commonwealth with Subjects as fast as they were cut off.[20]

There can be no doubt about our judgement about Wild; he is a Machiavel among thieves, far away from the image of the public servant which he pretends to be in reality. The facade is quickly removed by Defoe.

Comparing accounts of Wild's life and methods reveals a typical lack of concern for verisimilitude on the part of the different writers. While we tend to trust Defoe - since he is more skilful in guiding his readers to a judgement of the character - accuracy for him was not as strict as one might expect. Different authors quote different examples of Wild's activities; Smith, for example, insists he met Jane Sprackling whilst imprisoned for debt, 'who had a thorough Knowledge of all the Ill People of the Town, and had herself gone round the whole Circle of Vice'. Smith also cites two interesting examples of Wild's methods; first, a method of acquiring money for services rendered: Lady Godolphin has her chair stolen:

> Application was immediately made to *Wild*, who after taking his Fee, told the Inquirers, he would consider of it; and when they came again, he insisted on a pretty handsome Donation, which being comply'd with, he order'd the Chairmen not to fail of attending the Prayers at Lincoln's Inn Chapel the next Morning; when to their no small Surprize, and Satisfaction, they found their Lady's Chair, exactly in the Manner as it was when Stolen, under the Piazzas of the Chapel.[21]

This quotation makes it easier to see why the public were willing to pay Wild a fee for the recovery of stolen property. Wild must have known the whereabouts of most of the stolen goods; attempting to recover property through the normal processes of the law would mean considerable delay - and, in the end, the goods would no doubt be destroyed. Part of Wild's reputation must have rested on his ability to return property in perfect working order; and for the sake of a few pounds, and little aggravation, why not use the service?

Smith also describes Wild's vendettas against those who refuse to comply with the laws of the gang. He has several robbers killed, and preserves his good name as a citizen by apprehending several thieves: the latter serving as a reminder of the punishment for defaulters. After one robbery:

> (he was) inform'd of the Haunts of James Wright, one of the Persons concern'd in the Fact. He apprehended him in the Queen's Head Tavern on *Tower-Hill* brought him to *Newgate*, and being convicted of other Robberies in *Middlesex*, he was executed at Tyburn; which proved a beneficial Jobb to *Jonathan*, who besides the Lord *Bruce*'s Gold Watch, that was found in *Wright*'s Pocket, had the whole Reward, as given by Act of Parliament, for the Apprehending and Convicting of a Highwayman.[22]

These actions are typical of Wild, although the authenticity of the actual events are difficult to verify. This hardly matters as so many reports are available concerning the efficient, cynical methods of the man. Earlier writers, then, seem more interested in communicating the supposed nature of the man rather than in developing political parallels which were to be so prominent only a few years later. Wild was able to vindicate his methods: Defoe 'quotes' from Wild in prison:

> 1. The publick Good (is served), in taking and apprehending the most open and notorious Criminals; and 2. The procuring and restoring the Goods again to the right Owners, which had been stolen from them either by Fraud or Violence.[23]

Defoe described Wild as a Machiavel in one pamphlet, and the above reasoning justifies the description; by playing down his role as a receiver of goods and a controller of thieves, he seems to believe himself to be performing a valuable public service; Wild's hypocrisy is never glossed over by Defoe, or, indeed, any of his biographers.

The final example of Wild's complete ruthlessness also comes from Defoe. Wild anticipated nineteenth-century crime by taking poor children from the streets and training them in crime; Defoe comments:

> But which is still worse than all the rest, I have several Stories by me at this Time, which I have particular Reasons to believe are true, of Children thus strolling about the Streets in Misery and Poverty, whom he has taken in on pretence of providing for them, and employing them; and all has ended in this *(viz.)* making Rogues of them. *Horrid Wickedness* his Charity has been to breed them up to be Thieves, *and still more Horrid* several of these his own *foster Children*, he has himself caused afterwards to be apprehended and Hang'd for the very Crimes he first taught them how to Commit.[24]

So the condemnation of Wild is complete. A heartless, thankless robber who stooped to any means for material gain. Wild's manner and his lust for power gained him a place in the minds of his contemporaries as a symbol 'of brutal, unjust authority', as Howson describes him.[25] This authority was seen not just as a threat to the thieves themselves, but an extension of political authority: the major politician of the day, Walpole, was viewed as a robber figure by his opponents. The highwayman, Jack Sheppard, was a more popular figure. He gained his support by condemning the activities of such a man as Wild. Sheppard and Wild had several confrontations, Wild being responsible for the former's arrest on numerous occasions. Defoe gives Sheppard these words:

> I have often lamented the scandalous Practice of Thief-catching, as it is call'd and the publick Manner of offering Rewards for stolen Goods, in Defiance of two several Acts of Parliament; the Thief Catcher lives sumptuously, and keeps publick Offices of Intelligence. Those who forfeit their Lives every Day they breathe, and deserve the Gallows as richly as

any of the Thieves, send us as their Representatives to Tyburn once a Month: thus they hang by Proxy, while we do it fairly in Person.[26]

These sentiments are designed to carry as much sympathy as possible for Sheppard, and turn the readers away from the representative of absolute power over which the ordinary citizen has no control. While it is true that Wild was a brutal manipulator of others, Sheppard was hardly the innocent victim that contemporary accounts make him appear. Sheppard appealed to the public, possibly because of his 'small size, dapper appearance and cool wit : a perfect Cockney Sparrow'. In fact, he was a 'cold, unscrupulous, vengeful guttersnipe ... Yet when he betrayed his companions (as his brother had betrayed him), begged for his life, or made blasphemous jokes, the public applauded with delightful admiration'.[27] The truth was that Sheppard served a useful purpose to the people who wrote about him in that he defied authority, and defied it more successfully than anyone else. By playing down Sheppard's true character, and empha- sising the nasty traits in Wild's, Defoe and others were able to capture a market and make occasional satiric points about the political administration of the day.

Sheppard becomes, in the eyes of the prevailing ideology, a kind of anti- Wild, a man who defied an unfair authority. The truth of the matter hardly enters into it, for Sheppard was used as a convenient metaphor against which to place Wild. As Foucault notes, Sheppard (the 'condemned man'):

> found himself transformed into a hero by the sheer extent of his widely advertised crimes ... Against the law, against the rich, the powerful, the magistrates, the constabulary or the watch, against taxes and their collectors, he appeared to have waged a struggle with which one all too easily identified.[28]

As Sheppard fought the administration, so the latter fought back:
> Now Mr Sheppard's long and wicked Course seemingly draws towards a Period. Mr Kneebone (robbed by Sheppard) having apply'd to Jonathan Wild, and set forth Advertisements in the Papers, complaining of his Robbery. On Tuesday the 22nd of *July* at Night *Edgworth Bess* was taken in a Brandy-shop near Temple Bar by *Jonathan Wild*; she being much terrify'd, discovered where *Sheppard* was: A Warrant was accordingly issued ...[29]

Wild had to break any opposition to his absolute authority: it would take only one person to ruin the stranglehold which he had over the underworld. Sheppard's dapperness and his Cockney cheek pushed Wild to the limits, and Sheppard's death - ironically only a few months before Wild's own, and by the same method - must have been seen as a triumph for the 'establishment'. Defoe is outspoken in his condemnation of Wild. 'Who can think of such a thing', he writes, 'without a just Abhorrence, who can think it to be any less that the worst sort of Murder; such was the Life, and such the Practise of this wretched Man'.[30]

Reactions to Wild's capture and his eventual execution also bear a remarkable contrast to the reactions of the mob on the execution of Sheppard. Defore tells of his transportation to Tyburn, in an open cart:

here was nothing to be heard but Cursings and Execrations; abhorring the Crimes and the very Name of the Man, throwing Stones and Dirt at him all the way, and even at the Place of Execution ... the Mob ... call'd furiously upon the Hangman to dispatch him, and at last threatened to tear him to pieces, if he did not tye him up immediately.[31]

Defoe also adds details in another account of his journey to the gallows:

so far had he incurred the Resentment of the Populace, that they pelted him with Stones, etc. in several Places, one of which, in *Holborn* broke his Head to that Degree that the Blood ran down plentifully; which Barbarity, tho' as unjustifiable as unusual, yet may serve to deter others from treading his Steps, when they find the Consequences so universally odious. At the place of Execution, the People continued very outrageous, so that it was impossible either for *Jonathan* or any of the rest to be very composed.[32]

Other accounts confirm this vilification: the *Newgate Calendar* reports that the crowd 'execrated him as the most consummate villain that had ever disgraced human nature',[33] while Smith notes that Wild's body 'was so contaminated with venereal Performances with lewd Women, that it was perfectly rotten long before he died'.[34] Perhaps the comment owes more to Smith's imagination than to medical history, but it is a touch that Smith's audience would take as indicative of Wild's life: rotten, stinking and corrupt.

Finally, the following elegy sums up the reactions of most people on the death of Wild. The language amusingly combines eighteenth-century diction and the language of the broad-sheet ballad:

What mournful Muse must aid me in my Verse,
To pin on Jonathan's dark sable Hearse?
I know in Lethe I must dip my Pen
To write against the very worst of Men;
For none (I think) can write of him so well,
But what is brought from the Confines of Hell ...

Then Snot and Snivel throw about his Grave
And with Old-Nick may Soul and Body have.[35]

The activities of Wild took him into the realms of complex administration Making money by organising other people to do the work for him, Wild symbolized to many people the new order in public life. The political administration had taken on, for opponents of the government of the day, a remarkable parallel with the pursuits of Wild and his cronies. The brunt of the satiric and personal attack fell on the 'prime minister', Robert

Walpole. Walpole's administration became an operation with Walpole the manipulator of events for his own ends. Walpole's enemies never forgave him for his accumulation of a vast fortune during his period of Paymaster General, nor did they forgive him for his domination of the political scene until the mid 1740s. Because of the hitherto unprecedented acquisition of power, his friends and enemies alike began to call him the 'Great Man'. It was no coincidence that Wild also became known by the same name - especially by Walpole's enemies of course. Defoe makes an oblique reference to Walpole in his preface to the life of Wild. The readers of his tract, he claims, 'will see deeper Stratagems and Plots form'd by a Fellow without Learning or Education, than are to be met with in the Conduct of the greatest Statesmen, who have been at the Heads of Governments'.[36] At the time of writing, Walpole was still at the head of government, but the reference would have been taken by all of the readers.

Fielding's *Jonathan Wild* exploits the convention of the 'Great Man' and the 'Hero', removing by satire any pretensions to greatness that Wild may have had. The political purpose remains somewhat in the background; although the reader must be aware that the 'Great Man' under discussion is Walpole as well as Wild, specific parallels between the two are not pressed; Fielding allows his readers to draw their own conclusions. A reading of *Jonathan Wild* reveals Fielding the moralist, as each incident provokes an antagonistic reaction against the main character. Fielding's concern in the novel is similar to his concern as a magistrate: to reveal the corruption beneath the surface and to destroy it as far as possible; he attempted this through the law, and through the weapon of ridicule. Fielding states his aim:

> We would not therefore be understood to affect giving the Reader a perfect or consummate Pattern of human Excellence, but rather, by faithfully recording some little Imperfections which shadowed over the Lustre of those great Qualities which we shall here record, to teach the Lesson we have above mentioned, to induce our Reader with us to lament the Frailty of human Nature, and to convince him that no Mortal, after a thorough Scrutiny, can be a proper Object of our Adoration.[37]

The words 'perfect', 'Excellence' and 'great' are overshadowed by 'Imperfections', 'shadowed' and 'Frailty'. Wild becomes more than frail as the novel progresses - a heartless, immoral illiterate who uses any opportunity for his own financial gain.

Fielding is not as deadly serious as the other biographers who wrote tracts and pamphlets on the lives of villains. Fielding must have been aware of the numerous accounts of the lives of criminals, but he remains aloof from the aims of the Ordinary, or indeed of Defoe. He parodies elements, but turns the biography to a political and social purpose. It is necessary, he argues, 'to step a little backwards' in biographies to supply background to the subject. Fielding is not content with stepping only as far back as his subject's childhood; he creates for Wild a whole family tree of roguery:

> Mr Jonathan Wild, or Wyld, (for he himself did not always agree in one method of spelling his Name), was descended from the great Wolfstan Wild, who came over with Hengist, and distinguished himself very eminently at that famous Festival where the Britons were so treacherously murdered by the Saxons; for when the word was given, i.e., *nemet cour Sexes, take out your Swords*, this Gentleman, being a little hard of Hearing, mistook the Sound for *nemet her Sacs, take out their Purses*; instead therefore of applying to the Throat, he immediately applied to the Pocket of his Guest, and contented himself with taking all that he had, without attempting his Life. (p.6).[37]

Greatness and eminence are an established part of Wild's background as, it seems, is stupidity. The tradition continued to the next Wild, who lived in the reign of Henry III; this man, (Longfinger by name), 'Could without the knowledge of the proprietor, with great ease and dexterity, draw forth a man's purse from any part of his garment where it was deposited', (p.6).[37] and so the tale continues until Wild's birth, as though Wild were not responsible for his actions: the stain on his character was a result of his background. For confirmation of this, one need look no further than his mother, who, 'during her whole pregnancy constantly longed for everything she saw; nor could she be satisfied with her wish unless she enjoyed it clandestinely ... she had at this time a marvellous glutinous quality attending her fingers, to which, as to birdlime, everything adhered that she handled'. (p.9).[37] Whereas the conventional criminal biography gave details of the subject's birth and early years only briefly, Fielding's account delves into seemingly irrelevant realms, but it becomes important in the irony as a whole. True, Wild could not help his background, coming as he did from a stock of thieves, but this has nothing to do with the development of Wild's psychology: Defoe mentioned deprived childhoods in his own fiction, but Fielding has none of this; in fact he makes it quite clear that Wild had every opportunity in education, his father taking 'all imaginable care of his instruction' until he is ready to fend for himself in the world.

Fielding's point is one with which Defoe would have agreed: wilful criminals should be recognised, and punished to the full extent of the law. The compilation of details about Wild's background is used to emphasise the degradation of the man through no cause exterior to himself: the Wilds are thieves because they are thieves. Jonathan is a thief-taker because that is his natural inclination.

> If an Orchard was to be robbed (at school), Wild was consulted, and, though he was himself seldom concerned in the Execution of the Design, yet was he always Concerter of it, and Treasurer of the Booty, some little Part of which he would now and then, with wonderful Generosity, bestow on those who took it. He was generally very secret on these Occasions; but if any

offered to plunder of his own Head, without acquainting Master Wild, and making a Deposit of the Booty, he was sure to have an Information against him lodged with the Schoolmaster, and to be severely punished for his Pains.

Obviously, this forms a parallel with his later life and activities, and Fielding's point that Wild's actions are those of a peevish schoolboy is a pertinent one. Described in this light, his comrades appear as foolish as he is exploitative; but, like the criminals in Wild's later dealings, they are caught in the trap, the only escape being Newgate - or its equivalent.

Fielding is of course bending the truth - in fact he hardly adheres to it at all in his satiric attack on Wild at this point. Defoe reports that Wild's father died early:

> ... leaving four or five small Children for the Widow to bring up and subsist, 'tis no wonder if their Education was no better taken care of. As for Jonathan, he show'd early Signs of a forward Genius, and, whilst a Boy, would commit a thousand little Rogueries among those of the same or a superior Class.

The difference is contained in the word 'report': Defoe is attempting to place facts before us in as dispassionate a way as possible, and all details are significant in the drive towards a balanced judgement. Fielding does not require a balanced judgement: his study is an ironic attack by a novelist on a threatening part in society, and any details to enhance the attack are justifiable. Fielding is much more free to add or subtract details as he sees fit, and also at liberty to include personal comments to tip the balance firmly against Wild.

Wild's associations with women are mentioned by Smith and Defoe; neither of them seem particularly complimentary about those creatures. Fielding, true to this ironic epic style, gives Wild a girl-friend, the chaste Laetitia Snap:

> Her lovely Hair hung wantonly over her Forehead, being neither white with, nor yet free from Powder; a neat double Clout, which seemed to have been worn a few Weeks only, was pinned under her Chin; some Remains of that Art with which Ladies improve Nature shone on her Cheeks; her Body was loosely attired, without Stays or Jumps, so that her Breasts had uncontrolled Liberty to display their beauteous Orbs, which they did as low as her Girdle; a thin Covering of a rumpled Muslin Handkerchief almost hid them from the Eyes, save in a few Parts, where a good-natured Fold gave Opportunity to the naked Breast to appear. (pp.26/7).[37]

The lady seems well-matched to the noble aspirations of Wild, but, like Wild, she persists in the facade of respectability; she repels Wild's advances while at the same time allows favours to one Tom Smirk:

> (Wild was) transported to Freedom too offensive to the nice Chastity of Laetitia, who was, to confess the Truth, more indebted to her own Strength for the Preservation of her Virtue than to the awful Respect of her Lover ... for at the Ends of her Fingers she wore Arms, which she used with such

admirable Dexterity, that the hot Blood of Mr Wild soon began to appear in several little Spots on his Face ... She then proceeded to talk of her Virtue, which Wild bid her carry to the Devil with her, and thus our Lovers parted. (pp.27/8).[37]

When we discover all, as to preserve the Fidelity of our History we must, when we relate that every Familiarity had passed between them, and that the FAIR Laetitia (for we must, in this single Instance, imitate Virgil when he drops the *Pius* and the *Pater*, and drop our favourite Epithet of chaste), the FAIR Laetitia had, I say, made Smirk as happy as Wild desired to be. (p.30).[37]

The problem of irony never enters into these passages: clearly, Fielding is adopting a mock-heroic style to indicate the precise nature of Wild's character and of his relationships. The touch that Fielding includes of making Wild a loser in love, and indeed deceived by it, adds to the humour that is built up against him. Wild, a deceiver himself, and a character who should be able to judge other deceivers, is duped by a woman as harsh and calculating as he is with others. Laetitia is hardly given the status of heroine of course; the ironic parallel with Virgil emphasises that Wild and Laetitia deserve each other, but only in battle.

Having established a firm basis for a judgement of the nature of Wild, Fielding goes on to give examples of his methods and of how his mind works. Defoe described Wild as a Machiavel and Fielding puts thoughts into Wild's mind that suggest a close resemblance to Machiavellian reasoning. Wild divides mankind into two;

those that use their own Hands, and those who employ the Hands of others. The former are the base and rabble; the latter the genteel Part of the Creation ... (the latter) is that noble and great Part who are generally distinguished into *Conquerors, absolute Princes, Statesmen,* and *Prigs* (thieves). Now all these differ from each other in greatness only - they employ *more* or *fewer* Hands. And Alexander the Great was only *greater* than a Captain of one of the Tartarian or Arabian Hordes, as he was at the head of a larger Number. In what then is a single *Prig* inferior to any other great Man, but because he employs his own Hands only; for he is not on that Account to be levelled with the base and vulgar, because he employs his Hands for his Use only. Now, suppose a *Prig* had as many Tools as any prime Minister ever had, would he not be as great as any prime Minister whatsoever? (pp.42/3).[37]

The irony assumes several forms in this passage. Fielding continues the ironic parallel with other great figures, drawing the reader more closely into Wild's psychology - for it is Wild himself at this point who presses the point that he - the prig - is to be compared with Alexander. The satire against the leaders of the state is an obvious reference to Walpole, himself attacked for gaining the status of a 'prime' minister in the government, and the irony of the redefinition of the word 'great' combines the two leaders of men, Walpole and Wild, in the minds of the readers. It also emphasises Fielding's concern with the proper use of epithets: an unquestioning acceptance of a simple word can lead to a single person gaining a reputation which is undeserved; it can also give the person in question an inflated opinion of himself, as Wild has here.[39]

Fielding gives another of his villains, Mammon, similar sentiments in his poem *The Vernoniad*. This passage summarises Wild's attitude. Mammon, a thinly disguised Walpole, is speaking:

> Nature 'twixt Men no other Bounds hath set
> Than that of Sums - the little and the great.
> Nor is it reckoned scandalous, to be
> A Rogue. The Scandal lies in the Degree;
> A little Robber meets my Disregard,
> A great One my Embraces and Reward;
> And Laws the little Rogues alone pursue,
> As Floods drown those not able to swim thro'.[40]

This selfish, egotistical attitude is typical of Wild: he 'embraces and rewards' himself, and, from what one knows of the life of Wild, he was contemptuous of the 'little rogues' who worked for him. He too, would 'drown' the rogues who refused to comply with his demands. Fielding sums up Wild's Machiavellian attitude thus:

> With such infinite Address did this truly great Man know how to play with the Passions of Men, to set them at Variance with each other, and to work his own Purposes out of those Jealousies and Apprehensions which he was wonderfully ready at creating by means of those great Arts which the vulgar call Treachery, Dissembling, Promising, Lying, Falsehood, etc., but which are by great Men summed up in the collective Name of Policy, or Politics, or rather Politrics; an Art of which, as it is the highest Excellence of human Nature, perhaps our great Man was the most eminent Master. (p.64).[37]

The ironic purpose is once more made quite clear - and the repetition of the 'great man' theme brings Wild and Walpole into close alliance. If Wild loses in his attempts to seduce and exploit Miss Snap, because of her own willingness to fight back and her refusal to be conquered, he certainly gains a noble victory in his involvement with the Heartfree family. Heartfree is a naive believer in the dignity and honesty of human nature; ripe, then, for a cynic like Wild to exploit. Thomas Heartfree 'married a very agreeable women for love', a notable contrast to Wild's lascivious attempts on Laetitia, and they run a jewellry business. Fielding describes his character in terms which are intended to invite our sympathy, and which also openly serve as a contrast with the character of Wild:

> Heartfree ... was of an honest and open Disposition. He was of that Sort of Men whom Experience only, and not their own Natures, must inform that there are such Things as Deceit and Hypocrisy in the World, and who, consequently, are not at five-and-twenty so difficult to be imposed upon as the oldest and most subtle. He was possessed of several great Weaknesses

of Mind, being good-natured, friendly, and generous to a great Excess. (p.46).[37]

Heartfree's character, so much the antithesis to that of Wild, remains as static as this throughout the novel. It must do so, since the novel is concerned with the conflict between the Machiavellian and Christian instincts. Heartfree has to learn that there are such people as Wild in the world, but Fielding cannot allow him to retract from any of his beliefs; the dignity of man, at the expense of Wild's reputation, must win through. As Mrs Heartfree says, after she has escaped from the lecherous intents of various sea captains, 'providence will sooner or later procure the felicity of the virtuous and innocent'. (p.161).[37]

A belief in a benign destiny for those who uphold the faith of 'good heart' is the underlying message that the novel possesses. The contrast between the philosophy of Heartfree and that of Wild is made explicit by Fielding on several occasions. Wild persuades Heartfree to pay for some jewels, and then robs him of them. 'This double method of cheating the very tools who are instruments to cheat others is the superlative degree of greatness, and is probably, as far as my spirit crusted over with clay can carry it, falling little short of diabolism itself. (p.51).[37] If Heartfree is the Christian, Wild is the devil. With this contrast, Fielding is running into a difficulty that he did not foresee; is the suggestion that Christians are simple, trusting souls, with little or no insight into behaviour and motives, necessarily an accurate one? Are only the Snaps of this world the ones who will triumph over the Wilds? Fielding does not answer these questions, except to allow destiny to run its course and, at the outcome, it will be seen that the virtuous will survive. Fielding does not really need to answer the questions, since they are not only subsidiary ideas attached to the main one of denouncing Wild. By sticking to this task, Fielding does let himself over-simplify the character of Heartfree. It is not that the reader is asked to sympathise totally with him, but merely to recognise that such characters can exist, and are open to the methods that Wild prescribes. Irwin raises a point on similar lines:

> A Marxist might accuse him of being too timid to draw the conclusion of his social observations. But the point is rather that he has not realised just how fundamental is the variance between the Christian morality he is everywhere concerned to recommend, and the practice, if not the theory, of the current English social system.[41]

An interesting point, and one to which it is difficult to reply in absolute terms. True, Fielding does not write explicitly about this variance but the strong desire for reform which he had, both in practice as a magistrate, and in theory as a novelist, does push Fielding closer to a position in which he can indicate a solution. He is surely not arguing that we can all become like Heartfree, just as we cannot become like Tom Jones, but a truer recognition of the social set-up will reveal to his audience the widespread hypocrisy of many of its members. A gradual change to a society of 'good hearts' is not possible: Fielding would recognise that villainy, like poverty, is an integral part of his society, and his task was to open man's eyes to it, and control it as dutifully as possible.

In order to drive home the satirical point as fully as possible, Fielding employs devices which go beyond the technique of the novelist. Fielding's aim is satire, and not just of Wild and Walpole. He was aware that he was fictionalising the popular criminal biographies, and concerned himself with a parody of many of the techniques used by their authors. This meant that he could fuse fiction with facts, the fusion deepening the satiric purpose. Wild's cleverness - a word used earlier to describe Wild and many of his contemporary rogues - is one which, like Cartouche's, was a corrupt version of the normal associations of the word. Fielding captures this in the ironic repetition of 'greatness'. Beyond this, Wild had little to recommend him in the way of brains; consider the following letter, from Wild to Laetitia:

> MOST DIVINE AND ADWHORABLE CREETURE, - I doubt not but those IIs, briter than the son, which have kindled such a flam in my hart, have likewise the faculty of seeing it. It would be the hiest preassumption to imagin you eggnorant of my loav. No, madam, I sollemly purtest, that of all the butys in the unaversal glob, there is none kapable of hateracting my IIs like you. Corts and pallaces would be to me deserts without your kumpany, and with it a wilderness would have more charms that haven itself. For I hop you will beleve me when I sware every place in the universe is a haven with you. I am konvinced you must by sinsibel of my violent passion for you, which, if I endevored to hid it, would be as impossible as for you, or the son, to hid your buty's. I assure you I have not slept a wink since I had the hapness of seeing you last; therefore hop you will, out of Kumpassion, let me have the honour of seeing you this afternune; for I am, with the greatest adwhoration,

> Most deivine creture,
> Your most passionate amirer, adwhorer, and slave,
> JOHATHAN WYLD (p.100)[37]

This is certainly one way of ridiculing Wild, but it is based on fact. Howson notes that Wild was not skilful at grammar or spelling, judging from his surviving letters.[42] The point is even more forceful when the letter is taken in context: Fielding emphasises Wild's school days, his father keeping him there for as long as possible. The truth - as Defoe records it - that Wild had little education, would detract from Fielding's point: the novelist picked up points of fact that were useful to him, whereas the biographer attempted to adhere to the facts, choosing those which could command popular attention. Style is also involved: whereas Fielding's purpose is ironic, Defoe's is much more straight-forward. Having acknowledged these points, it should also be noted that the similarities between the two techniques are important factors in any consideration of the novel:

by using the tradition in which he was writing to satiric ends, Fielding expanded that tradition, and combined it with a different tradition - ironic, political prose - to produce a work which went beyond the two.

A favourite device of the biographers of the day was to present the condemned man's words from prison, either recorded by the writer himself or noted by the Ordinary: both found the device a lucrative one. Fielding is no exception, and presents 'a dialogue between the Ordinary of Newgate and Mr Jonathan Wild the Great; in which the subject of death, immortality, and other grave matters, are very learnedly handled by the former':

> Jonathan: Faith, Doctor, I remember very little of your Inferences; for I fell asleep soon after your naming your Text. But did you preach this Doctrine then, or do you repeat it now in order to comfort me? ... Faith, Doctor well minded. What say you to a Bottle of Wine?
>
> Ordinary: I will drink no Wine with an Atheist. I should expect the Devil to make a third in such a Company, for, since he knows you are his, he may be impatient to have his Due.
>
> Jonathan: It is your Business to drink with the Wicked, in order to amend them.
>
> Ordinary: I despair of it; and so I consign you over to the Devil, who is ready to receive you.
>
> Jonathan: You are more unmerciful to me than the Judge, Doctor He recommended my Soul to Heaven; and it is your Office to shew me the Way thither.
>
> Ordinary: No: the Gates are barred against all Revilers of the Clergy.
>
> Jonathan: I revile only the wicked Ones ... (p.164/5).[37]

The irony here is that it is Wild who appears to be preaching, rather than the Ordinary. In a desperate attempt to make Wild see the error of his ways, the Ordinary pleads with him to regard his punishment as just, and exemplary; Wild's reaction is to offer him a glass of wine. Wild remains impervious to any suggestions that he should feel morally guilty for his actions; the Ordinary is almost like all the others: Wild uses him, for his company means that he can drink punch, which induces sleep. The Ordinary is almost another Heartfree in that, despite having his eyes open to the wickedness surrounding him, he enters into relationships with the villains in an attempt to save their souls. Wild's was sold to the devil long ago; again, the association between Wild as the devil, opposing the good Christian forces here represented by the Ordinary, is a by now familiar one.

Wild's final act of greatness is at his execution; Fielding had a ready-made piece of satire here, in reality. The behaviour of the crowd at Wild's execution has already been shown; Fielding had to add very few embellishments:

When he came to the Tree of Glory, he was welcomed with an universal Shout of the People, who were there assembled in prodigious Numbers to behold a Sight much more rare in populous Cities than one would reasonably imagine it should be, viz. the proper Catastrophe of a great Man. But though Envy was, through Fear, obliged to join the general Voice in Applause on this Occasion, there were not wanting some who maligned this Completion of Glory, which was now about to be fulfilled to our Hero, and endeavoured to prevent it by knocking him on the Head as he stood under the Tree, while the Ordinary was performing his last Office. They therefore began to batter the Cart with Stones, Brickbats, Dirt, and all manner of mischievous Weapons ... The Ordinary being now descended from the Cart, Wild had just Opportunity to cast his Eyes around the Crowd, and to give them a hearty Curse ... Wild leaves the World as he entered it: contemptuous of those whom he regards as beneath him, those only worthy of Exploitation.

Throughout the novel, then, Fielding takes biography as the jumping-off point, and uses Wild's life in order to make a political and social point. Typical of Fielding also is that he is making a human point: people like Heartfree must be protected against the cynical selfishness of Wild. Corruption spreads itself through society as a whole:

the chief (corruption) is the tendency by many, notably those born into high stations, to assume that the distinctions among people are moral rather than social; to forget that all men are equal before God and their consciences; to think, like Wild, and other vicious great men, that the weaker orders are chattels of a different sort from ourselves, not people whose passions, desires, and situations demand their sympathy.[43]

Wild remains opposed to any sympathetic, Christian consideration for any of his victims. The ruthlessness with with he carries out his plan is devoid of human sentiment. Fielding is urging the reader to consider the implications of this: both the moral and the social connotations are inextricably combined in a book which, beneath the humour, contains a serious critique of the contemporary social situation.

NOTES

1. See P. Linebaugh, 'The Ordinary of Newgate and His "Account" in *Crime in England*, edited by Cockburn, op. cit., pp.247-250.
2. See Defoe, *A Narrative of the Proceedings in France*, (London, 1724), *The History of the remarkable Life of John Sheppard* (London, 1724), *A General History of the Pyrates* (London, 1724), *An Effectual Scheme for the Immediate Preventing of Street Robberies* (London, 1731).
3. See Pat Rogers, *The Augustan Vision* (London, 1974), pp. 99-104 passim.
4. Quoted by E. P. Thompson *Whigs and Hunters* (London, 1975), p.270.
5. Pat Rogers, 'The Waltham Blacks and the Black Act', *The Historical Journal*, XVIII, 3, 1974, 465-486.

6. W. A. Speck, *Stability and Strife. England 1714-1760* (London, 1977), pp.59-60.

7. Thompson, op. cit., pp.196-7.

8. Douglas Hay, P. Linebaugh and E. P. Thompson (eds), *Albion's Fatal Tree* (Harmondsworth, 1977), p.13.

9. Ibid., p.61.

10. G. R. Elton, 'Introduction' in Cockburn (ed), op. cit., pp.4/5.

11. F. W. Chandler, *The Literature of Roguery* (Boston, 1907), pp.155-6.

12. Quoted by Gerald Howson, *Thief-Taker General. The Rise and Fall of Jonathan Wild* (London, 1970), p.166.

13. Ibid., p.67-8 and p.75.

14. Ibid., p.89.

15. Defoe, *The Life of Jonathan Wild. From His Birth to his Death* (London, 1725), pp.17-18. This appears in J. R. Moore's *A Checklist of the Writings of Daniel Defoe* (Bloomington, Indiana, 1962) as no. 468 and is hereafter cited as Moore, 468.

16. Defoe, *The True and Genuine Account of the Life and Actions of the Late Jonathan Wild* (London, 1725), p.13. Moore (op. cit.) no. 473.

17. *The Newgate Calendar* (op. cit., p.75).

18. Ibid., p.78.

19. Moore, 471, p.16.

20. Ibid., pp.30-31.

21. Smith, op. cit., p.5.

22. Ibid., p.10.

23. Moore, 473, p.15.

24. Ibid., pp.32-3.

25. Howson, op. cit., p.6.

26. Moore, 468, pp.15/16.

27. Howson, op. cit., pp.224/5.

28. Michael Foucault, *Discipline and Punish* (London, 1977), p. 67.

29. Moore, 468, p.14.

30. Moore, 473, p.34.

31. Ibid., p.39.

32. W. Lee (editor), *Daniel Defoe: His Life and Recently Discovered Writings*, 3 vols. (London, 1869), vol. III p.389.

33. *The Newgate Calendar*, op. cit., p.110.

34. Smith, op. cit., p.22.

35. Ibid., p.23.

36. Moore, 471, pp.v-vi.

37. Fielding, *The History of the Life of the Late Mr Jonathan Wild the Great* (London, 1932), p.4. All references to this edition acknowledged by page nos. in the text.

38. Moore, 471, p.2.

39. See C. J. Rawson, *Henry Fielding and the Augustan Ideal Under Stress* (London, 1972): p.229.

40. Fielding, *The Vernoniad* in *The Complete Works of Henry Fielding*, edited by W. E. Henley, 3 vols. (London, 1903), vol II, p.53.

41. Michael Irwin, *Henry Fielding. The Tentative Realist* (Oxford, 1967), p.49.

42. Howson, op. cit., p.11.

43. Morris Golden, M *Fielding's Moral Psychology* (Cambridge, Mass. 1966), p.100.

CHAPTER 6

Fielding - The Plays

A close analysis of Fielding's plays in such a study as this presents several difficulties. First, one is tempted to discuss the plays as though they were written with particular characters and incidents in mind, while at the same time acknowledging that Fielding was concerned primarily with the general manners and morals of the age. Second, the explicit references in *The Grub-Street Opera* or *Tom Thumb* may tempt the reader into attributing political motives and satiric intentions to Fielding when, in fact, an examination of his whole career reveals a man who could shift allegiances as time and fortune demanded. An analysis may also be influenced by knowledge of Fielding's work as a magistrate. While this approach cannot be dismissed entirely, it proves unsatisfactory when placed in the context of the whole of Fielding's canon: his plays are not simply biographical documents. Then, having dismissed the bases from which a study of the plays could be made, the reader finds himself in the difficult position of attempting to form another base in order to establish a satisfactory reading: in other words, even such apparently straightforward plays may lead us into questioning a set critical approach, while at the same time any reading must be able to assert the value of the plays themselves. Critical commentary, too, must not find itself in the unenviable position of creating a reading which ignores the most significant aspects of the plays; that is, they are entertainments designed to make points and those points must be immediately identifiable to an audience. While Fielding seems to have written his plays on an *ad hoc* basis, general themes and attitudes do emerge; the critic's task is to examine these and to suggest how they may be viewed as a part of the literary and political denunciation of the times. Fielding's plays remain interesting because of a commitment to general social and moral standards - ones with which a contemporary audience would sympathise but which also relate to the discussion concerning politics and the standards set by politicians. Here possibly an answer to the problems set out above may be reached: by accepting Fielding's changing circumstances and by accepting too that he may not have been writing a consistent thesis, the plays may be viewed as a comment on the demands that an audience placed upon an author and as indications of the way in which a satirist could effectively communicate and reflect a general dissatisfaction.

If Fielding's aim is to present the habits of the human species, to discuss general human affections and foibles, to indicate man's weakness in the face of a wicked world and to show how the weaknesses are counterbalanced by virtues, then we should not be confused if the plays refuse to align themselves to the general literary attack upon specific political figures.

While the form of at least one of his plays - *The Grub Street Opera* - owes much to Gay, the content reveals that general rather than specific attacks dominate the proceedings. The writing has always a general social or political potency, expressed in terms which stand in broad relation to the language of Fielding's contemporaries. In *The Coffee-House Politician* the character of Worthy appears; he has little or nothing to do with the main action, which concerns the corruption of Squeezum, a lecherous magistrate. Being distanced from the action allows him - and Fielding - to make the point:

> Golden Sands too often clog the Wheels of Justice, and obstruct her Course; the very Riches, which were the greatest Evidence of his Villainy, have too often declared the Guilty innocent ... I long to see the Time when here, as in Holland, the Traveller may walk unmolested, and carry his Riches openly with him.[1]

The lack of specific allusion is a deliberate ploy on Fielding's part for it allows both the reader and the author a considerable leeway. It allows a broad interpretation relating to the general corruption of the times and the importance attached to money; and it enables the specific allusion to the law to be taken up and developed by anyone who cares to do so. While refusing to name any identifiable characters, the text allows a multiplicity of interpretation by its very openness. It can be seen as either a light, entertaining view of the corruptibility of human nature or it can be seen as a comment upon the times themselves. Either way, the audience must take the point that they - and their rulers in London - are a part of the real action upon which the play claims to be a comment.

In this way the audience is directed towards itself and towards questioning the value of the society in which it lives. In many of the plays, Fielding skirts around the edge of political satire, preferring instead that the audience should identify the social, political and the occasional literary references and to interpret them as they see fit. No Walpole sitting in the gallery would applaud the satire in order to blunt its purpose, but he may be made to feel uncomfortable by the nature of the references. *The Author's Farce* has several examples of this kind: in the second act, Jack Pudding announces the performance of a puppet show:

> This is to give Notice to all Gentlemen, Ladies and Others, that at the Playhouse opposite to the Opera in the Haymarket this Evening will be performed the whole puppet Show called *The Pleasures of the Town*, in which will be shown the whole Court of Dullness, with Abundance of Singing and Dancing.[2]

While no-one would claim that this is a profound comment on the nature of the times, it does signal Fielding's methods and intentions. We read here of a 'puppet show' suggesting humour and farce and suggesting too that the overriding significance of the show will be entertainment ('abundance of singing and dancing'); but inserted in the middle of the speech are the words '*The Pleasures of the Town*' and 'the whole Court of Dullness'. The audience is never far away from the corruption of the City of London, nor from the intrigues of the Court, nor from the literary world of Dryden and Pope. If the standards by which one lives and from which one chooses the examples as to how to live are eroded by the indecencies of the time, then it is the duty of the 'entertainment' to reveal this and to suggest a culprit.

Because the play is entertaining and because it assumes the form of *The Beggar's Opera*, Fielding's task is not difficult. The combination of these together with familiar allusions allow lightness and seriousness to mix. One of the songs, to the tune of 'Lillibalero' reads:

> But would you a wise Man to Action incite,
> Be Riches proposed the Rewards of his Pain,
> In Riches is centred all human Delight,
> No Joy is on Earth but what Gold can obtain.
> If Women, Wine,
> Or Grandeur fine
> Be most your Delight, all these Riches can,
> Would you have Men flatter?
> To be rich is the Matter;
> When you cry, he is rich, you cry a great Man.[3]

In parallel with Gay's song, riches are seen to be of paramount importance, for riches mean success and, more importantly and more obviously to an eighteenth-century audience, riches mean 'greatness'. Gay's words, concerning the transient nature of friendship when money is at stake are translated by Fielding into the need for money if one is to be labelled 'great', or, without labouring the point, if one wishes to become recognised in politics. Taking the two songs together, the suggestion is also present that friendship and politics are simply not part of the same world.[4]

A closer examination of another play which is more firmly set in the corrupt town reveals that Fielding was definitely concerned with communicating the parallels between the theatre and society. His task was to expose the vices of the town and to introduce language which would reflect the status of the city and which would at the same time introduce a sophisticated literary parallel. The play under discussion, *The Covent Garden Tragedy*, operates through a series of stock characters who were easily identifiable to a contemporary audience. The prologue makes this clear:

> For what are Kings and Heroes Faults to you?
> But these Examples are of general Use.
> What Rake is ignorant of the King's Coffee House?
> Here the old Rake may view the Games h'as known,
> And Boys hence dread the Vices of the Town:
> Here Nymphs seduc'd may mourn their Pleasures Past,
> And maids, who have their Virtue, learn to hold it fast.[5]

The object is to present the general types of human nature and, by denying that the play is about the 'great', Fielding draws the parallel which he purports to be denying. The play is a parody of Ambrose Philips *The Distrest Mother*, itself a translation of Racine's *Andromaque*. Philips' play lent itself to parody, with its long moralistic speeches and its final death bed scene of doomed lovers. Fielding parodies the classical modes by claiming inspiration from the gods but he writes about 'Rakes and Whores'. While many of the personal references have become obscure, the general point of the play remains as clear as it was at the first performance and centres around the parallel between the respectable members of the City and those who seem to be ere parasites upon it. By removing the play to Covent Garden - a familiar setting for whores in eighteenth-century London - and by particularising the setting in a brothel, Fielding could pinpoint some of the vices of the time. The play's main character is Punchbowl, 'the distressed mother' (actually the Madam of a brothel) who controls the actions in her 'court'; it is no accident that the word 'Punch' appears as an integral part of her name, for Fielding makes explicit parallels between the role of the 'mother' and that of the statesman. They both have one large thing in common: the need to make money in order to survive and to thrive. The statesman, surrounded by the aura of respectability has a much easier life; the bawd has every right to complain:

Who'd be a Bawd in this desperate Age
Who'd for her Country unrewarded toil
Not so the Statesman scrubs his platful Head,
Not so the Lawyer shakes his unfeed Tongue,
Not so the Doctor guides the doleful Quill.[6]

The common assumption is that the motives of self-interest are the driving force behind the court and the underworld. As Gay had already stated ironically 'we should protect and encourage cheats, since we live by them'; they inhabit the same world and are guided through it to success and to greatness. There is a double irony present in Fielding's play: first, the parallel between the money-makers, and, second, the fact that bawds are experiencing difficulties when they are providing a valuable service. The danger is that emotional involvements may prevent the proper conduct of their trade: Lovegirlo, a customer, flatters Kissinda so much that she begins to feel emotions:

Oh my Lovegirlo, I must hear no more,
The Words are strongest Poison to my Soul;
I shall forget my Trade and learn to dote ...
Thou know'st too well a Lady of the Town
If she give way to Love must be undone.[7]

She is very much aware of the need to adhere closely to the rules of her trade, and to avoid the individual relationships that would inevitably lead her into a situation that would be less than professional. The ironic 'Lady' reminds the audience of the references to high society in the prologue and also to Punchbowl's opening speech.

What is needed in the professional world of harlotry and the city is a correct balance between personal involvement and a sense of the value of property and the importance of trade and business. This seems to have been achieved by Stormanda in her relationship with Bilkum; it is less than fully romantic but it does have an economic basis:

Stormanda : Dost thou forget the Time,
When shiv'ring on a wintry icy Morn,
I found thy coatless Carcase at the Roundhouse,
Did I then not forget my proper Woes,
Did I not send for help a Pint of Gin,
To warm th' ungrateful Guts ...
... Did I not picket a Pocket or a Watch,
A Pocket pick for thee?

Bilkum : Have I not for thee ...
Robbed the Stage-Coach?[8]

The association between robbery, whoring, customers and possessions is one which appears throughout the play. To maintain a mistress is to maintain a possession, and it must be kept properly, at all costs. Relationships must be economic, whether they are the personal ones of master and mistress or the strictly business ones of lawyer and statesman. The epilogue sums this up neatly:

And virtuous Women, tho' they dread the Shame,
Let 'em but play secure, all love the Game,
For tho' some Prude her Lover long may vex,
Her Coyness is put on, she loves your Sex...

In short, you (men) are the Business of our Lives,
To be a Mistress kept, the Strumpet strives,
And all the modest Virgins to be Wives.
For Prudes may cant of Virtues and of Vices,
But faith we only differ in our Prices.[9]

The audience is brought back into the world of reality, and the overt message is that the scenes before us have been a comment on the hypocritical nature of those who profess 'honesty' or 'greatness' but whose economic and social motives are the same as those who profess profanity and materialism. Loose morals are a part of the city life and there is no way that the two may be disassociated. This last point was occasionally missed by contemporaries of Fielding. 'Prosaicus' argues:

how was I surprized to see the most notorious Bawds, Pimps, and Whores, brought on the Stage to please as polite an Audience as ever I saw ... Where

115

is the Humour of the Bawdy-House scene to any but a Rake? Or that of ... Stormanda to any Woman, but those of the Town?[10]

Almost accidentally, the critic has uncovered something which underpins the whole play, and much of Fielding's other works. By the tacit acknowledgement that there is a gap between the audience and the scenes in the play, the critic is arguing that the theatre may shock and surprise an audience and that it may even clarify issues which have been hitherto obfuscated. The obfuscation would be here the seeming separation between two ways of life; however, the parallels between them are so clear when stated in this way that we are amused by the antics and yet we may also maintain that they are a comment on the ruling classes of the time. What the latter affirm and what they perform are contradictory: the action denies the surface message. On the stage, the action *performs* the message with the result that clarity emerges. No wonder Prosiacus was a little confused: he seems to be unable to view the matching of two opposites as a valid comment upon ontemporary events. If Fielding's contribution to the critical comment on his time rested there, he would no doubt have escaped the wrath of the Walpole government and he might even have allowed the theatre to continue its life after 1737. Fielding seems to have become increasingly concerned with corruption at court and there are increasing signs that he was becoming politically more adventurous while at the same time wishing to experiment with the form of the theatre. In the *Tragedy of Tragedies*, he shows corruption spreading throughout the court. The play is a rewritten version of *Tom Thumb*; the two plays overlap at several points and may be considered as one piece. Certainly, in the second play, Thumb and Walpole are brought quite closely together: Tom is referred to as 'the Great' at one point, while modern editions note that the quarrel between Thumb and Grizzle over love-matches at court is a burlesque of a contemporary political issue.[11] Such minutiae of detail place Fielding firmly within the general satiric tradition and ally him closely to the technique of Gay. Several of the speeches reveal attitudes towards contemporary politics, and the language in which they are expressed show that comedy communicates the message and that Fielding enjoys the gusto which the free form of the theatre allows him: almost everything can be represented and almost any language employed. The Queen, having fallen in love with Tom, cries for him; the King has little sympathy:

Ha what wrinkled Sorrow
Sits, like some Mother Demdike, on thy Brow?
Whence flow those Tears fast down thy lubber'd Cheeks,
Like a swoln Gutter, gushing through the Streets?

While on the marriage of Tom and Huncamunca he gives them the following blessing:

Long may ye live, and love, and propagate,

116

Till the whole Land be peopled with *Tom Thumbs*.
So when the *Cheshire* Cheese a Maggot breeds,
Another and another still succeeds;
By thousands and ten thousands they encrease,
Till one continu'd Maggot fills the rotten Cheese.[12]

The images of the gutter and maggots are familiar ones to readers of the *Dunciad* and we are here invited to inhabit the same world. Tom will gain control and he will eventually riddle through society until it becomes dominated by him. The propagation of his kind - by any means from bribery to promises of favour - will ensure that city life will spread. Then the whole state will swell out with degeneracy until it becomes accepted as the norm. The speeches are not as localised as they may at first appear, for Fielding is placing into the mouth of the King words which produce an image in the mind of the audience which correlates with his own view of social conditions.

If Tom Thumb represents Walpole in particular, then he also represents power in general; moreover, he is power in the guise of a dwarf. In *The Tragedy of Tragedies* the King refers to Tom as 'the Great Tom Thumb/The little Hero, Giant-killing Boy,/Preserver of my Kingdom'.[13] The ironic fusion between greatness and littleness is acted out in the lays by means of scenes which show Tom's desire to possess. There are scenes which indicated that power over a court or a country may be symbolically represented by dominance in a relationship. In both plays, Tom gains power over the Queen and she is then rejected. In the first play, the Queen is downcast:

For what's a Woman, when her Virtue's gone?
A Coat without its Lace; Wig out of Buckle;
A stocking with a Hole in't - I can't live
Without my Virtue, or without Tom Thumb.
Then let me weigh them in two equal Scales,
In this Scale put my Virtue, that, Tom Thumb,
Alas Tom Thumb is heavier than my Virtue.[14]

In the second play, Glumdalca, queen of the giants, falls for Tom, but she is rejected by him in favour of Huncamunca; Glumdalca's speech is more aggressive:

Left scorn'd, and loath'd by such a Chit as this;
I feel the Storm that's rising in my Mind,
Tempests and Whirlwinds rise, and rowl and roar.
I'm all within a Hurricane, as if
The World's four Winds were pent within my Carcase.
Confusion, Horror, Murder, Guts and Death.[15]

Tom's use of power and his abuse of people for his own ambition is, then, part of the cycle about which Fielding was writing in many of his works: possession implies surrender; it implies a usurpation of one set of values over another. If the second set of values proves corrupt, then the corruption spreads itself into all corners of the person, or state, that is possessed. If the corruption goes unchecked, then it will eventually engulf the innocent. So, in *Tom Thumb* and *The Tragedy of Tragedies*, we are not simply witnessing a burlesque of certain conventions of heroic tragedy; instead Fielding wishes to explore the nature of the role of the theatre: if it is not merely to constitute 'entertainment' (and therefore be divorced from any relevant contemporary issues) but also to act as a comment, the question arises: how best to combine the two, and how best to discover what the potential of the theatre may be? Ian Donaldson has a succinct comment; he argues that Fielding 'implies that the contemporary uncertainty on theatrical matters may be paralleled by our uncertainty on moral and political matters; in each case we have not sufficiently considered the true meaning of greatness: hence on the theatrical stage and on the stage of life a dwarf may pass as a hero'.[16] Politics and the stage had to be inextricably linked and both seemed a reflection of the other. We are not sure whether we have ever left the public gallery.

In *The Grub-Street Opera* the political correspondence with the stage is made even more apparent. The characters in the play are directly related to political personalities of the day. Sir Owen Apshinken is George II; Master Owen is his son, the Prince of Wales; Lady Apshinken is Queen Caroline; Robin, a servant, is Walpole, with Sweetissa as Molly Skerrit, Walpole's mistress and later his wife. The life in an upper-class household parallels the life at court: both the igh and the low squabble and cheat, and in this play, too, Fielding comes closest to the form of the *Beggar's Opera*. It is in this play that Fielding is able to exploit fully the openings which Gay had shown the theatre to have. Owen's 'Air' in Act I introduces the high/low comparison and the theatrical comparison too:

The worn-out Rake at Pleasure rails,
And cries, 'tis all idle and fleeting;
At Court, the Man whose Int'rest fails
Cries, all is Corruption and Cheating:
But would you know
Whence both these flow,
Tho' so much they pretend to abhor them?[17]

Gay had a similar message at the beginning of the *Beggar's Opera* and once more we are in the seemingly narrow world of thieves and intrigue at court. But that is part of the ironic point: if the court itself cannot rise above pettiness and corruption then the rest of society must inevitably be in danger of being absorbed by their attitude. Robin's cynical message is a crude attempt to emphasise this point:

For rich and poor
Are Rogue and Whore,
There's not one honest Man in a Score
Nor Woman true in twenty four.[18]

Like Gay in the *Beggar's Opera*, Fielding varies his stance so that we can be at once shocked and amused by the characters. Walpole, cynical about the manipulations that were possible to maintain and secure power, was reputedly sentimental to the point of ridiculousness over one person. Here, Robin attempts to charm Sweetissa:

> Oh my Sweetissa thou art straighter than the straightest Tree - sweeter than the sweetest Flower - thy Hand is white as Milk, and as warm; thy Breast is as white as Snow and as cold - Thou art to sum thee up at once, an Olio of Perfections. ... thy Face is brighter than the brightest Silver. Oh could I rub my Silver to be as bright as they dear Face, I were a Butler indeed[19]

Robin and Walpole can be figures of fun, and yet at the same time they must be taken seriously. Walpole has been able to control the nation's purse strings and its politics; Robin has been successfully stealing the family silver. Amusing though both may be in their personal relations, they are adept at acquiring a fortune by corrupt means. Robin, however, argues from a different standpoint: the times themselves are corrupt; mankind is by definition a gallery of rogues and cheats:

The heads of all professions thrive, while the others starve.

Air

Great Courtiers Palaces contain
While small ones fear the Gaol,
Great Parsons riot in Champagne,
Small Parsons sot on Ale;
Great Whores in Coaches gang
    Smaller Misses
    For their Kisses
Are in Bridewell bang'd;
While in vogue
Lives the great Rogue.
Small Rogues are by dozens hang'd.[20]

The message is similar to the whole of the *Beggar's Opera*; the contrast between small and great is indeed a true one, provided that an inversion is made so that the hypocrisy of greatness is recognised. In *The Grub-Street Opera*, Fielding ironically places true messages in Robin's mouth - that the times are rotten, for example - while at the same time offering no solution to the rottenness. The aptly named Puzzletext says 'if Robin the Butler hath cheated more than other People, I see no other Reason for it, but because he hath more Opportunity to cheat'.[21] That is the inversion that we are asked to accept and the irony of thw whole play may be unravelled from that point: is the audience to be implicated in the attack or should the professions be singled out? Is Robin a manipulator,

119

buffoon and a thief? So too the role of the theatre becomes extended as the audience takes on board the succession of ironies. Part of the problem in answering the above question lies in the fact that there is no political commitment in the play, nor in Fielding's work as a whole; it is, as Goldgar points out, a 'politically cynical rather than a politically committed play'.[22] It is because of this that the text remains puzzling; the enigma is underlined by the ending as the couples are united in harmony:

> Couples united,
> Ever delighted
>   May we ne'er disagree
> First we will wed,
> Then we'll to bed;
> What happy Rogues are we [23]

The couples complete the action by celebrating their happiness and the audience is invited to share in the joys, which is not difficult to do for the festivity and *joie de vivre* of the characters is apparent from their language and their activities. At the same time the audience must also be aware that a deeper purpose is operating and one which may disturb the laughter. Gay had similar doubts about the efficacy of a committed moral attack, for who would listen in such times? In his *Fables*, he writes:

> I grant Corruption sways Mankind,
> That Int'rest too perverts the Mind,
> That Bribes have blinded common Sense,
> Foil'd Reason, Truth and Eloquence;
> I grant you too, our present Crimes
> Can equal those of former Times.
> Against plain Facts shall I engage,
> To vindicate our righteous Age?
> I know, that in a modern Fist,
> Bribes in full Energy subsist:
> Since then these Arguments prevail,
> And itching Palms are still so frail,
> Hence Politicians, you suggest,
> Should drive the Nail that goes the best;
> That it shows Parts and Penetration,
> To ply Men with the right Temptation.[24]

Gay has to acknowledge that the age is corrupt and so the problem remains - how to combat the corruption and yet at the same time to indicate that the age is redeemable and that the world of the *Dunciad* is not a *fait accompli*. Mankind may be swayed by the force of money but those with power should be above the temptations of materialism. The politician remains the darkest of characters; in Fielding's terms he is a Machiavelli, dedicated to his own art of manoeuvring on the political stage:

the meanest, lowest, dirtiest Fellow, if such a One should ever have the Assurance, in future Ages, to mimic Power and browbeat his betters, will be as able as Machiavel himself could have been to root out the Liberties of the bravest People.[25]

Power is used to destroy the very liberties that gave it strength in the first place and the common man will suffer. Wild browbeats his betters as did Walpole. Fielding's way of dealing with this was, in the words of the First Player in *The Historical Register*, 'to have a humming Deal of Satire, and I would repeat in every Page that Courtiers are Cheats, and don't pay their Debts, that Lawyers are Rogues, Physicians Blockheads, Soldiers Cowards ...[26] Satire is expository, it is 'humming' and it rails against all those who assume the form of office without discharging its function. *The Historical Register*, anarchic though it appears to be, has many poignant lines which indicate the nature of Fielding's thought about the politics of the time. Its significance for the theatre lies in its use of contemporary, personal references which read as though Fielding was crowding his lines with as many hits as possible. Scores against Theophilus Cibber, son of Colley, as manager of the Fleetwood Theatre, are paralleled by the satirical strokes against Walpole, now an actor-manager who oversees and controls the political stage of England. In Act III, Medley, the author of a play, discusses the casting of Shakespeare's *King John* with 'Apollo' (Walpole) and 'Ground-Ivy' (Colley Cibber). Ground-Ivy insists that the play be re-written to accommodate the audience and himself and that he will overcome his own unpopularity by sweet words to the audience:

Ground-Ivy: Why I'll tell them (the audience) that the former (the actors) only tread on my Heels, and that the greatest among the latter (the authors) have been damned as well as myself; and after that, what do you think of your Popularity ...

Apollo: Let them hiss. Let them hiss and grumble as much as they please, as long as we get their Money.

Hedley; There, sir, is the sentiment of a Great Man, and worthy to come from the great Apollo himself.[27]

The symbolic union in thought between Cibber and Walpole is one of the most significant scenes in the whole of Fielding's theatrical canon. It is now explicit that the theatre comments directly upon issues and person-alities and that it may be used as a vehicle whereby these may be attacked. The playwright's job has moved from the generalised attack on the times to the specific attack on individuals; and the playwright's imagination has brought in the management-of-theatre and management-of-nation idea the forefront. The union in thought between the two characters centres around their insensitivity towards their audience and their utter of selfishness in their conduct. The minds of the people may be moulded or, if not, then those in power may have sufficient power to enable their own wishes to prevail. Under threat, measures other than persuasion could be employed. This was confirmed a few months after the *Historical Register* was written when the Licensing Act came into force. Fielding, soon to write in mild support of the Walpole government, was, in 1736/7, one of its arch opponents.

NOTES

1. Fielding, *The Coffee House Politician*, V:5, in *Complete Works*, edited by W. E. Henley, 16 vols. (London, 1903), vol.II, pp. 145/6.
2. Fielding, *The Author's Farce*, edited by Charles B. Woods (London, 1967), II, viii, pp. 34/5.
3. Ibid, III, Air VIII, p. 56.
4. There is another reference to the 'great man' in the revised edition of the play. Punch says to Luckless 'Punch is very well known to have a very considerable Interest in all the Corporations in England; and for Qualifications, if I have no Estate of my own, I can borrow one ... (but I could) turn great Man; that requires no Qualification whatsoever.' (Ibid. p. 98). As Sheridan Baker has noted, Punch and Walpole ('fat guts') were often equated in this period. See 'Political Allusion in Fielding's *Author's Farce, Mock Doctor* and *Tumble-Down Dick'* (PMLA, Vol. LXXVII, June 1962, 221-231).
5. Fielding, *The Covent Garden Tragedy* (London, 1732), p. 12.
6. Ibid. I i. The edition is confused in the correlation between its collation and its pagination; this is reference B1r, paginated 1.
7. Ibid. I, 9, C2r, paginated 11.
8. Ibid. II 2, D1r, paginated 17.
9. Ibid. Epilogue, p. 13.
10. Quoted by Ronald Paulson and Thomas Lockwood (editors), *Henry Fielding: The Critical Heritage* (London, 1969), pp. 41/2.
11. The issue is probably that of Walpole's quarrel with Townshend over the Treaty of Seville; Glumdalca is the Queen of Spain. See L. J. Morrissey's 'Introduction' to his edition of *Tom Thumb* and *The Tragedy of Tragedies* (California, 1970).
12. Ibid. I 3, p. 25 and II 8, p. 35. The last speech also appears in *The Tragedy of Tragedies*, II 8, p. 79, spoken by a parson.
13. Ibid. I 2, p. 54.
14. Ibid. I 6, p. 28.
15. Ibid. II 8, p. 75-6.
16. Ian Donaldson, *The World Turned Upside Down* (Oxford, 1970), p. 190.
17. Fielding, *The Grub-Street Opera*, edited by L. J. Morrissey (Edinburgh, 1973) I, 4, p. 33.
18. Ibid. I, 9, p. 41.

19. Ibid. I, 6, p. 37-8.
20. Ibid. II, 5, p. 58.
21. Ibid. III, 14, p. 81.
22. Bernard A. Goldgar *Walpole and the Wits* (University of Nebraska Press, Lincoln, 1976), pp. 110-112.
23. *The Grub-Street Opera*, op. cit. III, 15, p. 85.
24. Gay, *Fables*, 1738. Fable IX, lines 1-16 in *Poetry and Prose* op. cit, I, pp. 410/1.
25. Fielding, *Dedication to the Public* in *The Historical Register for the year 1736* and *Eurydice Hissed*, edited by William W. Appleton (London 1968), p.8.
26. Ibid. I, p. 13.
27. Ibid. III, p. 43.

Postscript: Fielding's social comments and his work as a magistrate

By 1748, Fielding had become Justice of the Peace for Westminster. Like most people around him, he was appalled by the increase in the amount of crime and he was determined to do something about it. He was fighting not only against the underworld, but also against an attitude of the public, who seemed to regard many of the criminals as heroes fighting against a corrupt system. Highwaymen were often viewed as princes of the underworld, despite revelations of their characters and methods by Defoe, Fielding and others. But they retained a high esteem amongst ordinary members of the public:

> It is difficult to understand why they had so glamorous a reputation in the eighteenth-century and, indeed, why their image has been so romanticised ever since ... Their place in the public's estimation was well-recognised, as for example, their right to travel in the first cart whenever they were among a batch of prisoners making a final journey from Newgate gaol to the gallows at Tyburn.[1]

Fielding attempted to counter the upsurge in crime, and the popularity of the criminals, through his position as a magistrate and through his power as a writer.

By 1748, it had become generally accepted that crime was on the increase and that measures were necessary to combat it. The *London Magazine* of December 1748, reports that 'not only pickpockets, but street-robbers and highwaymen are grown to a great pitch of violence at this time, robbing in gangs, defying authority, and often rescuing their companions, and carrying them off in triumph'. This may be seen as part of the general fear of lawlessness, as the time seemed to be rapidly approaching when some kind of reform would be necessary.[2]

The major work which developed from the concern for lawlessness and the one which instigated a great deal of serious thought about its defeat was *An Inquiry into the Causes of the late Increase of Robbers*, first published in 1751. In this work, Fielding exposes what he considers to be the major causes of crime and suggests certain remedies. The 'Introduction' to the *Inquiry* outlines the contemporary evil and the danger which it poses for the ordinary citizen:

> The great Increase of Robberies within these few Years is an Evil to me appears to deserve some Attention; and the rather as it seems (tho' already become so flagrant) not yet to have arrived at that Height of which it is capable and which it is likely to attain: For Diseases in the political, as in the natural Body, seldom fail going on to their Crisis, especially when nourished and encouraged by Faults in the Constitution. In fact, I make no doubt, but that the Streets of this Town, and the Roads leading to it, will shortly be impassable without the utmost Hazard; nor are we threatened with seeing less dangerous Gangs of Rogues among us, than those which the Italians call Banditti.
>
> Should this ever happen to be the Case, we shall have sufficient Reason to lament that Remissness by which this Evil was suffered to grow to so great a Height. All Distempers, if I may once more resume the Allusion, the sooner they are opposed, admit of the easier and the sager Cure. The great Difficulty in extirpating desperate Gangs of Robbers, when once collected into a Body appears from our own History in former Times. France hath given us a later Example in the long Reign of Cartouche, and his Banditti; and this under an absolute Monarchy, which affords much more speedy and efficacious Remedies against these political Disorders, than can be administered in a free State, whose forms of Correction are extremely slow and incertain, and whose Punishments are the mildest and the most void of Terror in any other in the known world. For my own Part, I cannot help regarding these Depredations in a most serious Light; nor can I help wondering what a Nation so jealous of her Liberties, that from the slightest Cause, and often without Cause at all, we are always murmuring at our Superiors, should tamely and quietly support the Invasion of her Properties by a Few of the lowest and vilest among us: doth not this Situation in Reality level us with the most enslaved Countries? If I am to be assaulted, and pillaged, and plundered; if I can neither sleep in my own House, nor walk the Streets, nor travel in safety; is not my Condition almost equally bad whether a licenced or unlicenced Rogue, a Dragoon or a Robber be the Person who assaults and plunders me?[3]

We are plunged into the world of Johnson's *London*, a world of a diseased body politic and a lawlessness that could only be associated with savagery. Yet the state of affairs is one encouraged by those who manipulated the law. Even after the days of Walpole, crime and power are seen as intimately linked. Babington notes the activities of footpads:

> Footpads were as callous as they were daring. They would often hamstring the persons they had robbed by cutting the sinews of their legs in order to prevent their escape. It was small wonder that Smollett felt constrained to

124

write 'thieves and robbers are now become more desperate and savage than they have ever appeared since mankind was civilised'.[4]

Smollett's concern that London may be degenerating into savagery is one which is shared by Fielding, who has set himself up as a typical ordinary citizen who desires a peaceful domestic life. The reproach which he aims at his countrymen for their seeming lack of care and compassion and who merely rail at authority rather than support it, strengthens his position as a magistrate; the appeal is one to common sense and the need for justice in a declining state.

Having stated his views about the country, Fielding proceeds to examine the ways in which crime may be dealt with and how to deter the potential criminal. The argument commences with statements of general social concern and Fielding outlines the degradation to which certain members of society are reduced. This degradation is often the result of the consumption of cheap gin:

> The intoxicating Draught itself disqualifies them from using any honest Means to acquire it, at the same Time that it removes all Sense of Fear and Shame, and emboldens them to commit every wicked and desperate Enterprize. Many Instances of this I see daily: Wretches are often brought before me, charged with Theft and Robbery, whom I am forced to confine before they are in a Condition to be examined; and when they have afterwards become sober, I have plainly perceived, from the State of the Case, that the Gin alone was the Cause of the Transgression, and have been sometimes sorry that I was obliged to commit them to Prison.[5]

The problem had become increasingly acute as the century had progressed. In 1725 there were 6,000 places where one could buy gin, and by 1750 there was one 'public house' to every fifteen private houses in the City of London and one public house to every four private ones in St Giles.[6] The places of the highest proportion of 'public' to 'private' were also the areas which contained the highest rate of crime.

Fielding, as one of the few conscientious magistrates, saw that a distinction could be drawn between those who stole in order to buy gin and those who were part of the structure of the organized gangs. The gangland bosses had more power than any magistrate, and, while acknowledging that gin-drinking constituted a threat to the morals and health of the nation, it was only a part of the system of a corrupt, yet highly organised, hierarchy of crime.

Any criminal, whether it was a gangland boss or a petty thief, could cock a snook at the law:

> If a Pickpocket steal several Handkerchiefs, or other Things, to the Value of twenty Shillings, and the Receiver of these, knowing them to be stolen, is discovered, and both are indicted, the one as Principal, the other as Accessory, as they must be; if the Jury convict the Principal, and find the Goods to be of as high Value as a Shilling, he must receive Judgement of

Death; whereas, by finding the Goods (which they do upon their Oaths) to be of the value of tenpence, the Thief is ordinarily sentenced to be whipped, and returns immediately to his Trade of picking Pockets, and the Accessory is of course discharged, and of course returns to his Trade of receiving the Booty. Thus the Jury are perjured, the Public highly injured, and two excellent Acts of Parliament defeated, that two Miscreants may laugh at their Prosecutors, and at the Law.[7]

There may be, Fielding argues, some provision within the law for the control of crime but that is simply not enough; the law is ineffective in practice, and so must be seen as futile and indeed in a laughable state.

Fielding believes that the receivers of stolen goods - the inheritors of the tradition of Jonathan Wild - are by no means popular with the public. The blemish on society is a 'deplorable evil' which must be defeated. He identifies the two sources of the problem: first, the ack of effective methods of prosecution, and second, the complicity of the public:

The principal Defect seems, to me, to lie in the extreme Difficulty of convicting the Offender; for, 1. Where the Thief can be taken, you are not at Liberty to prosecute for the Misdemeanour.

2. The Thief himself, who must be convicted before the Accessory is to be tried, cannot be a Witness.

3. Without such Evidence, it is very difficult to convict of the Knowledge that the Goods were stolen: which, in this Case, can appear from Circumstances only. Such are principally, first, Buying Goods of Value, of Persons very unlikely to be the lawful Proprietors. Secondly, buying them for much less than their real Value. Thirdly, buying them, or selling them again, in a clandestine Manner, concealing them, etc. None of these are commonly liable to be proved.[8]

Fielding goes on to make several suggestions; he appeals to the 'sense of parliament' to introduce laws to deal with these defects, while at the same time indicating that his suggestions stem from common sense and a common identity with the general public. The problem is a 'stubborn mischief' but may be overcome:

First, Might it not be proper to put an effectual Stop to the present scandalous Method of compounding Felony by public Advertisements in the Newspapers? Might not the inserting of such Advertisements be rendered highly criminal in the Authors of them, and in the Printers themselves, unless they discover such Authors?

Secondly, Is it impossible to find any Means of regulating Brokers and Pawnbrokers? if so, what Arguments are there against extirpating entirely a set of Miscreants, which, like other Vermin, harbour only about the Poor, and grow fat by sucking their Blood?

Thirdly, Why should not the receiving of stolen Goods, knowing them to be stolen, be made an original Offence? by which means the Thief who is

often a paltry Offender in comparison of the Receiver, and sometimes his
Pupil, might, in little Felonies, be made a Witness against him.[9]

If other magistrates were corrupt, then Fielding clearly is not; he
identifies himself with the victims, dismisses the brokers as 'vermin' and
by doing so he hopes to gain sympathy from his audience. The law must
not be allowed to be regarded as distant and inhuman, or detached from
the realities of the harshness of contemporary conditions.

A lack of belief in the efficacy of the law - and a belief in the corruptibility
of it - had allowed criminals to be free. Fielding appeals to the common
sense and reason of the reader in order to establish the truth of the matter,
which is that the gangland bosses must be seen as 'vermin'. The vocabulary
is significant since it stablishes a firm base in the mind of the reader from
which to reject criminals, their way of life, and their basis of power.

Fielding was also aware that the law had to have a compassionate side.
He regarded English justice as far superior to any which he had studied
on the continent, for it upheld the principle that every accused person had
the right to defend himself, it had established the system of trial by jury
and it had also an appeal system built into it. Criticism of the system had
to be seen to be both permissible and reasonable:

> To make, therefore, such an Application (i.e. Proof of Innocence after
> sentencing) on behalf of injured Innocence is not only laudable in every
> Man, but is a Duty, the Neglect of which he can by no means answer to
> his own Conscience; but this, as I have said, is to be done in a proper and
> decent Manner, by a private Application to those with whom the Law hath
> lodged a Power of correcting its Errors and remitting its Severity; whereas
> to resort immediately to the Public by inflammatory Libels against the
> Justice of the Nation, to establish a Kind of Court of Appeal from this Justice
> in the Bookseller's Shop, to re-examine in Newspapers and Pamphlets the
> Merits of Causes which, after a fair and legal Trial, have already received
> the solemn Determination of a Court of Judicature, to arraign the Conduct
> of Magistrates, of Juries, and even Judges, and this even with the most
> profligate Indecency, are the Effects of a Licentiousness to which no
> Government, jealous of its own Honour, or indeed provident of its own
> Safety, will ever indulge or submit to.[10]

The quotation suggests duty is a sense of what is right and a civilised code
of behaviour. The press, already guilty of permitting advertisements for
stolen goods, cannot be relied upon for objective judgement. A civilised
way of protesting is contrasted with the hysteria that may break out from
the popular press; by establishing this contrast, Fielding is acknowledging
the contentiousness that existed and he must also be indicating that the
basis of power needed to be shifted away from those who he associates
with villainy - thief-takers and politicians - onto those who he associates
with common-sense and reason, namely, himself. At every turn, he is the
reasonable man:

If none of these Methods be thought possible or proper, I hope better will be found out. Something ought to be done, to put an End to the present Practice, of which I daily see the most pernicious Consequences; many of the younger Thieves appearing plainly to be taught, encouraged, and employed by the Receivers.[11]

Moreover, the calm, analytical tone renders even more effective the message he is attempting to convey. Part of the answer may lie in history, and the civilised man, having access to this information, is able to communicate it:

> There is no Part of our ancient Constitution more admirable than that which was calculated to prevent the concealment of Thieves and obbers. The Original of this Institution is given to Alfred, at the End of his Wars with the Danes, when the English were very much debauched by the Example of those Barbarians, and betook themselves to all manner of Licentiousness and Rapine. These Evils were encouraged, as the Historians say, by the vagabond State of the Offenders, who, having no settled Place of Abode, upon committing any Offence, shifted their Quarters, and went where it was difficult to discover them. To remedy this Mischief, therefore Alfred having limited the Shires or Counties in a better Manner than before, divided them into Hundreds, and those again into Tithings.[12]

The appeal here is to tradition, to custom and to order, in contrast to the barbaric laws and customs of the invaders. England needs to return to a peaceful existence, both internally and externally. Robbers of whatever order constitute a threat to the security of the nation.

Fielding continues his survey of the laws relating to vagabonds until he reaches his own time. The law stipulated that there should be no habitation of foreign parishes without registration, but it was difficult to administer and, of course, not everyone was prepared to conform. Fielding's concern is to rid the streets of the contamination:

> though most of the Rogues who infest the public Roads and Streets, indeed almost all the Thieves in general are Vagabonds in the true Sense of the Word, being Wanderers from their lawful Place of Abode, very few of them will be proved Vagabonds within the Words of this Act of Parliament. These Vagabonds do, indeed, get their Livelihood by Thieving, and not as petty Beggars or petty Chapmen; and have their Lodging not in Alehouses, etc. but in private Houses, where many of them resort together, and unite in Gangs, paying each 2d per night for their beds.[13]

The trouble with the law was that it allowed such rogues to wander the streets without providing sufficient check against them. At this stage, it is worthwhile pausing and considering Fielding's precise position for there is a contradiction here which is inherent in it. While he must try to encourage respect for the law, his examination of it reveals it to be inadequate, and while he may write in high terms about civilisation and the moral health of the nation, one only has to turn to his plays, or to newspaper accounts or to his own attitude towards the genuine rogues to realise that the England that Fielding envisages may exist only in the imagination. The reality resides in ridding the place of a corruption which stems from the hierarchy, and a hierarchy of which Fielding himself was a member, if not an adherent. Again, the genuine rogues provide a serious problem, not in their apprehension but in their definition; Fielding, who wishes to be seen as a kind of liberal humanist, betrays the kind of dilemma that the doctrine contains:

> I can add, what I myself once saw in the Parish of Shoreditch, where two little Houses were emptied of near seventy Men and Women; amongst whom was one of the prettiest Girls I had ever seen, who had been carried off by an Irishman, to consummate her Marriage on her Wedding-Night in a Room where several others were in Bed at the same Time.

> If one considers the Destruction of all Morality, Decency, and Modesty; the Swearing, Whoredom, and Drunkenness, which is eternally carrying on in these Houses, on the one Hand, and the excessive Poverty and Misery of most of the Inhabitants on the other, it seems doubtful whether they are more the Objects of Detestation or Compassion.[14]

To detest or to feel compassion is a dilemma which Fielding was never able to resolve; he seems to have tried to content himself with objective assessments of the cases as they were brought before him, using the law as an outline rather than an absolute:

> In conjunction with other justices of the peace, he also revoked licences for the sale of spirits; and tried to end all unlawful traffic in gin, though he found the law inadequate for the purpose. Profane swearers on the street were hauled into his court, and fined or sent to Bridewell, that he might check 'the licentious insolence of the vulgar'. Vagrants who appeared honest were discharged; the sick were recommended to the care of the overseers of the poor; and the rest were bound to good behaviour or sent to the house of correction until they could be removed to the parishes where they belonged.[15]

The overall view of Fielding must be of a man caught in an impossible position, and of a man with few if any allies. Who else among the magistrates attempted to analyse cause and effect, and who else cared to much as Fielding? His attempts to discriminate against those who were vermin and those who were genuinely in need of compassion are signs that he wished to change the way of thinking of those in power; he found himself administering laws which he found over-harsh and lacking in discrimination.

Footpads and highwaymen continued to flourish and the latter, especially, retained their place in the popular imagination; perhaps his dilemma as to the nature of the society reveals why. Fielding failed to comprehend the appeal:

> No Hero sees Death as the Alternative which may attend his Undertaking with less Terror, nor meets it in the Field with more imaginary Slory. Pride,

which is commonly the uppermost Passion in both, is in both treated with equal Satisfaction. The Day appointed by Law for the Thief's Shame is the Day of Glory in his own Opinion. His Procession to Tyburn, and his last Moments there, are all triumphant; attended with the Compassion of the Meek and Tenderhearted, and with the Applause, Admiration, and Envy, of all the bold and hardened.[16]

That he failed to comprehend is understandable when placed in context of the kind of people he was faced with as a magistrate. And as an author - who appealed to the imagination of his public, as well as to their common sense - he attributed the qualities of the robber to the social climate. What he cannot get to grips with is the fact that the rogues have an opposite interpretation, which both depends on Fielding's and contrasts with it: namely, that the highwayman is an adventurous anarchist, willing to rob those who have robbed others, in the name of justice.

Fielding's ideal of justice is best represented in *A Journey from This World to the Next*. The examples of true justice which Fielding gives in the work conform largely to the idea as presented in the *Inquiry*. In this text, several people are judged by Minos as they attempt to enter Elysium. Fielding notes that 'those who were guilty of some very heinous crimes ... were hustled in at a little black gate, whence they tumbled immediately into the bottomless pit.'[17] A neat mythological arrangement, perhaps, but not one which bore much relation to the conviction and treatment of contemporary criminals. Minos acts as an ideal judge, humane and dispassionate and equipped with an innate ability to detect the truth; a spirit approaches Minos, begging that

he might not go to the bottomless Pit: he said he hoped Minos would consider that, though he had gone astray, he had suffered for it - that it was Necessity which drove him to the Robbery of eighteenpence, which he had committed, and for which he was hanged - that he had done some good Actions in his Life - that he had supported an aged Parent with his Labour ... that he had ruined himself by being Bail for his Friend. At which Words the Gate opened, and Minos bid him enter, giving him a Slap on the Back as he passed by him.[18]

The ideal world of Elysium welcomes those who show themselves to be of good heart and who are civilised or who have been civilised. They have shown respect for the law and deserve sympathy because their individual circumstances demand it. Fielding summed up his attitude in the following manner:

Actions are their own best Expositors; and though Crimes may admit of alleviating Circumstances, which may properly induce a Judge to mitigate the Punishment; from the Motive, for Instance, as Necessity may lessen the Crime of Robbery, when compared to Wantonness or Vanity.[19]

There may be alleviating circumstances and the need for fine discrimination - such as that which Fielding possessed, and which resulted from a civilised view of the world - was a 'Necessity' for the magistrate, and, by implication, those who commanded the magistrate to action.

NOTES TO POSTSCRIPT

1. Antony Babington, *A House in Bow Street. Crime and the Magistracy, (1740-1881* (London, 1969): p.18.
2. Quoted by Wilbur L. Cross, *The History of Henry Fielding*, 3 vol. (New Haven,1918): II, P.250: and Martin R. Zerker, *Fielding's Social Pamphlets* (California,1966): Chapter 2, passim.
3. Fielding, 'An Inquiry into the Causes of the late Increase of Robbers' in *Works*, op.cit.*Legal Writings*: pp.19/20.
4. Babington, op.cit.p.17.
5. *Legal Writings*,p.34.
6. See J.L. & B. Hammond, *Poverty, Crime, Philanthropy in Johnson's England*, edited by A.S.Turberville, 2 vols. (London,1933):I,p.312 and Donald Low, *Thieves' Kitchen* (London, 1982): p.14.
7. Henley, (ed.), op.cit. p.80.
8. ibid., p. 81.
9. ibid., pp 81/2.
10. Fielding, 'A clear State of the Case of Elizabeth Canning' in *The Works of Henry Fielding*, edited by Leslie Stephen, 10 vols. (London, 1882): VI,'Essays and Legal Cases' p.373.
11. Henley (ed.), op.cit. p.82.
12. ibid., p.83.
13. ibid., p.96.
14. ibid., pp.96/7.
15. Cross, op.cit. II, p.281
16. Henley (ed.), op.cit. pp.121-4.
17. Fielding, *A Journey from This World to the Next*, edited by Claude Rawson (London, 1973): pp. 31/2.
18. Ibid., pp. 33/4.
19. Fielding, 'Essay on the Knowledge and Characters of Men' in *Miscellanies* edited by Henry Knight Miller (Oxford, 1972) p. 163.

CHAPTER 7

Alternatives and Parallels

1. The State in the Past

The metaphor of the crime which is perpetrated by one man until the whole of the nation becomes corrupt was a convenient one for contemporary satirists, but those who were more optimistic found that they were confronted with a problem: the satiric view of the age was essentially destructive, and few, with the possible exception of the exiled Bolingbroke, could provide an alternative which would enable the country to recover from its lapses and to re-affirm itself as a glorious example of honesty, trade, and industry. It may have appeared that the age offered nothing to those who hoped for a better future; the possibility seemed to be emerging that England was permanently contaminated.

Those writers with a more optimistic propensity decided to create, from this chaos, an emerging order. The basic idea was to show that despite the corruption that may be inherent in any court or in any political circle, there are honest, upright men who refuse to sell their principles or their country for the sake of power and who represent the ideal which fights against insidious cynicism. Bolingbroke had attempted to suggest that there was an alternative ideology to follow, but he had been incapable of providing specific examples or practices from the contemporary scene which could serve as a definite alternative. Other writers faced the same problem, and tried to overcome it by looking into the past. Recent English history was too dangerous and the analyses of it were too inconsistent for it to supply examples of proper courtly behaviour, so writers, and dramatists in particular, removed the action in both place and time. Past times may have been corrupt but optimism is possible since history showed that no court could be totally corrupt: it had to be a reflection of the society to which it belonged and observation suggested that good men were available, and struggling against the manipulators of power. The history need not be factual, since, as in Gay, the imaginative world provided general metaphorical parallels which could be translated into specific ones by the audience. What some dramatists were arguing was that the depression which many felt in the fact of such enormous crimes was one which had a remedy. The perpetual struggle is summed up in a speech by Portius, in Addison's *Cato*. Portius, Cato's son, speaks of the conflict between his father and Caesar:

> The Dawn is over-cast, the Morning lours,
> And heavily in Clouds brings on the Day,
> The great, the important Day, big with the Fate
> Of *Cato* and of *Rome* - our Father's Death

Would fill up all the Guilt of Civil War,
And close the Scene of Blood. Already Caesar
Has ravaged more than half the Globe, and sees
Mankind grown thin by his destructive Sword:
Should he go further, Numbers would be wanting
To form new Battles, and support his Crimes.
Ye Gods, what havoc does Ambition make
Among your Works.[1]

The conflict is between Caesar who perpetrates crimes and Cato who
is viewed as the true defender of the State. Caesar exploits the resources
of the State in order to boost his own position and he is determined upon
any course of action that will enable him to remain in power. So, he may
declare war when necessary and he may destroy others, but the warfare
and destruction are aimed at only one goal, which is that of self-preser-
vation. Civil strife is used by him for the same end. Cato proves to be the
hero in the sense that he regards the policies of Caesar as bad; he is
prepared to fight against them from within the state system. He wishes to
preserve the structure of the state but to replace its leaders, since, within
the present framework of the court, there are enough men who would
prove honourable:

Cato: Trust me Lucius,
      Our civil Discords have produced such Crimes

      Such monstrous Crimes, I am surprised at Nothing.
      - O Lucius, I am sick of this bad World

      The Day-light and the Sun grow painful to me.[2]

The play, written in 1713, does not deliberately foreshadow any of the
ensuing debate on the nature of the crime in which politicians indulged
nor does it deliberately set out to castigate a previous Tory administration.
Certainly, some of Addison's contemporaries thought it had political
undertones, but Addison asked several high-ranking Tories to read it,
while Swift was invited to attend rehearsals, and few objections to its
political content were made.[3] The objective in this chapter is not to revive
the debate about any specific political content, but to indicate that, in times
which were acutely sensitive politically, such a play could be seen to
occupy a certain general position. That stance is of a country searching
for former glory whilst under the shackles of a self-seeking administration.
Cato is an example of the kind of searching that was taking place and
what the theatre had to offer in the way of political comment. There is,
after all, an ideology at work and one which is produced by the times in
which the play was written.

Cato also serves as an introduction to other works of the period; as well
as representing the conflict between the 'country' and the 'city', certain

dramatists turned to the past to examine political behaviour and, in turn, to pass comment. The quotations from and general discussion about *Cato* are useful in order to introduce two plays by David Mallet, whose concerns are broadly the same as those of Addison. Mallet was dismissed by Johnson, and his reputation has hardly been augmented since then. While a painstaking analysis of Mallet's plays would do little to enhance his standing, the plays are interesting from the point of view of their representation of a society in conflict and the possible solution to that conflict.

Mallet's *Mustapha*, written in 1739, deals with the attempts of Rustan, the grand Vizier of the court of Solyman, to create a conflict etween Solyman and his son, Mustapha; he is aided by Roxolana, the Empress. There is, as Felicity Nussbaum says, a partial parallel between the intrigues which are perpetrated by Rustan and those which Walpole employed in the court of George II in order to maintain power both over the court and in the country.[4] Both Rustan and Walpole were seen as types of the kind of minister who would exacerbate any tension in order to achieve personal ambition. In the play, Rustan is aware that human nature is corruptible and that power hastens suspicion and the necessity for intrigue; his methods are to exploit the weaknesses rather than search for goodness:

> I, at Times,
> Have thrown out Hints, Insinuations, Doubts,
> Some dark and distant, some more plain and near:
> And from such fruitful Seeds is springing up
> A Harvest to our Hopes. The Sultan now,
> Declining to th' Infirmities of Age,
> Is lapsing to its Vices; quick Distrust,
> Umbrage at rising Excellence, but chief
> At signal same in Arms. He fears his Son:
> And in the Hearts of Kings, by Years made gloomy,
> From Fear to Hate the Progress is not slow.[5]

The Sultan, whose political insight is in decline, is to have his weakness exploited for the sole purpose of personal aggrandisement. Rustan is opportunistic and acts through principles or ideology other than the ones of pragmatic arrangement. The view of human nature is cynical and the view of the nature of politics is Machiavellian. Conduct within the court is governed by preserving the facade of politeness while plotting for one's personal ambition. The court circle is, then, inward-looking, and it is quite clear from Rustan's speech that the Sultan himself, through his association with the court, is capable of total misjudgement when faced with the intrigues of Rustan and Roxolana. Rustan warns Solyman about his son's pride and Roxolana advises him to watch Mustapha carefully.

Mustapha is the alternative to intrigue; he is wary of the court, naive about how it works, and yet aware of the possibilities lurking therein. He is capable of speaking the truth, a quality which is admirable in a man, but no asset at court; he says to his friend, Achmet:

> Bred in Camps,
> Trained in the gallant Openness of Truth
> That best becomes a Soldier; thou, my Friend,
> Art happily a Stranger to the Baseness,
> The Infamy of Courts. Achmet, the Caspian
> When terrible with Tempest, is less fatal
> To the frail Bark that plows it, than a Court
> To Innocence and Worth ...
> ... A Vizar, meanly cunning, coolly cruel,
> Grown old in Arts of Treachery and Ruin,
> Pursue me, hunt me down [6]

The oppositions and the contrasts are clearly established here. They are between evil and good, the selfish and the simple, the man of intrigue and the man of truth, the politician and the soldier, the static life at court and the active one outside it. The conflict is also between two views of human nature: one which states that the process of statesmanship leads to corruption, and the other ideals which expand beyond personal ambition. Rustan says he is driven by 'Dire Ambition' and his court is dark and secret:

> We are not yet secure.
> Fond Nature may return, and baffle all
> Our labour'd Schemes - Ambition deadly Tyrant
> Inexorable Master what Alarms,
> What anxious Hours, what Agonies of Heart,
> Are the sure Portion of thy gaudy Slaves?
> Cruel Condition Could the toiling Hind,
> The shivering Beggar, whom no Roof receives,
> Wet with the mountain Shower, and crouching low
> Beneath the naked Cliff, his only Home;
> Could he but read the Statesman's secret Breast,
> But see the Honors there, the Wounds, the Stabs,
> From furious Passions and avenging Guilt:
> He would not change his Rags and Wretchedness,
> For gilded Domes and Greatness [7]

If the quotation is taken in isolation, then the meaning of the speech comes close to the ideas expressed by Mandeville: human nature is inherently bad and power is a conspiracy; the two are engaged in a continual struggle and the stronger of the two emerges as victor, while goodness and benignity of temperament mean little. In Mandeville, there is no such thing as an honest heart:

136

These were call'd Knaves, but bar the Name,
The grave Industrious were the same:
All Trades and Places knew some Cheat,
No calling was without Deceit.[8]

Mallet's point is somewhat different however, for struggling against Rustan is Mustapha; Mustapha represents the potential heroism in man. The ideal of the court has been attacked by such as Rustan and it has found itself in a position which approaches villainy but Mustapha remains untarnished. Mustapha is outward, open and active, opposed to the closed interior world of the court. Rustan is only active in an insidious way, when he is seeking personal gain and when driven on by ruthless ambition. Mallet's point is essentially optimistic, for the life of the court does not inevitably depend upon a Machiavelli who is determined to win at all costs: principles may be seen to survive, and the Rustans of the court must be resisted. Mallet's play is almost a morality in type, as the struggle between good and evil continues; the struggle is for power and for the heart and mind of the court. Another character, Zanger, Mustapha's brother, is approached by Rustan and asked to take part in the conspiracy; Zanger reacts:

> Thou earth-born Slave
> I thought to have restrain'd me - but thy Baseness
> Arouses me beyond Dissembling. - No:
> Thy Counsel perish with thee - Heaven is he,
> Are such as he the Men whom Princes trust?
> And must the Fate, the Safety or Destruction
> Of millions, each less guilty than himself,
> Hang on the Breach of one whom thou must hate?[9]

The fate of the court and the fate of the country rests with people like Rustan. The moral here is not wholly pessimistic since the prince seems detached from the corruption, although he may be affected by it, and the ordinary citizen is given a kind of noble innocence which raises him above villainy and yet makes him subservient to it. Those such as Rustan may influence statesmen or even hold power, but there is an opposition to them also. The court, although not inherently corrupt, will continue to be involved in a struggle between the forces of dark and light. What must come first is the country, and adherence to duty must be held paramount in the mind of any prince.

If Mustapha and Zangar represent the noble forces at work against evil, then the ideal of the prince is represented in another play, *Alfred: A Masque*. Although it is even less specific in reference than *Mustapha*, there are several speeches which reveal the stately ideal and the need for humility in the task of running the State. The humility comes from a simpleness of heart which is closely associated with the country ideal. In a masque, the shepherds represent this open and honest 'country-ness', and in the play, Corin, a shepherd, argues from a position which dissociates him from the taints of politics and which establishes the ideal position:

> are we poor?
> Be Honesty our riches. Are we mean
> And humbly born? The true Heart makes us noble.
> These Hands can toil; can sow the Ground and reap
> For thee and thy sweet Babes. Our daily Labor
> Is daily Wealth.[10]

The virtues of the shepherd must be shared by the King, who must also be willing to fight against those who are attempting to destroy the nobility of the court and the country. Alfred sees 'his country laid in ruins,/His subjects perishing beneath the sword/Of foreign war' and he promises to do his duty:

> If not to shelter useful Worth, to guard
> His well-earn'd Portion from the Sons of Rapine,
> And deal out Justice with impartial Hand;
> If not to spread, on all good Men, thy Bounty,
> The Treasures trusted to me, not my own;
> If not to raise anew our English Name,
> By peaceful Arts that grace the Land they bless,
> And generous War to humble proud Oppressors:
> Yet more: if not to build the public Weal,
> On that firm Base which can alone resist
> Both Time and Chance, on Liberty and Laws;
> If not for these important Ends ordain'd
> May I ne'er poorly fill the Throne of *England*[11]

The excess of chauvinism may not be to the taste of a modern audience nor does the verse contain literary merit, but it has another function which is that it serves to emphasise the nobility of kingship. The leader should be sensitive to the needs of his public and aware of the potential greatness of the country which he rules. In a play which has 'Rule Britannia' as its climax, we are not entitled to great depths of ambiguity and subtlety, but we are entitled to place it within the larger framework of the search for an ideal within the new political context. The ideal, in all Tory writers, was to be found in the reconstruction of the past; a past which was at once simpler than the present and yet at the same time one which contained similar conflicts between the selfishness of the individual politician and the needs of the state. Alfred's final speech sums this up; no doubt Bolingbroke would have approved of the sentiments:

> O may the Toils, I yet must undertake,
> The slumbering Genius of this Isle awake.
> Revive her Worth, relume her antient Flame,
> That shun'd no Danger in the Road to Fame
> That saw no Terrors, but in sure Disgrace

And only turn'd aside, from what was base
Yet, tho Heaven mean all Humankind to bless,
From his own Labors Man must draw Success:
Each Head, Heart, Arm, combin'd in one great View,
Their Country's good, unweary'd, to pursue,
But, from his Zenith, should they once descend;
Should all their Aims in venal Poorness end:
Lost is the Nation, deaf to Glory's Call
And, with fallen Virtue, Freedom too must fall![12]

Mallet was not alone in incorporating these noble (or naive) sentiments into his plays; several minor dramatists attached morals to their plays, and did so in such a manner as to refer directly to the times, yet, by keeping the action of the plays at a distance, they avoided the direct relevance of *The Beggar's Opera* for example and avoided also any political interference even though the plays may have been a general censure of politics. In James Thomson's *Agamemnon*, for example, several of the speeches read almost as though they were written as commentaries on the meaning of Mallet's plays; the language is contemporary, the action historical and, as in Mallet, the message is clear:

Important is the Moral we wou'd teach:
(Oh may this Island practise what we preach)
Vice, in its first Approach, with Care to slum;
The Wretch, who once engages is undone.
Crimes lead to greater Crimes, and link us streight
What first was Accident, at last is Fate:
The unhappy Servant sinks into a Slave;
And Virtue's last sad Strugglings cannot save.[13]

Once again, any discussion relating the meaning of these lines to any contemporary political significance must be a general one. The lines are 'Bolingbroke' in character and sentiment; they yearn for a past age of innocence in which words and (by implication from the ensuing action) political deeds were to be judged at their face value. Like Mallet, Thomson is determined to produce a play with a general moral, a morality about human nature when engaged in political actions at Court. Drama is seen as a vehicle for teaching, with the ideology once more placed at the general level of the requirements that a prince needs for the successful government of the state. 'Crimes', a word so popular in the theatre as to require no explanation as to its significance, have corrupted the State and reduced its people to slaves; the people are, as in Bolingbroke's pamphlets, struggling for freedom against an oppressive regime. The court is a place of intrigue in which 'We must not wear the Soldier's honest Face'.[14]

Thomson's and Mallet's attempts at drama take the general implications of the philosophy of Bolingbroke concerning the present political climate in the State and translate it into references to the past, while sharing the Tory concern for the present.

2. The State in the Present

Not all writers looked to the past for a means whereby to draw attention to the present age. Many decided, along with Pope, Swift and Gay, that a direct satiric assault was necessary. This meant that audiences were invited to share the attack, but were not able to discover where an answer lay to the problems which the writers were confronting. The alternative may well have been found by the writers themselves as they employed wit as a weapon and suggested that laughter and thought were a part of human nature and constituted an alternative to the corrupt hearts with which they were surrounded. The prologue to John Kelly's play, *Timon in Love*, begins:

> Ladies and Gentlemen since all Transgression
> Is promis'd Pardon, when it makes Confession,
> Knows that our Play, a Sheaf of Foreign Gleaning,
> Dreads to be damn'd, for its Excess of Meaning.
> What tho', to court kind Judges, our Translator
> Has let loose Scandals and unbridled Satire
> Vain are his Arts: - That Play was built for Sinking,
> Where none can laugh, but at th' Expence of Thinking:
> In a free Nation, 'tis too like Subjection,
> To pay (for Mirth) both Money and Reflexion.[15]

We may perhaps be thankful that the author acknowledges the 'Sheaf of Foreign Gleaning' and that he refuses to claim any great merit for the play; what the reader may also notice is the reference to satiric 'Sinking' and the general lightness of tone in which the passage is written. Kelly insists that laughter and revelation are intricately combined and that the 'free Nation' must support such a linkage.

After the Prologue, the plot moves towards its Classical subject: it deals with the attempts by Mercury (Aspasia) to seduce Timon into falling in love with Eucharis. There are occasional speeches which deal with money and its position in the world and it is in these that the significance of the plot for a contemporary audience is revealed. In Act II, Pierot explains to Socrates the value of money and why he, Pierot, wants so much:

> I am rich, and I am told Man that is rich May be every thing he will; that Gold will purchase Wit, Birth, Honour, Titles, Reputation, and all that's valuable in the World.

While in Act III Aspasia sings the following 'Air' on Gold:

> Cast your Eye thro' ev'ry Nation
> Learn the Idols of the Crowd
> 'Tis the rich that are all the Fashion,
> Not the Noble, Great and Good.
>
> If your Gold will then procure you,
> All that Birth and Wisdom can,

What in Life can more allure you?
What can form a happier man?[16]

Gold is equivalent to Birth which in turn is equivalent to Nobility; one
may buy oneself anything and money comes to *mean* 'respectability' (in
an ironic, *Beggar's Opera*, way) for the rich are superior. Here, the
analogy with Gay must end, for in *Timon in Love* the method of acquiring
riches is never mentioned and so the examination of any contemporary
issues is brought to an abrupt halt. It would be unfair to demand that
Kelly produce anything more, for the intention behind the play is stated
in the prologue. The implication is that the Court is corrupt but the
structure of the plot diverts attention away from a consideration of this,
on to Timon falling in love. The suggestion is that there is another world,
which is away from the court and inside the 'heart', where the honest
alternative may be found.

The more one mentions money and corruption then the more the analogy
with Walpole and his government comes into focus. Popular ballads were
usually much more explicit and open about the character of the man, and
they reflect the feeling that the state had become corrupted by one man
and by one obsession:

Good People draw near
And a Tale you shall hear,
A story concerning one *Robin*,
Who, from not worth a Groat,
A vast Fortune has got,
By Politicks, Bubbles and Jobbing.

But a few Years ago,
As we very well know,
He scarce had a Guinea his Fob in;
But, by bribing of Friends
To serve his dark Ends,
Now worth a full Million is *Robin*.

Each Post he had fill'd
With Wretches unskill'd,
In all other Arts except Fobbing;
For no man of Sense
Would ever Commence
Such prostitute Creatures of Robin.

By the same worthy Means
We have B (ishop)s and D (ean)s
As dull as blind *Bayard* or *Dobbing*,
That both Church and State
Draw near to their Date
By the excellent Measures of Robin ...

(2 verses omitted)

141

As oft hath he said,
That our Debts should be paid,
And the Nation be eas'd of her Throbbing;
Yet on tick we still run,
For the true Sinking Fund
Is the bottomless Pocket of *Robin*.[17]

The idea is clear and it relates closely to many of the others already discussed in this chapter: the State only exists for the fulfilment of one man, who has managed to inveigle himself into the structure of the State, to find those who are most ready to accept his methods and to suborn them. There seems no credible opposition here, as the State, the Church and the economy are subsumed under the interests of Walpole. As in so many direct attacks, an alternative was difficult to provide; there may be an underlying ideology, but it is one which never attempts to achieve a general philosophical status. Satirists, especially in the 1730s, had to confine themselves to almost desperate attacks on Walpole himself. An example of such a satirist is James Miller, who regarded Pope as the civilised man fighting against the corrupt regime of Walpole; it is not that Pope engages in any kind of active combat, but that he is a symbolic presence. *Are These Things So?* is supposedly an attack by Pope on Walpole:

That thus the *Fountain* of *Britannia's* Health
Source of her Grandeur, Liberty, and Wealth,
Polluted by your *all-corrupting* Hand,
With rank Infection deluges the Land;
Parent at once of *Want* and *Luxury*,
Of open Rapine and dark Treachery;
The knave's *Elixir*, and the Just Man's *Bane*,
Food to the *Locust*, *Mildew* to the *Swain*;
Pouring on those who once in *Goshen* dwelt;
More deadly Plagues than Aegypt ever felt.[18]

Britain has become a totally corrupt island; Walpole rejects any form of traditional values, and assigns himself instead to the establishment of a regime dominated by plagues, darkness and treachery. 'Liberty' and 'Health' are no longer part of the structure of the State; they are no longer part of the vocabulary of the poet, either, except in an ironic sense or when used to introduce their opposites. The State at present is rotten, and the rottenness is perpetuated in order to preserve a status quo.

The pamphlet was followed by a reply, in which the Great Man attempts to defend himself; entitled *The Great Man's Answer to Are these Things So?*, it takes the form of a dialogue between *E. M.* (Pope) and *G. M.* (Walpole):

E.M.: If none thy baleful Influence will withstand,

Go forth, Corruption, Lord it o'er the Land;

142

If they are thine for better and for worse,
On them and on their Children light the Curse.

G.M.: *Corruption*, Sir - pray use a milder Term;

'Tis only a Memento to be firm;
The times are greatly alter'd - Years ago,
A Man would blush the World his *Price* should know:
Scruple to own his Voice was to be bought;
And meanly minded what the Million thought;
Our Age more *Prudent*, and *Sincere* is grown,
The Hire they *wisely* take, they *bravely* own;
Laugh at the Fool, who let's his Conscience stand,
To barr his Passage to the promis'd Land;
Or sway'd by Prejudice, or puny Pride,
Thinks *Right* and *Int'rest* of a different Side.

G.M.: Furies My *thousand Bank*, Sir,
E.M.: Thus I Tear
Go, blend *Corruption*, with *corrupting* Air.
G.M.: Amazing Frenzie Well, if this won't do,
What think you of a *Pension*?
E.M.: As of You.
G.M.: A *Place* -
E.M.: Begone.
G.M.: *A Title* -
E.M.: is a Lie
When ill conferred.
G.M.: A Ribband.
E.M.: I defie.[19]

Pope is the representative of the honest, ordinary citizen who defies the
attempt to corrupt his honesty and so offers some hope that civilised
standards of behaviour will be preserved. The cynical materialism of
Walpole may be an historical event but it may disappear with the
overthrow of the Great Man. Two aspects of the attack emerge here: it is
convenient for Miller (disguised as Pope) to represent 'the poet' as the
preserver of standards, since, on the surface, Pope had removed himself
from the intrigue of the court and had constructed a world in Twickenham
which symbolised a continuity of standards and a consistent pattern of
behaviour; but Pope was just as capable of intrigue as Walpole, as any
friend - and enemy - of Pope could testify, and both were men of
extreme energy who had to fight to preserve what they believed in. The
contemporary poet (Miller) when castigating the State in its present form,
has difficulty in suggesting an alternative hich is credible in absolute terms,
for specific details may emerge which detract from his argument. This is
where the general ideology as represented in the plays already discussed
may score over the direct attacks. Although the plays never achieve the
same kind of immediate response from their audience, they have the

advantage of suggesting a general ideology and mode of behaviour that is free from taint while at the same time they are relatively free from political involvement and so may escape political censure.

Secondly, the date of Miller's attack should be noted: 1740. By that time, Walpole had been in power for two decades and the assaults upon him appeared to have been fruitless. There was a feeling that whatever techniques were employed, no writer would be able to shift Walpole from his entrenched position; hence the stance taken is much more direct for there was nothing to lose and possibly something to gain by stating quite explicitly the distinction between what was regarded as civilised and what was not: no political stand was necessary. The message was to get rid of Walpole and then establish (or re-establish) a different form. The language reflects the attitudes; Walpole's ideology could only be destroyed by abuse, since he had out-manoeuvred all others in their attempts to establish alternatives:

Lo where he stands, amidst the *servile Crew*;
Nor Blushes stain his Cheek with crimson Hue,
While dire *Corruption* all around he spreads,
And every ductile Conscience captive leads:
Brib'd by his Boons, behold the *venal* Band,
Worship the *Idol* they could once command:
So Britain's now, as Judah's Sons before,
First raise a GOLDEN CALF, and then adore.[20]

The feeling that wit was necessary in order to sustain and enhance the message has disappeared; Walpole is an object to be vilified and attacked; he is no longer an object of fun or an object which has a certain entertainment value. The language has become dour; the age has become tainted and the nation has become totally materialistic. Values which could be relied upon in the past and which had an intrinsic merit have been turned on their head, until opposite values apply to both words and institutions:

Well - of all the Plagues which make Mankind a Sport,
Guard me, ye Heav'ns from that worst Plague - a Court.
'Midst the mad Mansions of Moorfields, I'd be
A straw-crown'd Monarch, in mock Majesty,
Rather than Sovereign rule Britannia's Fate,
Curs'd with the Follies and the Farce of State.
Rather in Newgate Walls, O let me dwell,
A doleful Tenant of the darkling Cell,
Than swell, in Palaces, the mighty Store
Of Fortune's Fools and Parasites of Power.
Than Crown, ye Gods be any State my Doom,
Or any Dungeon, but - a drawing Room.[21]

Power resides in the court and the drawing room, but the relationship between those who hold power is an incestuous mockery of any ideal that had held sway in the past. The palace has been replaced by Newgate's cells and the monarch is a dummy, controlled by the whims of those who have reduced the machinations of government to a farce. The attack is satiric but it is a bitter satire; the author vilifies the corruption but implies too that he can see no alternative; the language suggests a darkness over the state that admits no light.

The works discussed in this chapter do not, in traditional criticism, enter into serious consideration; they may be regarded as minor or of academic interest only. But a departure from the great works of the early eighteenth-century reveals the underlying feeling that the times had become devastated by corruption and that honesty had disappeared. The works reveal, too, how politically sensitive the times actually were and how authors, especially dramatists, were striving to pass comment upon political institutions without actually criticising directly the regime under which they were living. By including references to other countries, authors were inviting their audiences to draw parallels with contemporary moral and political life; any references to an 'ideal' statesman would require an audience to consider whether a criticism was being made of those politicians who dominated the times, but none of the material was exact and precise. The poets had an answer: provided, of course, that the question was concerning the nature of the attack to be launched; they left no room for ambiguity and, like the government itself, fought with whatever weapon they found at their disposal. The fear was that the apparent contamination had spread so far as to be irremoveable. Tories looked to the past to create an imaginary ideal, and they could only hope that the future would be a radical break with the present:

> There have been Men indeed splendidly wicked, whose Endowments threw a Brightness on their Crimes, and whom scarce any Villainy made perfectly detestable, because they never could be wholly divested of their Excellencies; but such have been in all Ages the great Corrupters of the World, and their Names to be no more preserved than the art of murdering without Pain.[22]

NOTES

1. Joseph Addison, 'Cato', I i, in *Miscellaneous Works* edited by A. C. Guthkelch (London, 1914), p.355.
2. Ibid. IV iv, pp.405/406.
3. See Bloom, *Joseph Addison's Sociable Animal*, op. cit. pp.97/8.
4. See Introduction, *The Plays of David Mallet*, edited by Felicity A. Nussbaum (New York, 1980).
5. David Mallet, 'Mustapha', IV i, Ibid. p.4 (B2v).

6. Ibid. II i, p. 17 (Dir).

7. Ibid. III iv. p. 41 (Gir).

8. Bernard Mandeville, *The Fable of the Bees*, edited by F. B. Kaye, 2 vols. (Oxford, 1924) I, pp.19/20.

9. 'Mustapha', op. cit., III v p.44 (G2v).

10. David Mallet, 'Alfred: a Masque', in *Works*, 3 vols. (London, 1759), III I i, p.10 (B5v).

11. Ibid., I vii, pp.24/5 (B12v - Cir).

12. Ibid., III, p. 69 (D11r - D11v).

13. James Thomson, *Agamemnon*, (Dublin 1738), Prologue, A3r.

14. Ibid., II iv. p.18 B4v.

15. John Kelly, 'Timon in Love : or The Innocent Theft', in *Classical Subjects II*, edited by W. H. Rubsamen (New York, 1974: reprint of London, 1733), p.A3v.

16. Ibid., II vi. p. 35 (D2r) and III viii, pp. 42/3 (D5v - D6r).

17. Percival, op. cit., pp.15/16.

18. James Miller, *Are These Things So?*, (London, 1749: reprinted as Augustan Reprint Society, no 153, Los Angeles, 1972), p.5.

19. Ibid., p.8 and p.13.

20. Paul Whitehead, *The State Dunces*, (London, 1733), p.4.

21. Paul Whitehead, 'Manners. A Satire', in *The Works of The English oets* (London, 1810), vol.XVI, p.210.

22. Samuel Johnson, The Rambler, 31 Mar.1750. Quoted in *Novel and Romance, 1700-1800. A Documentary Record*, edited by Ion Williams (London, 1970).

CHAPTER 8

Language

The question which is most usually posed when considering how an argument (or discourse) achieves its effects is 'what is this piece of writing trying to do' or 'how is the discourse structured in order to achieve its effects?'[1.] This chapter will attempt to examine the variety of argument that was put forward during the period and which was directed, largely, by those who regarded the Whigs as untrustworthy and dishonest. As the reign of Walpole progressed, the arguments became more hostile and the language more bitter. As opponents of Walpole began to realise that he was likely to retain power despite their protestations and that chaos, dullness and darkness seemed to be covering all, then the language reflected the increased feelings of bitterness and helplessness. As the language of the aristocrat faded, that of the merchant began to take control until the stockjobber emerged as the one who defined the temper of the age: pragmatic at best, opportunistic and unprincipled at worst.

For convenience, the chapter is divided into three: the first part deals with some aspects of prose, the second with poetry and drama while the third considers some of the techniques of persuasion that were employed.

1. Prose

At the beginning of the century the Whig and Tory conflict, although a real one, had by no means achieved the proportions that were to follow. The major crisis which split the two parties was the War of the Spanish Succession and the desire of the Tories to begin peace negotiations. The Tories suspected that the Whigs wished to prolong the war through personal need rather than national interest. Swift was at the centre of the debate, but other, often anonymous, tracts appeared which, while making clear their exact political allegiance, did not utilize the methods that were to become prevalent as the years went by. The following, written in 1710, is a *'Warning to the Voters of Cockermouth not to choose Whigs'*:

> We can't but be very surprised and concerned to hear (that) a Man of your Temper, Sense and (as we hoped) well affected to the Established Church should at this Time so far start aside as to associate with Separatists and Schismatics and assisting of them in the choice of Members for the next British Parliament, as if that Party were not strong enough already with the Help of their Scotch Friends, Peers, Commissioners and Representatives ... Though his Grace my Lord Duke (of Somerset) himself (who has been a very bountiful Benefactor to your Borough) should now knowingly recommend to you a Person of republican principles (James Stanhope), one that would not allow her present Majesty any hereditary Title, that would be for clipping and paring the Prerogative of the Crown, and for the erecting

147

new Schemes of government in order to ruin and undermine our present happy Constitution and Establishment in Church and State ... can you think yourself under any Obligation to make Choice of Men for your Representatives whom you have any Reason to fear are of such dangerous Principles? As for my Lord Wharton ... they always have him sure both upon Principles and Interest, and they need not fear his deceiving of them by his recommending any of contrary Sentiments. It's true that both these great Lords have been wonderfully kind to your Town. What, then? Are you for that obliged to sacrifice your Conscience?

The Queen, God bless her, no doubt has very good Reasons for the Changes she made in her Ministers of State and for the Dissolution of the Parliament. Many think she has been long under a Kind of Restraint and no free Agent (not to say insulted) in the Throne, and that she found her sacred Person, Crown and Dignity in Danger from Men of base, disloyal, and republican Principles. If so, where is the Prudence, Policy or good Manners to her Majesty or our Nation to promote to the Interest and Design of such who may again distress her and all her good Subjects?[2]

Although the piece is partisan in character, it has none of the exuberance or malice that later writers who were more cynical and more bitter were to utilise to such effect. The appeal here is to reason and logic, expressed in terms that are designed to affect the man who is accustomed to weighing up issues and debates in a cool and steady manner. The accusations against the Whigs, that they may be 'separatists and schismatics' is one which is stated but never pushed to an extreme of vituperation. The oppositions which are established are simple ones and ones which are designed to influence a reader to vote Tory without appearing at all hysterical against the Whigs. The Tories are in favour of unity (as opposed to faction); they are supporters of the Crown, a familiar metonymy to contemporary readers, and they favour the continuation of the association between Church and State. The particular principle of allowing the monarch to change minister is also touched upon, establishing the Tories' belief in the constitution and heir adherence to traditional modes of governmental practice. These simple oppositions were also used to state the Tory ideology, without any apparent reference to the Whigs; in the following case, the language is restrained and balanced while the manner is subservient:

We have learned the Duty of our inferior Stations than to inter-meddle in the weighty Affairs of Government. But when your Majesty shall judge it expedient to summon a new Parliament, we promise to choose such Representatives as shall be unsuspected of having any Inclination to Change; Gentlemen of known Affection to your Majesty's Person, Title and Prerogative, and at the same Time careful to preserve the just Rights and Liberties of the Subject; determined by a Principle to maintain the Doctrine, Worship and Discipline of the Church of England, and by a true Christian Moderation to continue that Indulgence which our Laws have granted to Consciences truly scrupulous; willing to contribute to the carrying on of the War, whilst

148

absolutely necessary, and ready to oncur in such Measures as may most tend to procure a speedy, safe and lasting Peace.[3]

Clearly, the Borough of Westbury had every intention of remaining conservative, pro-monarchy, Christian (Church of England variety), law-abiding and peaceful. No doubt her Majesty was as pleased with this 'Profession of Tory faith', as she would have been to receive the protestation from George Granville in which he sets out the principles of behaviour which he will follow:

> To support Monarchy and the Church for which so many of our Ancestors have sacrificed their Lives and Fortunes together to establish the Protestant Succession beyond any Possibility of Dispute.

> To restore the Credit of the Nation, which her Majesty has so happily retrieved by the late Exercise of her royal Authority.

> To carry on the War against France with such Vigour and such Intentions as may produce a safe, honourable and speedy Peace.[4]

The language and the argument follow a similar pattern to the passages already discussed: the advantage of this extract is that it itemises in the simplest possible form the nature of contemporary conservativism and it shares the language and attitude of many Tory tracts. The order of the argument is also significant, as it moves from establishing the general principle of adherence to Church and State, while the final statement is a reminder that the author has contemporary politics in mind which may be linked with Tory ideology. The manner is once more servile and the language confirms and supports the Tory faith and never challenges any of its traditions. The language also disguises the political nature of the events in which Granville and other Tories were participating, for the prose is set out and is expressed in an ordinary manner, as though the only possible gentlemanly course of action would be to vote Tory or to join their ranks. It disguises the fact that the Tories were themselves engaged in political manoeuvring in just the same way as the Whigs and they were acutely aware of the opposition and of the dangers that the Whigs and the rising Walpole presented.

In 1712, Walpole was expelled from the House of Commons and imprisoned; in the 1713 election however, he was returned to parliament by the electors of King's Lynn. His speech of acceptance presents an interesting contrast in language and emphasis:

> Gentlemen -

> I cannot but think myself entirely obliged to you for the Favours bestowed on me this Day. But more especially I think myself particularly bound to offer you my most hearty Thanks for your Kindness in electing me after that malicious Prosecution of me, inasmuch as you were pleased to stand by me, because you dare to be honest in the very worst of Times; and this Act of yours will render this Corporation famous to the later Posterity. The

149

late Parliament (from whom no Good could be expected, nor no Good came) addressed her Majesty to use her Interest with all foreign tates to remove the Pretender from their Dominions, but this hath been so well complied with that he is at present removed as near us as the Power of France can place him. Gentlemen - her Majesty was pleased to tell us (as you all know) a Year past that Dunkirk should be demolished, but one Stone is removed, and the Completion of that Work is deferred till Christmas, and whether it will then be demolished we have no Certainty. And as to the Terms of Peace, I dare be bold to affirm that had the King of France beaten us, as we have done him, he would have been so modest as to have given us better Terms than we have gained after all our glorious Victories. Gentlemen - we have some Reason to think that the ensuing Parliament will tread in the same Steps with the former, but assure yourselves we will struggle hard for our Religion and Liberty.[5]

The first emphasis is on practical politics: Walpole had been 'maliciously prosecuted' the year before and he here reminds his audience of the exact nature of Tory policy towards their opponents. Despite its high ideals, the Tory party is not above such action; however, Walpole cannot be seen to be simply attacking the Tories on a personal issue, so he moves on quickly to the present attempts at peace negotiations, despite the great victories that had been achieved and despite promises that had been made. The emphasis throughout is on practical politics, for ideals to Walpole seem embedded in action, not simply words. At the end of the passage he concedes that 'religion and liberty' will be struggled for but it is a by-product of practical politics rather than any ideology that will be firmly adhered to and practised. Naturally, an election address and a letter from a Tory are, in formal terms, two different things which anticipate two quite distinct audiences, but they serve as examples of the kind of way in which the opponents thought and, consequently, hoped to act. The language and manner, too, reveal a stance from which political action would derive and from which attacks could be launched on the opposition: Bolingbroke, over twenty years later, was still echoing the earlier Tory arguments and ideals, while Walpole was moving on to deal with situations as they stood or as he had created them.

It is Swift to whom one must turn for examples of the most effective anti-Whig rhetoric; *The Examiner* reveals much about Swift's Tory position but it reveals too the usage of rhetoric for political purposes. Swift's methods are simple, and a re-examination of some passages will reveal some of the methods which he employed.

The first, familiar to all readers of *A Tale of a Tub* or *The Battle of the Books* is the personification of certain contemporary issues; these issues may be general in character but they have particular political leanings:

Liberty, the Daughter of Oppression, after having brought forth several fair Children, as Riches, Arts, Learning, Trade, and many others; was at last delivered of her youngest Daughter, called FACTION; whom Juno, doing the Office of Midwife, distorted in its Birth, out of Envy to the Mother; from whence it derived its Peevishness and Sickly Constitution. However, as it is often the Nature of Parents to grow most fond of their youngest and disagreeablest Children, so it happened with Liberty, who doated on this Daughter to such a Degree, that by her good Will she would never suffer the Girl to be out of her Sight. As Miss Faction grew up, she became so termagant and froward, that there was no enduring her any longer in Heaven. Jupiter gave her warning to be gone; and her Mother, rather than forsake her, took the whole Family down to Earth. She landed first in Greece, was expelled by degrees through all the Cities by her Daughter's ill Conduct; she fled afterwards to Italy, and being banished thence, took shelter among the Goths. with whom she passed into most Parts of Europe; but being driven out every where, she began to lose Esteem; and her Daughter's Faults were imputed to her self: So that at this Time she hath hardly a Place in the World to retire to. One would wonder what strange Qualities this Daughter must possess sufficient to blast the Influence of so divine a Mother, and the rest of her Children: she always affected to keep mean and scandalous Company; valuing no Body, but just as they agreed with her in every capricious Opinion she thought fit to take up; and rigorously exacting Compliance, although she changed her Sentiments ever so often. Her great Employment was to breed Discord among Friends and Relations; and make up monstrous Alliances between those whose Dispositions least resembled each other. Whoever offered to contradict her, although in the most insignificant Trifle, she would be sure to distinguish by some ignominious Appellation, and allow them to have neither Honour, Wit, Beauty, Learning, Honesty or common Sense. She intruded into all Companies at the most unseasonable Times; mixt at Balls, Assemblies, and other Parties of Pleasure; haunted every Coffee-House and Bookseller's Shop; and by her perpetual Taling filled all Places with Disturbance and Confusion. She buzzed about the Merchant in the Exchange, the Divine in his Pulpit, and the Shopkeeper behind his Counter. Above all, she frequented Publick Assemblies, where she sat in the Shape of an obscene, ominous Bird, ready to prompt her Friends as they spoke.[6]

The political motive is clear and has already been discussed; on the level of rhetoric, Swift wishes to place certain things in the foreground. Certainly, the passage is a fable and it conforms to the simple pattern of such a tale while revealing its political significance. Swift has an advantage of course: any reader who picked up *The Examiner* would expect to read a pro-Tory tract, and so Swift has a ready-made audience and one which would be receptive to the message; the method - of fable and of explicit parallel - becomes important because of the expectations that the reader has. These expectations - that the Whigs will be attacked, or the Tories defended, or both - is both confirmed and denied. It is confirmed after the fable has been related for the author - who now becomes a political commentator rather than a narrator of a well-known story - asks 'the Undertakers for the late Ministry to take notice of' the 'true Interest and Constitution of their Country' since 'Faction' appears to be taking over. However, Swift confines himself to these general comments, for he changes his stance and asks 'what are the true Characteristicks of a Faction?' The expectations of the reader are fulfilled at this point in a general sense only, for the commentator refuses to identify specific instances of Faction, preferring instead to llow the reader to draw his own conclusions. Now, it may be argued that Swift is also denying the reader full satisfaction by exactly the same method: there is no overt political message, at least on the surface; everything operates on a level of general abstraction and there are no facts which the reader may retain to bring forward in any other, coffee-house argument. What the reader is trying to do is extract meaning from the passage which will confirm his Toryism and which will be useful ammunition against a Whig opponent; Swift will not allow the reader to read and memorise however: he is invited to think politically and to invent arguments for himself. As the passage progresses, Swift asks rhetorical questions in order to emphasise his point and to place demands upon the reader once more:

> If the present Ministry, and so great a Majority in the Parliament and Kingdom, be only a Faction; it must appear by some Actions which answer the Idea we usually conceive from that Word. Have they abused the Prerogative of the Prince, or invaded the Rights and Liberties of the Subject? Have they offered at any dangerous Innovations in Church or State? Have they broached any Doctrines of Heresy, Rebellion or Tyranny? Have any of them treated their Sovereign with Insolence, engrossed and sold all Her Favours, or deceived Her by base, gross Misrepresentations of Her most faithful Servants? These are the Arts of a Faction; and whoever hath practised them, they and their Followers must take up with the Name.[7]

The challenge is to identify meaning, for Swift returns to one of his favourite themes which is the use and abuse of words and their meanings and the consequences of this upon thought and action. The political purpose of the passage is clear - to identify the party which constitutes a faction and to support the one which represents unity - but the means are equally important. Language must for Swift represent truth - here, a political truth. Its persuasive forces will only be properly realised if its proper function is adhered to.

It is only at the end of the argument that Swift returns to the fable that he has already told, but in an oblique manner:

> It is usually reckoned a Whig Principle to appeal to the People; but that is only when they have been so wise as to poison their Understandings beforehand; Will they now stand to this Appeal, and be determined by their Vox Populi, to which Side their Title of Faction belongs? And that the People are now left to the natural Freedom of their Understanding and Choice, I believe our Adversaries will hardly deny. They will now refuse this Appeal, and it is reasonable they should; and I will further add, that if our People resembled the old Grecians, there might be Danger in such a Tryal. A pragmatical Orator told a great Man at Athens, that whenever the People

were in their Rage, they would certainly tear him to Pieces; yes, says the other, and they will do the same to you, whenever they are in their Wits. But, God be thanked, our Populace is more merciful in their Nature, and at present under better Direction; and the Orators among us have attempted to confound both Prerogative and Law, in their Sovereign's Presence, and before the highest Court of Judicature, without any Hazard to their Persons.[8]

Here, Greece and Athens are recalled from the fable with which Swift commenced the argument; he reminds the reader that he should return to the beginning in order to re-examine the story in the light of the judgement on the word 'Faction' that he has just pronounced, while at the same time he provides hints (or possibly clear indications) as to how the fable should be read.

Swift points the exact direction to take. The effect of the language is to invite the reader to ask questions about the nature of such words as faction and to demand that he interprets the passage and works upon it, rather than expect the answer to be provided by either a narrator or a political commentator. The rhetoric is the argument; Swift invents a story as a means of persuasion, but he does not remain satisfied with that: he establishes his own credibility and appeals to the audience's sense of logic and reason. By the end of the piece Swift has drawn us into the rhetorical net of belief in him as a judge of contemporary events and their implications, and he has demonstrated his worth as a narrator of relevant material.[9]

An earlier *Examiner*, no. 16, deals with Marlborough and is dedicated to denouncing him as a man, as a general and as a representative of Whiggism. Again, this tract has been discussed in a different chapter, but at this point it is worth returning briefly to the argument in order to demonstrate its associations with and differences from the one already considered.

Swift's consideration of the successes and failures of Marlborough begins with an association which is suggestive of a complimentary historical parallel but which is designed to mislead:

I said in a former Paper (Numb. 13) that one specious Objection to the late Removals at Court, was the Fear of giving Uneasiness to a General, who hath been long successful abroad: And accordingly, the common Clamour of Tongues and Pens for some Months past, hath run against the Baseness, the Inconstancy and Ingratitude of the whole Kingdom to the Duke of Marlborough, in return of the most eminent Services that ever were performed by a Subject to his Country; not to be equalled in History. And then to be sure some bitter Stroak of Detraction against Alexander and Caesar who never did us the least Injury. Besides, the People who read Plutarch come upon us with Parallels drawn from the Greeks and Romans, who ungratefully dealt with I know not how many of their most deserving Generals: While the profounder Politicians, have seen Pamphlets, where

Tacitus and Machiavel have been quoted to shew the Danger of too resplendent a Merit.[10]

According to the beginning of the argument, Marlborough is a general who ranks amongst the classical generals; but the parallel is a disguise which is designed to establish the author as an honest, dispassionate narrator who is both learned in argument and knowledgeable in the classics, and thus better able to inform and instruct the reader. he argument is quickly turned on its head however, through the means of rhetorical questions which are asked in order to demonstrate the civilised manner in which Marlborough was treated in contrast with those heroic generals of the past: 'Hath he been tried for his Life, and very narrowly escaped? Hath he been accused of high Crimes and Misdemeanours? Has the Prince seized on his Estate, and left him to starve?' Swift's questions indicate that the Tory government is indeed composed of gentlemen and that its politics are not designed to punish one man for the crime of a whole previous administration:

> But the late Ministry was closely joined to the General, by Friendship, Interest, Alliance, Inclination and Opinion; which cannot be affirmed of the present; and the Ingratitude of the Nation lieth in the People's joining as one Man, to wish, that such a Ministry should be changed. It is not at the same Time notorious to the whole Kingdom, that nothing but a tender Regard to the General, was able to preserve that Ministry so long, until neither God nor Man could Suffer their Continuance? Yet in the highest Ferment of Things, we heard few or no Reflections upon this great Commander; but all seemed Unanimous in wishing he might still be at the Head of the Confederate Forces; only at the same Time, in Case he were resolved to resign, they chose rather to turn their Thoughts somewhere else, than throw up all in Despair. And this I cannot but add, in Defence of the People, with Regard to the Person we are speaking of; that in the high Station he hath been for many Years past, his real Defects (as nothing Human is without them) have in a detracting Age been very sparingly mentioned, either in Libels or Conversation; and all his Successes very freely and universally applauded.[11]

The argument is one which appeals to reason and which convinces the reader of the reasonableness of the Tory cause. 'The Reason of my stating this Account', Swift states afterwards, 'is only to convince the World, that we are not quite so ungrateful either as the Greeks or the Romans', but the 'only' here reads like a deliberate understatement, for Swift alludes to the practice of proper government and to the practice of proper generalship. No sooner has Swift stated his aim than he begins to expand upon it and draw the reader into the factual right of the argument; he proves that the 'Bill of Roman Ingratitude' (which he computes as 'ready Money in the General's Pocket') came to 94 11s. 10d. while that of the British came to 540,000; the conclusion must be that 'we are not yet quite so bad at worst, as the Romans were at best'.[12]

In this paper, irony is mixed with fact, and events are mixed with stories. Instead of inviting his readers to refer back to a fable or story with which he has begun his tract, he concludes with an everyday story concerning 'A Lady of my Acquaintance':

> A Lady of my Acquaintance, appropriated twenty six Pounds a Year out of her own Allowance, for certain Uses, which her Woman received, and was to pay to the Lady or her Order, as it was called for. But after eight Years, it appeared upon the strictest calculation, that the Woman had paid but four Pounds a Year, and unk two and twenty for her own Pocket: It is but supposing instead of twenty six Pounds, twenty six thousand; and by that you may judge what the Pretensions of Modern Merit are, where it happens to be its own Paymaster

The passage appeals to the reader since it expresses the political moral of the pamphlet in simple everyday terms and yet forces the reader into a position from which he must condemn the Lady and which forces him onto Swift's side in the argument; the jumble of figures which Swift has employed earlier has been made clear by a simple story which any reader may retain and which, from a rhetorical point of view, expresses exactly what a Tory would want to hear: it condemns Whiggery and those associated with it and sums up all the previous points without hesitation or fuss. Swift has proved himself an objective and reliable commentator once more, while his technique of narrating an event is designed to illustrate the points in an imaginative way, reinforcing the politics and stating them in a different form. The end is pre-determined; once more, it is the method that is the argument.

Swift's arguments are closely connected with the idea that Toryism protects the individual and the state and that the Whigs encouraged selfishness and the crime of faction. By the time that George Lyttelton came to write his *Political Tracts*, the emphasis had changed: the subtle techniques of the earlier Swift had not worked, Bolingbroke was writing in exile, and Walpole seemed finally and irrevocably in control. Lyttelton's *Letters from a Persian in England to his Friend at Ispahan* are not so consistent in argument, or indeed intention, as Swift's political prose, for they range over much of the eighteenth-century landscape, from stockjobbing to politics to opera. The importance of some of the arguments lies in the change of emphasis that may be detected in the use of language. The state of England is a sad one; the country seems to have changed stance and the pursuit of money has replaced the pursuit of Liberty:

> I perceive, Sir, you are very much cast down with the Bounds that have been set to your Authority: But perhaps you have not lost so much as you imagine. - The People are very proud of their own Work and look with great Satisfaction on the Outside of their new-erected Government; but those

who can see the Inside too, find every thing too rotten and superficial to last very long.

The two Things in Nature the most repugnant and inconsistent with each other, are the Love of Liberty, and the Love of Money: the last is so strong, among your Subjects, that it is impossible the former can subsist. I say, Sir, they are not HONEST enough to be FREE - Look round the Nation, and see whether their Manners agree with their Constitution. Is there a Virtue which Want does not disgrace, or a Vice which Riches cannot dignify? Has not Luxury infected all Degrees of Men amongst them? Which way is that Luxury to be supported? It must necessarily create a Dependance which will soon put an End to this Dream of Liberty. Have you a Mind to fix your Power on a sure and lasting Basis? Fix it on the Vices of Mankind; Set up private Interest against publick; apply to the Wants and Vanities of Particulars; shew those who lead the eople, that they may better find their Account in betraying than defending them: This, Sir, is a short Plan of such a Conduct as wou'd make you really superior to all Restraint, without breaking in upon those nominal Securities, which the Troglodites are more attach'd to a great deal than they are to the Things themselves. If you please to trust the Management to me, I shall not be afraid of being obnoxious to the Spirit of Liberty; for in a little while I will extinguish every Spark of it; nor of being liable to the Justice of the Nation, for my Crime itself shall be my Protection.[14]

A new status quo has arrived, and it is one which is designed to prevent freedom from flourishing and one which determines that mediocrity and crime will survive and that the state will remain one which promotes love of money, vices and crime. The metaphor of crime assumes great importance; crime has now become a controlling factor in the life of the nation, instead of something that may be fought against and overcome by steady, traditional democratic processes. The tone of the passage is one of depression, even of acceptance of this state of affairs. The mood of exhilaration, of joy in the fabrication of an argument that is present in Swift is not present here; all arguments have been rehearsed and proved useless in the face of Walpole's manoeuvrings. The truth of the matter is evident for all to see: nothing but dishonesty rules and the individual currency that ruled under Tory-ism has been not just devalued but replaced by the stock exchange and paper credit.

The new Whiggism has, then, produced an economic order which the landed gentry not only finds unacceptable, but also practically incomprehensible. To attack Whiggism was to attack an economic system that depended on paper and upon bargaining and which encouraged shifty, double-dealing practices; the suspicion that the new order was typified by these practices was confirmed after the collapse of the South Sea Company, an economic fiasco which saw Walpole escape unscathed, but which ruined many of those who had ventured into the land of economic opportunism. The bursting of the South Sea Bubble also showed that luck played a great part in modern economic survival: those who had tradition behind them were just as likely to fall whilst speculating as those who wished to become the 'nouveaux riches', while the latter had an equal chance of attaining a similar financial status to their social superiors. It all seemed so much of a jungle, that those who wished to attack the new order found themselves using language which reflected their feelings that the world was becoming more savage and less human; possibly simply more competitive. The prose work which most clearly suggests this attitude is *Cato's Letters* by Trenchard and Gordon. The collected Letters were published in 1724, and they depict the country as being infested with disease for which there seems no cure; there is a conspiracy amongst the jobbing companies, who are 'cannibals feeding on the body politic' and who have no sense of duty and therefore no sense of freedom:

> I think it would have been a Symptom of Wisdom in us, to have chosen rather to fall by the Hand of God, than by the execrable Arts of Stockjobbers: That we are fallen, is a sorrowful Truth, ot only visible in every Face you meet, but in the Destruction of our Trade, the Glory and Riches of our Nation, and the Livelihood of the Poor.[15]

The jobbers have upset the balance of power and they have confirmed by their actions that they are in no way interested in the principles of the 1688 revolution which conferred a certain kind of freedom upon men and which seemed to guarantee a nation in which trade flourished and the country grew rich. The revolution also suggested that the country should remain conservative in principle. The balance of power has been altered, but is now in the hands of an unrecognizable enemy - he is no longer human, no longer a member of any particular party of faction, but he is simply a 'jobber' and he may be found in all walks of society. Hence allegiances changed and no-one could be sure that he would remain in power - or wealth - from one day to the next; attacks could come from any quarter:

> A Man robb'd in his House, or on the Highway, receives from the Law all possible Satisfaction: He has the Restitution of his Goods again, where it can be made; and he has the Life of the Offender, if he can be apprehended; and then there is plentiful Reward given for every such Apprehension. By this salutory Method, Vengeance is at once taken for the Crime committed, and a terrible Example made of its Author, to prevent its Repetition ... The Ruin is general, and every Man has the miserable Consolation to see his Neighbour undone; for as to that Class of Ravens, whose Wealth has cost the Nation its All, as they are manifest enemies to God and Man, no Man can call them his Neighbours; they are Rogues of Prey, they are Stock-Jobbers, they are a Conspiracy of Stock-Jobbers ... Your Terror lessens, when you liken them to Crocodiles and Cannibals, who feed, for Hunger, on human Bodies.[16]

The 'Crime' metaphor again appears and its significance need not be dwelt upon; suffice it to say that the crime which the jobber commits is no crime at all in the eyes of the law; 'real' criminals, however, are harmless compared with the cannibalism of the jobbers whose activities are sanctioned by the state and who are associated with those highest in the State. Politicians have become birds of prey, no longer seen as supporting any principle but seen as members of a conspiracy which works against the state and which encourages and then feeds on corruption in it:

> If this mighty, this destructive Guilt, were to find Impunity, nothing remains, but that every Villain of a daring or Avaricious Spirit may grow a Great Rogue, in order to be a Great Man; When a People can no longer expect Redress of publick and heavy Evils, nor Satisfaction from publick and bitter Injuries, hideous is the Prospect they have before them.[17]

Again, the vocabulary of the Great Man and its association with outright destructive villainy need not be dwelt upon, except to state that the metaphor was becoming more widely used and that an automatic response to the phrase could be expected from those who read it. The clear identification, too, between the state and the sanctioning of rime is one which was becoming a common form of attack, all culminating in *The Beggar's Opera* and leading to Bolingbroke's theoretical Toryism.[18]

The vocabulary and stance which Trenchard is taking have an immediate appeal which lies on the surface. He is less difficult since the rhetorical effect need not be searched for and the vocabulary is designed to affect the reader in an immediate way, for it abuses the enemy and castigates the perpetrators of corruption rather than inviting the reader to engage himself with the text. The method is mostly solemn, yet it appeals to decency, honour, tradition and the feelings of freedom that the True-Born Briton surely held dear; no reasonable man could enjoy seeing corruption flourish, and surely, then, could not fail to respond to appeals such as the following:

> Make Use now, O worthy and free Britons make good Use of this present Dawn, this precious Day of Liberty, to recover once more that invaluable Privilege. Do not wildly chuse any One, who has given up, or attempted to give up your Birthrights; and above all, that Right which secures all the rest. Admit no Man to be so much as a Candidate in your Counties and Burroughs, till he has declared in the clearest Manner, and in the most express and solemn Words declared, his most hearty and vigorous Resolutions, to endeavour to Repeal all Laws which render you encapable to serve your King, or to punish Traitors, or to preserve your original and essential Rights.[19]

Well, quite; if Liberty is to be preserved, then why not use the simple powers of rhetoric in order to preserve it? The prose invites agreement on a surface level, while the vocabulary raises questions about the nature of the language employed to attack the government. These questions may be more readily attended to by an examination of the satiric methods employed in some of the poetry and drama of the period.

2. Poetry and Drama

Vocabulary connected with corruption in general and the eating away of the nation by a small group of unprincipled men is common enough in the period. This section will examine extracts from some of the poets and dramatists of the period.

Pope was very rarely explicit in his criticism of Walpole and Robino-cracy; he had to be careful: after all, he was both a Tory and a Catholic, and he had made sufficient personal enemies in his satires without inviting the wrath of the Whig administration. He was so often praised as being the antithesis to Walpole - country-loving, gentlemanly, Tory, intelligent - that he hardly needed to point out the corruption of contemporary Britain: he symbolised, for many, what England had been and what was now lost. That is not to say that he kept quiet: in one poem - *One Thousand Seven Hundred and Forty* - he examines the political and social scene and provides a review of those in power and those who aspired to it. In a sense, the poem is a private eaction to the political climate of 1740: although it was written in that year, the poem was not published until 1797:

O wretched B-----, jealous now of all,
What God, what Mortal, shall prevent thy Fall?
Turn, turn thy Eyes from wicked Men in place,
And see what Succour from the Patriot Race.
C-----, his own proud Dupe, thinks Monarchs things
Made just for him, as other Fools for Kings;
Controls, decides, insults thee every hour,
And antedates the Hatred due to Pow'r.[20]

Britain (B----- in the above) can no longer be associated with the pastoral world of innocence, for she is about to fall; Pope's appraisal is one which is shared by many other Tory writers; Britain no longer seems to contain any redeeming features, for even within the power structure, those who oppose Walpole (Carteret, or C-----) are doing so from selfish motives: they have no intention of re-establishing decency, honour or dignity but view others - Monarchs for example - as fit instruments to be used for the acquisition of political power. The 'Patriot Race' (the Tories) are themselves corrupt and divided since 'some of them ... had views too mean and interested to deserve that name'.[21] The *office* of administration has become corrupt, and whosoever attempts and then succeeds in entering the office becomes corrupt too:

The Plague is on thee, Britain, and who tries
To save thee in th' infectious Office *dies*.[22]

There is, of course, one source for all of this corruption, and that is to be found in the person of Walpole. Walpole has re-defined the values of the age. Walpole has established the precedence of money over anything, including honesty, tradition, free-speech and thought:

> But,'faith your very Friends will soon be sore,
> *Patriots* there are, who wish you'd jest no more -
> And where's the Glory? twill be only thought
> The Great man never offer'd you a Groat,
> Go see Sir Robert ------
>
> See Sir Robert - hum -
>
> And never laugh - for all my life to come?
> Seen him I have, but in his happier hour
> Of Social Pleasure, ill-exchanged for Pow'r;
> Seen him, unencumber'd with the Venal tribe,
> Smile without Art, and win without a Bribe.
> Would he oblige me? let me only find,
> He does not think me what he thinks mankind.
> Come, come, at all I laugh He laughs no doubt,
> The only diff'rence is, I dare laugh out.[23]

Laughter has not lost its place amongst those who are opposed to Walpole, but it is laughter against a Venal Tribe who control by bribery and corruption and assume that everyone else has the same values. These values are ones which subsume everything under the name of 'Power' and hich suborn all those who come into contact with them. Pope is quick to assert that his values - those of the country - have no price which the Great Man could afford or, indeed, one to which he could even relate or understand. Pope also has to face up to the fact that, despite the satiric attentions from both himself and other Scriblerus writers, Walpole has continued to hold power and his values seem to hold most forcefully:

> Down, down, proud Satire tho' a Realm be spoil'd,
> Arraign no mightier Thief than wretched *Wild*,
> Or if a Court or Country's made a Job,
> Go drench a pick-pocket, and join the Mob.[24]

The metaphor has arisen once more; Pope here extends the meaning to indicate the limits of the genre and yet also to insist the necessity for its continuation: in satire, the author is free to include language of bitter attack, to include direct and explicit references to the thievery of the administration and to malign the Court and Country. It provides a medium through which attacks may be carried out and it advances political thought.

The engagement in political activity may also mean that the author would be continually on the side of the Opposition, seeking an alternative to the life-style which seemed to be being thrust upon him. Pope's alternative is both general and specific. In specific terms, he can turn to those whom he regards as virtuous and of whose company he would be glad:

Yet think not Friendship only prompts my Lays;
I follow *Virtue*, where she shines, I praise,
Point she to Priest or Elder, Whig or Tory,
Or round a Quaker's Beaver cast a Glory.
I never (to my sorrow I declare)
Din'd with the MAN of ROSS, or my Lord MAY'R
Some, in their choice of Friends (nay, look not grave)
Have still a secret Byass to a Knave:
To find an honest man, I beat about,
And love him, court him, praise him, in or out.[25]

The Man of Ross, a familiar figure to readers of the *Moral Essays*, is once again praised as an example of proper behaviour and a man worthy of emulation. Goodness may be found in specific, nameable cases; it may also be found in a life-style - one such as his own in Twickenham for example - which removes one from direct involvement with activities of the city. The language alternates between the knavery of the city and the honesty of civilised conversation around the dining table, situated, one presumes, in the country.

Examples of the extremes to which the two alternatives led are common in the period and some have been quoted above (Chapter 7), but the more one reads the clearer the distinction becomes and it is more obvious where the focal points of attention lay. Two further contrasting examples may serve. Allan Ramsay's play *The Gentle Shepherd*, (1728) is a celebration of a past world, but one which really only existed in he mind of Ramsay himself. The country is defined in a prologue to each of the scenes; each prologue creates a mood and defines the atmosphere:

A snug Thack-house, before a Door a Green;
Hens on the Midding, Ducks in Dubs are seen.
On this Side stands a Barn, on that a Byre;
A Peat-Stack joins, and forms a rural Square.
The house is Glaud's; - there you may see him lean,
And to his Divat-Seat invite his Frien [26]

Ramsay pushes his audience far away from the world of the eighteenth-century city, into one which he constructs as an escape from it, and also one which reads almost as a pastiche of the Elizabethan 'green world'. His world is the regions of Scotland - as the vocabulary makes clear - and so forces the audience's attention onto something remote, even escapist. While Pope's pastoral were written with an intense awareness of their opposition - the city - Ramsay's play is an attempt at a lighthearted celebration of an imaginary world which has little meaning beyond the confines of the structure in which we find it: Ramsay refuses to point contrasts, he is comfortable in the pastoral and presents his subject-matter without commitment or, indeed, embarrassment.

In an attempt to discover references to the opposition, the reader must turn not to other works by the same author, but to different authors of

161

the same period. Pope was able to combine his love of the pastoral, his commitment to a country world, with his attitude towards politics; it was a combination which is part of the whole package of ideological commitment and value judgement. Other author's complement Ramsay's over-simplified escapism. George Lillo's *Fatal Curiosity* opens with a celebration of the pastoral; young Wilmot has landed in England after a particularly hazardous sea journey:

Oh England, England!
  Thou Seat of Plenty, Liberty and Health
  With Transport I behold thy verdant Fields,
  Thy lofty Mountains rich with useful Ore,
  Thy numberous Herds, thy Flocks, and winding Streams [27]

At the beginning of the play, the folk lore of England is celebrated; England still appears to be Merrie, but this interpretation turns out to be fanciful. The events of the play are worth summarising: Agnes, stepmother of Young Wilmot, and Old Wilmot, his father, have become poverty stricken during their son's absence; they also believe that their son is dead. They fail to recognise Young Wilmot on his return and they convey their grief to him. He entrusts them with a casket full of jewels. In turn, they conspire to kill 'the stranger' and Old Wilmot, goaded by Agnes, stabs his son. Agnes's reaction to possession of the jewels is significant:

Possesed of these,
  Plenty, Content, and Power might take their Turn,
  And lofty Pride bare its aspiring Head
  At our Approach and once more bend before us,
  A pleasing Dream [28]

Money becomes synonymous with power and, hence, with corruption, malevolence and selfishness. On the discovery of the truth, Old Wilmot kills Agnes and then himself. One of the weaknesses of the play is its derivational nature while it refuses to provide the reader with the political significance of its source. However, it fits in well with many of the other plays of the period as it reveals the essential corruption beneath the veneer of peace and respectability. The motivating forces behind action are once more selfishness and greed and the characters are inward-looking and hostile. The redeeming features are also suggested in the play since the pastoral is not destroyed, although Young Wilmot's interpretation of it - that it defines the character of the nation and its people - is shown to be false. While the audience may feel sympathetic towards the parents at the beginning - theirs after all is a real grief and a genuine mistake - the qualities which the characters eventually betray shifts the audience's stance. True, inconsistencies there are, but the idea behind the play of the actual existence of two worlds and two interpretations fits in well with many of the other works examined here. Money and the desire for it leads to corruption in both the state and the individual; the general feeling was that the times had become dominated by paper-values and that Walpole was a kind of monarch of Chelsea, determining what could or could not be done:

> 'Tis Money my Lads does all's to be done,
> 'Tis Gold that makes War, 'tis Gold makes it cease;
> The way to apply it, had some People known,
> 'Tis odds that 'ere this, they had bought us a *Peace*

> Yet it can't be deny'd,
>> They their utmost have try'd,

> And given large Earnest on every Side.
> Which tho' all proves in vain, yet 'tis certainly Thought,
> We shall have a *Peace* - when we're not worth a Groat[29]

If all this were true and generally accepted, why didn't Walpole fall from an apparently tottering position? The answer probably lies with the more pragmatic of writers of the period, who knew that the opposition to Walpole was itself split and was divided into factions. The opposition, too, consisted of a small group: despite the echoings of the group's sentiments in popular ballads, the form which the opposition employed and the language which it used would have alienated the majority of the population; the audience, although intellectual, was small, and even then it would be expected to agree with a Tory who was also a Catholic (Pope), who was alienated both politically and emotionally from many English people. The opposition also found a voice in Bolingbroke, but he was in exile and writing tracts which were hardly designed to appeal to the broad mass of the population. Fielding had excited some political movement but he found strict allegiance to the opposition difficult to adhere to; in fact, hypocrisy may have been as large a vice in the opposition camp as dishonesty was in the government's:

> Then leave Complaints: Fools only strive
> To make a Great and Honest Hive
> T'enjoy the World's Conveniences,
> Be form'd in War, yet live in Ease,
> Without great Vices, is a vain
> EUTOPIA seated in the Brain.
> Fraud, Luxury and Pride must live,
> While we the Benefits receive:
> Hunger's a dreadful Plague, no doubt,
> Yet who digests or thrives without?[30]

Many of the arguments of the opposition, and many of their theoretical and literary constructs, were 'seated in the Brain' and they remained there.

3. Techniques of Persuasion

In a sense, it is false to construct a separate section on 'techniques' simply because everything is a technique within itself: form, content, language, all these are 'techniques'. However, it is worth isolating a few more examples from Pope in order to investigate how the techniques come together to reinforce each other.

As Walpole's reign progressed, the satiric mode of writing became closely associated with those opposed to his rule; those who attacked the ministry were usually more subtle than the following passage might suggest:

> (Walpole has) a malicious, vindictive, sanguinary Nature; a saucy, insulting, over-bearing imperious Behaviour in Prosperity; a poor, low, wretched, mean, abject Spirit in Adversity; of a perfidious, impious atheistical Principle; remarkably addicted to Lying; an ignorant, forward, positive, inexperienced, headstrong, blundering Driver, despised, condemn'd, and hated by all his Master's faithful Servants.[31]

Such attacks, although achieving an immediacy unclaimed by the writings of other, intellectual, writers, could hardly claim to be the mainstay of the political opposition. After Bolingbroke, by 1738 a distant remote figure, it was Pope around whom politically intellectual attacks centre. Pope, although careful to avoid the vituperations that he could practise, made it clear where his political affiliations lay, though he was under no illusion about the nature of his role in the state:

> We Poets are (upon a Poet's word)
> Of all Mankind, the Creatures most absurd:
> The Season, when to come, and when to go,
> To sing, or cease to sing, we never know;
> And if we will recite nine Hours in ten,
> You lose your Patience, just like other Men.
> Then too we hurt our Selves, when to defend
> A single Verse, we quarrel with a Friend;
> Repeat unask'd; lament, the Wit's too fine
> For vulgar Eyes, and point out ev'ry Line.
> But most, when straining with too weak a Wing,
> We needs will write Epistles to the King;
> And from the moment we oblige the Town,
> Expect a Place, or Pension from the Crown.[32]

The position of the poet in society was one of which he was intensely aware and the passage reflects the subservient role which he is often forced to adopt, while at the same time he recognises that the role may be the limited, even useless one, of arguing about the nature of poetic taste in general. The poet may also discuss events or writings with a small group of people while the machine of the state continues to rumble on. The idea is to efface the image of the poet, to make him seem a harmless creature but at the same time disallow the argument that he is a useless figure: he is, after all, intimately connected with the Crown through his praise of it, the acceptance of a Pension from it or by his attacks upon it.

The more specific attacks occur in the *Epilogue to the Satires* in which Pope examines the role of satire while at the same time he employs its techniques to answer the questions. The examination of these Dialogues in previous pages may be added to by examining some of the more overt, personal statements which Pope makes about Walpole and about the nature of the age:

> (He) Has never made a Friend in private Life,
> And was, besides, a Tyrant to his Wife.[33]

The comment is in the line of the direct insult but, taken with Pope's other works, is an amusing comment on the nature of the technique of satire since Pope rarely uses such direct methods in his attacks. Instead, he shows the corrupt nature of the times and argues that satire is the most adequate weapon against his opponents and that his position as a poet is a sound, philosophical one:

> Ask you what Provocation I have had?
> The strong Antipathy of Good to Bad.
> When Truth or Virtue and Affront endures,
> Th'Affront is mine, my Friend, and should be yours.
> Mine, as a Foe profess'd to false Pretence,
> Who think a Coxcomb's Honour like his Sense;
> Mine, as a Friend to ev'ry worthy Mind;
> And mine as Man, who feel for all Mankind.[34]

Satire provides the perfect weapon with which the vices of the age may be confronted and the poet, by employing that mode, stands in a dignified position as protector of Truth and Virtue. Pope feels that the preservation of certain standards is a worthwhile enterprise; he invites the reader to agree with him by offering him no alternative with which to counter the argument, since Walpole is cruel on a personal level and he never attains any degree of political wisdom or maturity. The Poet has his art, his life-style and his method which stand as examples of what could be:

> O Sacred Weapon left for Truth's defence,
> Sole Dread of Folly, Vice and Insolence
> To all but Heav'n-directed Hands deny'd
> The Muse may give thee, but the Gods must guide.
> Rev'rent I touch thee but with honest Zeal;
> To rowze the Watchmen of the Publick Weal,
> To Virtue's Work provoke the tardy Hall,
> And Good the Prelate slumb'ring in his Stall.[35]

The technique is a means to an end, which is the preservation of standards, the upholding of proper behaviour and the encouragement of a sense of responsibility in those elected to serve ('the tardy Hall'). Pope is the reasonable man, asking proper questions but receiving only deception and corruption as an answer. The method is simply to present a persona of a free speaking yet upright man who can see what is wrong with the political opposition and who wins his argument by means of reason and sense.

It did not work; the truth of the matter was that the writing did not reach a sufficiently wide audience. As the *London Journal* of September 14, 1728, wrote "Satyr and Libelling have been practised from the Beginning of Letters in every Nation, yet I'd be glad to know what Vices they really do prevent."[36]

Pope knew this and compensated for it by an escape into another world where he could be sad and reflective and where he could consider a properly organised society run by true patriots:

> Those who shalt stop, where Thames' translucent Wave.
> Shines a broad Mirrour thro' the shadowy Cave;
> Where lingering Drops from Mineral Roofs distill,
> And pointed Crystals break the sparkling Rill,
> Unpolish'd Gemms no Ray on Pride bestow,
> And latent Metals innocently glow:
> Approach: But awful Lo the Aegerian Grott,
> Where, nobly pensive, St John sate and thought;
> Where BRITISH Sighs from dying WYNDHAM stole,
> And the bright Flame was shot thro' MARCHMONT's Soul.
> Let such, such only, tread this sacred Floor,
> Who dare to love their Country, and be poor.[37]

NOTES

1. See, for example, Stanley Fish, *Is There a Text in This Class?* (Cambridge, Mass, 1980) p.25f.
2. Quoted by Geoffrey Holmes and W. A. Speck (eds), *The Divided Society: Parties and Politics in England 1694-1716~* (London, 1967) pp. 104/105.
3. *The Humble Address of the Borough of Westbury to the Queen*, 14 Apr.1710. In Holmes and Speck (eds), ibid. pp. 126/7.
4. George Granville to the Sheriff of Cornwall, 29 Sep.1710,. ibid. p. 127.
5. ibid., p.129.
6. Swift, *The Examiner*, 8 Mar,1710, op. cit., pp.102/3
7. ibid., pp.104/5.
8. ibid., p.105.
9. Cp. Richard Cook, op. cit., ch 3 passim.
10. *Examiner*, 23 Nov.1710, op. cit., p.19.
11. ibid., p.20/1.

12. ibid., p.22/3.

13. ibid., p.24.

14. George Lyttelton, *Political Tracts 1735-1748* (New York, 1974), pp.60/1. This edition is a reprint of *Letters from a Persian* (London, 1735).

15. Trenchard and Gordan, *Cato's Letters*, 4 vols. (London, 1724), I, p.6.

16. ibid., I, pp.10/1.

17. ibid., I, p.14.

18. Cp. Isaac Kramnick, *Bolingbroke*, op. cit., p.248.

19. *Cato's Letters*, op. cit., II, p.178.

20. Pope, *One Thousand Seven Hundred and Forty*, ll. 1-8 in *Poems*, ed. Butt, op. cit., pp.827/8.

21. Pope, *Epilogue to the Satires*, Dialogue I, ibid., p.689, note 24.

22. Pope, *1740*, ll. 75/6, ibid,, p.830.

23. *Epilogue to the Satires*, Dialogue I, ll.23-36, *Poems*, op. cit, Pp.695/6.

24. Dialogue II, ll. 38-41,, ibid, p.696.

25. ibid., ll. 94-103, p.698.

26. Allan Ramsay, *The Gentle Shepherd*, (1728) prologue II i, in *The Works of Allan Ramsay*, edited by B. and J. W. Oliver (Edinburgh, 1953).

27. George Lillo, *Fatal Curiosity*, edited by W. H. McBurney (London, 1967), I iii, p.21, The play was first performed in 1736.

28. ibid., III i, p.41. There is more than a small debt to *MacBeth* in many scenes of the play.

29. *The Chelsea Monarch or Money Rules All* in Percival (ed.), *Ballads* etc, op. cit. pp.50/3.

30. Bernard Mandeville, *The Fable of the Bees*, edited by F. B. Kaye, 2 vols. (Oxford, 1924), I p.36.

31. *Robin's Panegyrick: or, The Norfolk Miscellany*, 1731. Quoted in *Introduction* to Roberts' edition of *The Grub-Street Opera*, op. cit., p.XIX.

32. Pope, *The First Epistle of the Second Book of Horace Imitated*, ll.358-371, in *Poems*, op. cit., p.648.

33. *Poems*, op. cit., p.699.

34. ibid., p.701.

35. ibid., p.702.

36. Quoted by Goldgar, *Walpole and the Wits*, op. cit., p.21.

37. *Poems*, op. cit., p.707.

CONCLUSION

The Opposition to Walpole was united and yet suffered at the same time from disunity. The fact that the latter outweighed the former made it possible for Walpole to remain in power for more than two generations, while the Great Man used his own political cunning to enable him to be the 'Prime Minister'.

The Tory Opposition was united in the sense that it was anti-Walpole, with all which that connotated. Walpole was not only corrupt politically but he was so close in character to the thief that the two merged at many points. Crime, with its close association with an underground world which had its own laws and which ran counter to the general interests of the nation, was used as a metaphor to express the changing nature of the times and used to show that the morality of the town was a fluid thing, with no fixed point of reference. The consequence of this was chaos, yet one which worked to the good of a minority of unscrupulous politicians. Lacking in scruple or a sense of tradition, Walpole had changed the definitions of morality and truth in order to justify his own ends and to ensure continuation of power. So the opposition seemed to have a firm base from which to work since they were solidly agreed about the nature of the times and about the character of the man who was leading the nation. They, too, seemed united in character themselves: intelligent, even intellectual, they moved in circles in which ideas were exchanged and new ways of attacking Walpole were focussed upon and encouraged. Satire and irony became the most prominent weapons and so they were united too in their belief in that method and about its power to reveal the truth about the age.

At this point the disunity of the opposition begins to become apparent. Satire may be an effective weapon, but it could not construct an alternative vision, for it was a weapon which was almost totally narrowly literary or intellectual in its appeal. Gay could expose the nature of the times on the stage, yet those who wrote of better things had to construct a world which had passed long ago, or, indeed, had only really existed in English mythology. The arcadian green world was a useful literary tool, but it had insufficient force to counter the world in which Walpole was living and which he had constructed. Bolingbroke's appeal was also to the past - and one which did seem to have a proper political construct. But Bolingbroke's ideas were, by 1735, outdated and they had faded from prominence.

The view that the ideas had faded, or were somehow irrelevant, is an important one for it links closely with the opposition as a disunited force. It is connected with the audience that the opposition attracted. The audience was not a wide one: in fact, after Swift and with the exception of *The Beggar's Opera*, the audience was other writers of a similar persuasion. In other words, Pope could admire Bolingbroke but Bolingbroke's prose was hardly designed to appeal to anybody other than an intellectual like Pope or those belonging to his circle. Bolingbroke was even more distant intellectually than he was physically, and anyway he was in no position to moralise about the times. Walpole, or one of his hirelings, had merely to point to the discrepancy between the man as rake and the man as a moralist to destroy the intellectual base to which Bolingbroke was trying to cling.

Moreover, the opposition was easily disunited by political tactics. Fielding may have written most effectively for the stage, but Walpole found he could hire him for his own purposes when the time came. True, it was fortuitous for Walpole that Fielding was in personal difficulties at the time, but nevertheless it did indicate that the literary opposition was not as steadfast in its principles as an examination of any one of its works would suggest.

Nor did the opposition have any argument against the usefulness of the merchant: although occasionally closely associated with the stockjobber and the attendant evils, the merchant brought wealth to the nation and if the stockmarket and the person of the jobber came as part of the package, then such things had to be. Mercantilism was a Whiggish ideology which had a practical appeal too:

Thorowgood:

> Methinks I would not have you only learn the Method of Merchandise and practice it hereafter merely as a Means of getting Wealth. 'Twill be well worth your Pains to study it as a Science, see how it is founded in Reason and the Nature of Things, how it has promoted Humanity as it has opened and yet keeps up an Intercourse between Nations far remote from one another in Situation, Customs, and Religion; promoting Arts, Industry, Peace, and Plenty; by mutual Benefits diffusing mutual Love from Pole to Pole.

Trueman:

> Something of this I have considered, and hope, by your Assistance, to extend my Thoughts much farther. I have observed those Countries where Trade is promoted and encouraged do not make Discoveries to destroy but to improve Mankind - by Love and Friendship to tame the fierce and polish the most savage; to teach them the advantages of honest Traffic by taking from them, with their own Consent, their useless Superfluities, and giving them in return what, from their Ignorance in manual Arts, their Situation, or some other Accident, they stand in need of.[1]

Gone were the days when the landed gentry had control and, therefore, possessed the material goods. The new mercantile class and, by association, the new government, was bringing wealth to the nation and to the individual. By the time the opposition had constructed their complaints and had realised that the times were crooked, it was too late: the opposition was commenting on events which had already taken place and the increasing despair of such writers as Pope indicated that they felt that they were losing the battle and that their criticisms and comments could only appeal to a small group of believers. We may now praise Walpole both for political astuteness and for providing the inspiration behind some of the greatest writing of the century.

Note

1. George Lillo, *The London Merchant*, edited by William H. McBurney (London, 1965), III i, p.40.

BIBLIOGRAPHY

Addison, Joseph *Miscellaneous Works*, ed. A. C. Guthkelch (London 1914).

Addison, Joseph *The Freeholder*, ed. James Leheny (Oxford, 1979).

Arbuthnot, John *The History of John Bull*, ed. Alan W. Baker and Robert A. Erickson (Oxford, 1976).

Armens, Sven M. *John Gay, Social Critic* (London, 1954).

Atherton, H. M. *Political Prints in the Age of Hogarth. A Study of the Ideographic Representative of Politics* (Oxford, 1974).

Babington, A. *A House in Bow Street* (London, 1969).

Baker, Sheridan 'Political Allusions in Fielding's *Author's Farce, Mock Doctor* and *Tumble-down Dick.*' (*PMLA*, LXXVII, 1962, 221-231).

Battestin, M. C. 'Fielding's Changing Politics and *Joseph Andrews*' (*P Q*, 39, 1960, 39-55).

Battestin, M. C. *The Providence of Wit* (Oxford, 1974).

Beasley, J. C. 'Portraits of a Monster: Robert Walpole and Early English Prose Fiction' (*Eighteenth-Century Studies*, 4, 1981, 406-431)

Beattie, J. M. 'The Criminality of Women in Eighteenth-Century England' (*Journal of Social History*, IX, 1975).

Beattie, J. M. 'The Pattern of Crime in England, 1600-1800 (*Past and Present*, 62, 1974).

Becker, C. L. *The Heavenly City of the Eighteenth-Century Philosophers* (New Haven, 1960).

Birkett, Sir Norman (editor) *The Newgate Calendar* (London, 1951).

Black, J. (editor) *Britain in the Age of Walpole* (London, 1984).

Black, J. 'An "Ignoramus" in European Affairs? (*British Journal for Eighteenth-Century Studies*, 6, no. 1, 1983, 55-65).

Blanchard, Rae (editor) *Tracts and Pamphlets by Richard Steele* (The Johns Hopkins Press, Baltimore, 1944).

Bloom, Edward A. & Lillian, D. *Joseph Addison's Sociable Animal* (Brown University Press, Providence, 1971).

Boas, F. S. *An Introduction to Eighteenth-Century Drama* (Oxford, 1952).

Bolingbroke, Henry St John *Historical Writings*, ed. Isaac Kramnick (Chicago, 1972).

Bolingbroke, Henry St John *Works* 4 vols. (Philadelphia, 1841).

Bolingbroke, Henry St John *The Craftsman* (London, 1736).

Bond, R. P. *Studies in the Early English Periodical* (North Carolina, 1957).

Braudel, Ferdnand *The Structures of Everyday Life. Civilisation and Capitalism 1500-1800* (London, 1982).

Brown, Homer O. 'The Displaced Self in the Novels of Daniel Defoe' (*ELH*, 38, 1971, 562-590).

Brown, S. C. (editor) *Philosophers of the Enlightenment* (The Harvester Press, Sussex, 1979).

Burgess, C. F. 'Political Satire: John Gay's *The Beggar's Opera*' (*Midwest Quarterly*, VI, 1965, 270-274).

Butt, John *Pope, Dickens and Others: Essays and Addresses by John Butt* (Edinburgh, 1969).

Byrd, Max *London Transformed, Images of the City in the Eighteenth Century* (Yale, 1978).

Cannon, John (editor) *The Whig Ascendancy. Colloquies on Hanoverian England* (London, 1981).

Carswell, John *From Revolution to Revolution: England 1688-1776* (London, 1973).

Carswell, John *The South-Sea Bubble* (London, 1960).

Centlivre, Susanna *A Bold Stroke for a Wife*, ed. Thalia Stathias (London, 1969).

Chandler, F. W. *The Literature of Roguery*, 2 vols, (Boston, 1907).

Cibber, Colley *Plays*, ed. Rodney L Hagley, 2 vols. (New York, 1980).

Cibber, Colley *Love in a Riddle* in *Classical Subjects II: Pastoral and Comedy*, ed. Walter Howard Rubsamen (New York, 1974).

Clifford, J. L. (editor) *Man versus Society in Eighteenth-Century Britain* (Cambridge, 1968).

Cockburn, J. S. (editor) *Crime in England 1500-1800* (London, 1977)

Coley, W. B. 'Henry Fielding and the Two Walpoles' (*P Q* 45, 1969, 157-178).

Cook, Richard I. *Jonathan Swift as a Tory Pamphleteer* (Washington, 1967).

Defoe, Daniel *The Complete English Tradesman* (London, 1726).

Defoe, Daniel *An Essay on the Regulation of the Press*, ed. J R Moore, (Oxford, 1958).

Defoe, Daniel *The History of the remarkable Life of John Sheppard* (London, 1724).

Defoe, Daniel *A Narrative of all the Robberies, Escapes, etc. of John Sheppard* (London, 1724).

Defoe, Daniel *The True and Genuine Accounts Of The Life and Actions of the Late Jonathan Wild* (London, 1725).

Defoe, Daniel *The Life of Jonathan Wild. From His Birth to His Death* (London, 1725).

Defoe, Daniel *Second Thoughts are Best* (London, 1728).

Defoe, Daniel *An Effectual Scheme for the Immediate Preventing of Street Robberies* (London, 1731).

Denning, Michael 'Beggars and Thieves' (*Literature and History* 8, no. 1, 1982, 41-55).

Dickinson, H. T. *Bolingbroke* (London, 1970).

Dickinson, H. T. *Liberty and Property: Political Ideology in Eighteenth-Century Britain* (London, 1977).

Dickinson, H. T. *Politics and Literature in the Eighteenth Century* (London, 1974).

Dickinson, H. T. 'Walpole and His Critics' (*History Today*, June 1972, 410-419).

Dickinson, H. T. *Walpole and the Whig Supremacy* (London, 1973).

Dobree, Bonamy *English Literature in the Early Eighteenth Century* (Oxford, 1959).

Donaldson, Ian *The World Upside Down* (Oxford, 1970).

Downie, J. A. *Robert Harley and the Press: Propaganda and Public Opinion in the Age of Swift and Defoe* (London, 1979).

Edwards, T. R. *This Dark Estate: A Reading of Pope* (Berkeley, 1963).

Ewald, William Bragg *The Masks of Jonathan Swift* (Oxford, 1954).

Fan, T. C. 'Chinese Fables and anti-Walpole Journalism' (*RES*, 25, 1949, 141-151).

Farrell, W. J. 'The Mock-Heroic Form of Jonathan Wild' (*Modern Philology*, lxiii, 1966, 216-226).

Fielding, Henry *Complete Works*, ed. W. E. Henley, 16 vols. (London, 1903).

Fielding, Henry *Miscellaneous Writings*, 3 vols (London, 1903).

Fielding, Henry *The Author's Farce*, ed. Charles B. Woods (London, 1967).

Fielding, Henry *The Covent-Garden Tragedy* (London, 1742).

Fielding, Henry *The Grub-Street Opera*, ed. Edgar V. Roberts (London, 1969).

Fielding, Henry *The Grub-Street Opera*, ed. J. Morrissey (Edinburgh, 1973).

Fielding, Henry *The Historical Register for the Year 1736* and *Eurydice Hissed*, ed. William V. Appleton (London 1968).

Fielding, Henry *Jonathan Wild* (London, 1932).

Fielding, Henry *A Journey from This World to the Next*, ed. Claude Rawson (London, 1973).

Fielding, Henry *The Opposition. A Vision* (London, 1742).

Fielding, Henry *Pasquin* (London, 1736).

Fielding, Henry *Tom Thumb* and *The Tragedy of Tragedies* ed. L. J. Morrissey (California, 1970).

Fielding, Henry *The Covent-Garden Journal*, ed. G. E. Jensen, 2 vols. (New Haven, 1915).

Fish, Stanley *Is there a Text in This Class?* (Cambridge, Mass. 1980).

Fisher, John Irwin and Donald C. Mell, jr *Contemporary Studies of Swift's Poetry* New Jersey, 1981).

Forbes, Duncan *Hume's Philosophical Politics* (Cambridge, 1975).

Forsgren, Adina *John Gay, Poet 'Of a Lower Order'* (Stockholm, 1971).

Foucault, Michael *Discipline and Punish* (London, 1977).

Fritz, P. & Williams, D. (Editors) *The Triumph of Culture: Eighteenth Century Perspectives* (Toronto, 1972).

Fritz, P. & Williams, D. *City and Society in the Eighteenth Century* (Toronto, 1972).

Gay, John *The Beggar's Opera*, ed. Edgar V. Roberts (London, 1969).

Gay, John *The Poetical, Dramatic and Miscellaneous Works of John Gay*, 6 vols. (London, 1795, reprinted New York, 1970).

Gay, John *Poetry and Prose*, ed. Vinton A. Dearing, 2 vols. (Oxford, 1974).

George, Dorothy *London Life in the XVIIIth Century* (London, 1925).

Goldgar, Bernard *The Curse of Party. Swift's Relations with Addison and Steele* (Lincoln, Nebraska, 1961).

Goldgar, Bernard *Walpole and the Wits* (Lincoln, Nebraska, 1976).

Hanson, L. W. *Government and the Press 1695-1763* (London, 1936).

Hart, Jeffery *Viscount Bolingbroke: Tory Humanist* (London, 1966).

Harth, Philip 'The Satiric Purpose of the Fable of the Bees' (*Eighteenth-Century Studies*, 4, 1969, 321-340).

Hatfield, Glenn W. *Henry Fielding and the Language of Irony* (Chicago 1968).

Hay, D., Linebaugh, P. and Thompson, E. P. (editors) *Albion's Fatal Tree* (London, 1975).

Hayward, Arthur L. (editor) *Lives of the Most Remarkable Criminals* (London, 1927).

Hecht, J. J. *The Domestic Servant in Eighteenth Century England* (London, 1956 and 1980).

Hilson, J. C., Jones M. M. B. and Watson, J. R. *Augustan Worlds* (Leicester, 1978).

Holmes, Geoffrey *British Politics in the Age of Anne* (London, 1967).

Holmes, Geoffrey and Speck, W. A. (editors) *The Divided Society. Parties and Politics in England 1694-1716* (London, 1967).

Hopkins, Robert H. 'Language and Comic Play in Fielding's *Jonathan Wild*' (*Criticism*, VIII, 1966, 213-228).

Howson, Gerald *Thief-Taker General: The Rise and Fall of Jonathan Wild* (London, 1970).

Humphreys, A. R. *The Augustan World* (London, 1955).

Humphreys, A. R. 'Fielding's Irony: Its Methods and Effects' (*RES*, 18, 1942, 183-196).

Irving, W. H. *John Gay. Favorite of the Wits* (North Carolina, 1940).

Irving, W. H. *John Gay's London* (Cambridge, Mass. 1928).

Irwin, Michael *Henry Fielding. The Tentative Realist* (Oxford 1967).

Irwin, W. R. *The Making of Jonathan Wild: A Study in the Literary Method of Henry Fielding* (New York, 1941).

Kelly, John *Timon in Love: or, The Innocent Theft* in *Classical Subjects II*, ed. Walter Howard Rubsamen (New York, 1974).

Kemp, Betty *King and Commons, 1660-1833* (London, 1959).

Kemp, Betty *Sir Robert Walpole* (London, 1976).

Kidson, Frank *The Beggar's Opera. Its Predecessors and Successors* (Cambridge, 1922).

Kramnick, Isaac *Bolingbroke and His Circle* (Cambridge, Mass. 1968).

Landa, Louis A. *Essays in Eighteenth-Century English Literature* (Princeton, 1980).

Langford, Paul *Walpole and the Robinocracy* (Cambridge, 1986).

Lee, Nathaniel *The Rival Queens*, ed. P. F. Vernon (London, 1970).

Lee, William (editor) *Daniel Defoe: His Life and Recently Discovered Writings* 3 vols (London, 1869).

Lillo, George *Fatal Curiosity*, ed. W. H. McBurney (London, 1967).

Lillo, George *The London Merchant*, ed. W. H. McBurney (London, 1965).

Levine, George R. *Henry Fielding and the Dry Mock* (The Hague, 1967).

Lock, F. P. *The Politics of 'Gulliver's Travels'* (Oxford, 1980).

Loftis, John *Comedy and Society: Congreve to Fielding* (Stamford, California, 1957).

Loftis, John *The Politics of Drama in Augustan England* (Oxford, 1963).

Low, Donald *Thieves' Kitchen* (London, 1982).

Lyttelton, George *Political Tracts 1735-1748* (New York, 1974).

Lyttelton, George *Works* (London, 1775).

Lyttelton, George *The Court Secret. A Melancholy Truth* (London, 1742).

Mack, Maynard *The Garden and the City* (Toronto, 1969).

Mallet, David *Plays*, ed. Felicity A. Nussbaum (New York, 1980).

Mallet, David *Works* 3 vols (London, 1759).

Mandeville, Bernard *An Inquiry into the Causes of the Frequent Executions at Tyburn* (London, 1725, reprinted Los Angeles, 1964).

Mandeville, Bernard *The Fable of the Bees*, ed. F. B. Kaye, 2 vols (Oxford, 1924, reprinted 1957).

McKendrick, N. (editor) *Historical Perspectives: Studies in English Thought and Society in honour of J. H. Plumb* (London, 1974).

McKendrick, N., Brewer, John and Plumb, J. H. *The Birth of a Consumer Society: The Commercialism of Eighteenth-Century England* (London, 1982).

Marshall, Dorothy *Eighteenth-Century England* (London, 1962).

Marshall, Dorothy *English People in the Eighteenth Century* (London, 1956).

Mazzeo, J. A. (editor) *Reason and Imagination* (New York, 1962).

Miller, James *Are these Things So? and The Great Man's Answer to Are these Things So,* (London, 1740, reprinted Los Angeles, 1972).

Moore, C. E. 'Whig Panegyric Verse, 1700-1760. A Phase of Sentimentalism' (*PMLA*, 41, 1926, 362-340).

Moore, J. R. *A Checklist of the Writings of Daniel Defoe* (Bloomington, Indiana, 1962).

Nadel, J. H. 'Bolingbroke's Letters on History' (*Journal of the History of Ideas*, 23, 1962).

Natan, Alex (editor) *Silver Renaissance. Essays in Eighteenth-Century English History* (London, 1961).

Nicoll, Alladyce *A History of Early Eighteenth Century Drama* (Cambridge, 1952).

Novak, Maxmillian E. *Economics and the Fiction of Daniel Defoe* (New York 1962).

Partridge, Eric *A Dictionary of the Underworld* (3rd edition, London, 1968).

Paulson, Ronald *Fielding*, (London, 1962).

Paulson, Ronald and Lockwood, Thomas (editors) *Henry Fielding: The Critical Heritage* (London, 1969).

Paulson, Ronald *Hogarth: His Life, Art and Times* (New Haven, 1971).

Percival, M. (editor) *Political Ballads illustrating the administration of Sir Robert Walpole* (Oxford, 1916).

Pike, L. O. *A History of Crime in England*, 2 vols. (London, 1873-6, reprinted New Jersey, 1968).

179

Plumb J. H. *The Growth of Political Stability in England* 1675-1725 (New York, 1967).

Plumb J. H. *Sir Robert Walpole. The King's Minister* (London, 1960).

Pope, Alexander *Correspondence*, Ed. George Sherburn, 5 vols (Oxford, 1956).

Pope, Alexander *Poems*, ed. John Butt (London, 1963).

Porter, Roy *English Society in the Eighteenth Century* (London, 1982).

Probyn, Clive T. (editor) *The Art of Jonathan Swift* (London, 1978).

Probyn, Clive T. (editor) *Jonathan Swift: The Contemporary Background* (Manchester, 1978).

Purney, Thomas *The Ordinary of Newgate. His Account of the Behaviour, Last Dying Speeches and Confessions of Four Malefactors* (London, 1725).

Radzinowicz, Leon *A History of English Criminal Law*, 4 vols. (London, 1948).

Ramsay, Allen *Works*, Ed. B. Martin and J. W. Oliver (Edinburgh, 1953).

Rawson, C. J. *Henry Fielding and the Augustan Ideal Under Stress* (London, 1972).

Realley, C. B. *The Early Opposition to Sir Robert Walpole* (Lawrence, Kensas, 1931).

Realley, C. B. *The London Journal and its Authors* (Lawrence, Kansas, 1935).

Reilly, Patrick *Jonathan Swift: the brave desponder* (Manchester, 1982).

Rivers, I. (editor) *Books and their Readers in Eighteenth-Century England* (Leicester, 1982).

Robbins, Caroline *The Eighteenth-Century Commonwealthman* (Cambridge, Mass., 1968).

Rogers, Pat *The Augustan Vision* (London, 1974).

Rogers, Pat *The Eighteenth Century* (London, 1982).

Rogers, Pat *Henry Fielding. A Biography* (London, 1979).

Rogers, Pat *Grub Street. Studies in Subculture* (London, 1972).

Rogers, Pat 'The Waltham Blacks and the Black Act' *(The Historical Journal*, XVIII, 1974, 465-486).

Ross, Angus (editor) *Selections from 'The Tatler' and 'The Spectator'* (Harmondsworth, 1982).

Ross, J. F. *Swift and Defoe: A Study in Relationship* (Berkeley, 1941).

Rubsamen, W. H. (editor) *The Beggar's Opera. Imitated and Parodied* (New York, 1974).

Rude, George *Paris and London in the Eighteenth Century* (London, 1970).

Rumbelow, David *I Spy Blue. The Police and Crime in the City of London from Elizabeth I to Victoria* (London 1971).

Said, E. (editor) *Literature and Society* (The Johns Hopkins Press, Baltimore, 1980).

Said, Edward W. 'Swift's Tory Anarchy' (*Eighteenth Century Studies*, 1, 1969, 48-66).

Sams, Henry W. 'An End to Writing about Swift' (*Essays in Criticism*, vol XXIV, 1974, 275-285).

Schultz, W. E. *Gay's Beggar's Opera. Its Content, History and Influence* (New Haven, 1923).

Scouten, Arthur H. (editor) *Restoration and Eighteenth-Century Drama* (London, 1980).

Shea, Bernard 'Machiavelli and Fielding's *Jonathan Wild*' *(PMLA*, 1 xxii, 1957, 55-73).

Smith, Capt. Alexander *Memoirs of the Life and Times of Jonathan Wild* (London, 1726).

Smith, Capt. Alexander *A Complete History of the Lives and Robberies of the Most Notorious Highwaymen*, ed. Arthur L Hayward (London, 1933).

Spacks, Patricia *John Gay* (New York, 1965).

Speck, W. A. *Stability and Strife, England 1714-1760* (London, 1977).

Steele, Richard *The Theatre, 1720* ed. John Loftis (Oxford, 1962).

Stephen, Leslie *History of English Thought in the Eighteenth Century* (London, 1962).

Styles, J. A. (editor) *An Ungovernable People. The English and their law in the Seventeenth and Eighteenth Century* (London, 1980).

Sutherland, Lucy 'The City of London in Eighteenth-Century Politics' in *Essays Presented to Sir Lewis Namier* (London, 1956).

Swift, Jonathan *Correspondence*, ed. Harold Williams, 5 vols. (Oxford, 1965).

Swift, Jonathan *Complete Prose*, ed. Herbert Davis et al, 14 vols. (Oxford, 1939-1959).

Swift, Jonathan *Prose Works*, ed. T. Scott, 12 vols. (London, 1897-1908).

Swift, Jonathan *Journals to Stella*, ed. Harold Williams, 2 vols. (Oxford, 1948).

Swift, Jonathan *Poetical Works*, ed. Herbert Davis (London, 1957).

Thomas, Donald *A Long Time Burning: The History of Literary Censorship in England* (London, 1969).

Thompson, E. P. *Whigs and Hunters* (London, 1975).

Thomson, James *Agamemnon* (Dublin, 1738).

Tobias, J. J. *Crime and Industrial Society in the Nineteenth Century* (London, 1967).

Trenchard and Gordon *Cato's Letters*. 4 vols (London, 1724).

Turberville, A. S. *Johnson's England* 2 vols (London, 1933).

Ward, Ned *The London Spy*, ed. Arthur Hayward (London, 1927).

Wells, J. E. 'Fielding's Political Purpose in *Jonathan Wild*' (PMLA, XXVIII, New Jersey, 1913, 1-55).

Whitehead, P. *Manners, A Satire* (1738) in *The Works of the English Poets* (London, 1810).

Whitehead, P. *The State Dunces* (London, 1733).

Wiles, R. M. *Freshest Advices: Early Provincial Newspapers in England* (Ohio, 1965).

Williams, Basil *The Whig Supremacy* (London, 1939).

Williams, Kathleen *Jonathan Swift and the Age of Compromise* (London, 1958).

Woods, Charles B. 'Notes on three of Fielding's Plays (*PLMA*, LII, 1937, 359-373).

Zirker, Malvin R. *Fielding's Social Pamphlets* (Berkeley, 1966).

INDEX

Addison, Joseph:
Agamemnon, 139
Cato, 133-135
Freeholder, The, 7, 8
Author's Farce, The; compared to *The Beggar's Opera*, 113

Beggar's Opera, The: v. Gay, John
Bolingbroke, (Henry St. John): Chapter 3, *passim*.
Works: *A Dissertation upon Parties*, 10, 50-54
Letters on the Study and Use of History, 49, 58-63
Letter to Wyndham, 52
On good and bad Ministers, 52-53
On the Policy of the Athenians, 58-63
Remarks on the History of England, 9
The Idea of a Patriot King, 54-58
and monarchy, 50-51, 52, 57
dislike of Whiggery, 59-60
on Divine Right, 56
letter to Swift quoted, 17-18, 58
his reputation, 63-65, 170
his views expressed in Mallet's *Alfred*, 138
playwrights and, 64-65

Cartouche, 67
Cato, 133-135
Cato's Letters, 4, 157-158
Centlivre, Susan: *A Bold Stroke for a Wife*, 71-73
Cibber, Colley:
Love in a Riddle, 11
The Refusal, 74-75
Clear State of the Case of Elizabeth Canning, A, 127-129
Coffee-House Politician, The, 112
Covent Garden Tragedy, The, 113-116
crime:
general, 78-79, 87-92, 157
increase in, 67-68
in London, 68-70
organisation of, 89
and stockjobbers, 70-75

Defoe, Daniel:
on crime, 87

on highwaymen, 67
on Sheppard, 96-97
on Jonathan Wild, 93-96, 98-99
Dissertation upon Parties, A: v. Bolingbroke.

Essay on the Knowledge and Characters of Men, 129-130
Examiner, The: Chapter 2 *passim* and v. Swift.

Fables: v. Gay, John.
Fate of Villainy, The, 75-76
Fielding, Henry:
on crime, 123-131
as a magistrate, 123-131
Jonathan Wild, 99-107
on Wild's background, 100-101
on Wild in prison, 106
on Wild at his execution, 106-107
criticised by contemporary reviewers, 115-116
works:
The Author's Farce, 112-113
The Coffee-House Politician, 112
The Covent-Garden Tragedy, 113-116
A Clear State of the Case of Elizabeth Canning, 127-129
Essay on the Knowledge and Characters of Men, 129-130
The Grub-Street Opera, 118-120, 164
The Historical Register, 120-121
An Inquiry into the Causes of the late Increase in Robbers, 123-127
A Journey from this World into the Next, 130-131
Tom Thumb, 116-117
The Tragedy of Tragedies, 116, 117-118
The Vernoniad, 103

Gay, John:
and crime, 67-70
and satire, 75, 78
plays suppressed by Walpole, 83
works:
The Beggar's Opera, 36, 50, 78-82
compared to *Timon in Love*, 141

183

Compared to *The Grub-Street Opera*, 118-119
Fables, 5, 120
The Mohocks, 76-79
Polly 82-84
Trivia, 4, 76-77

Historical Register, The, 120-121

Idea of a Patriot King, The, 54-58
Inquiry into the Causes of the late Increase of Robbers, 123-127

Johnson, Samuel:
  The Rambler quoted, 145
Journey from this World to the Next, A, 130-131

Kelly, John: Timon in Love, 140-141

Letters on the Study and Use of history, 49, 58-63
Licensing Act, The, 83
Lillo, George:
  Fatal Curiosity, 162-163
  The London Merchant, 170
Lyttelton, George:
  The Court Secret, 63-64
  Letters from a Persian, 155-156

Magistrates and magistracy, 123-131
Mallet, David:
  Mustapha, 135-136, 137
    and Walpole, 135
  Alfred: a Masque, 137-139
    and Bolingbroke, 138
Mandeville, Bernard: The Fable of the Bees, 137, 163
Marlborough, Duke of:
  attacked by Swift, 28-34
    as 'Marcus Crassus', 32-34
merchant, the, 4-8
Mohocks, The, v. Gay, John.
money, Chapter 1, passim, 162
monarchy: Chapter 2, passim,

Ordinary of Newgate, 87, 106

Philips, Ambrose, 64, 114
Polly, v. Gay, John.
Pope, Alexander:
  critic of the town, 3, 4
  and satire, 16, 164-166
  as participant in Are these Things so? 142-3
  as honest man, 142-143
  attacks Walpole, 159-160

and the pastoral, 166
works:
  Epilogue to the Satires, 159, 160, 165
  First Epistle of the second Book of Horace, 164
  1740, 159-160
  Moral Essays, 161
prostitution, 70
Public Spirit of the Whigs, The , v. Swift, Jonathan.

Ramsay, Allen; The Gentle Shepherd, 161-162

Sheppard, John:
  general, 96-97
  as 'opposite' of Wild, 96
  character, 97
  capture and execution, 97
Smollett, Tobias, 124-125
Steele, Richard:
  The Crisis, 38-39
    attacked by Swift, 40-42
  The Englishman, 74
  The Spectator, 5, 6, 7
  The Theatre, 7
stockjobbing, 70-75, 157-158
Swift, Jonathan:
  and monarchy, 17, 19, 30
  nature and origins of Whiggery, 17
  as a Whig, 20
  as a Tory, 15-16, 27
  on the division between Whigs and Tories, 18
  and trading, 23-24
  on stocks, 22-23
  War of the Spanish Succession, 19-20, 23
  attack on Marlborough, 28-34, 153-155
  attack on Walpole, 152-153
  attack on Wharton, 34-35, 36-7
  on lying, 35-37, 46
  his audience, 15, 42, 43-46
  fables, 44-5, 46
  letters to Stella, 46
  works:
    The Conduct of the Allies, 23-26
    The Examiner, 10-11, 16-23, 29-36, 43-44
    Letter to the October Club, 44
    The public Spirit of the Whigs, 39, 40-42, 43